P9-BZE-655

The.
Choice

The. Choice

EDITH EGER

with Esmé Schwall Weigand

RIDER

LONDON • SYDNEY • AUCKLAND • JOHANNESBURG

1 3 5 7 9 10 8 6 4 2

Rider, an imprint of Ebury Publishing,
20 Vauxhall Bridge Road,
London SW1V 2SA

Rider is part of the Penguin Random House group of companies whose
addresses can be found at global.penguinrandomhouse.com

Penguin
Random House
UK

Copyright © 2017 Edith Eger

Edith Eger has asserted her right to be identified as the author of this Work
in accordance with the Copyright, Designs and Patents Act 1988

First published in Great Britain by Rider in 2017
Published in the United States by Scribner, an imprint of Simon & Schuster, Inc,
1230 Avenue of the Americas, New York, NY 10020

www.penguin.co.uk

A CIP catalogue record for this book is available from the British Library

Hardback ISBN 9781846045103
Trade Paperback ISBN 9781846045110

Printed and bound in India by Thomson Press India Ltd.

For the five generations of my family—
my father, Lajos, who taught me to laugh;
my mother, Ilona, who helped me find what I needed inside;
my gorgeous and unbelievable sisters, Magda and Klara;
my children: Marianne, Audrey, and John;
and their children: Lindsey, Jordan, Rachel, David, and Ashley;
and their children's children: Silas, Graham, and Hale

Contents

CONTENTS

PART III: FREEDOM

PART IV: HEALING

Foreword

By Philip Zimbardo

Psychologist and professor emeritus at Stanford University, Phil Zimbardo is the creator of the famed Stanford prison experiment (1971) and author of many notable books, including the New York Times *bestseller and winner of the William James Book Award for best psychology book* The Lucifer Effect: Understanding How Good People Turn Evil *(2007). He is founder and president of the Heroic Imagination Project.*

One spring, at the invitation of the chief psychiatrist of the U.S. Navy, Dr. Edith Eva Eger boarded a windowless fighter jet bound for one of the world's largest warships, the USS *Nimitz* aircraft carrier, stationed off the California coast. The plane swooped down toward a tiny five-hundred-foot runway and landed with a jolt as its tailhook caught the arresting wire and stopped the plane from careening into the ocean. The only female aboard the ship, Dr. Eger was shown to her room in the captain's cabin. What was her mission? She was there to teach five thousand young Navy men how to deal with the adversity, trauma, and chaos of war.

On countless occasions, Dr. Eger has been the clinical expert brought in to treat soldiers, including Special Operations Forces, suffering from post-traumatic stress disorder and traumatic brain injuries. How is this gentle grandmother able to help so many military personnel heal from the inner brutality of war?

Before I met Dr. Eger in person I called to invite her to give a guest lecture to my Psychology of Mind Control class at Stanford. Her age and her accent made me picture an old-world babushka with a headscarf tied under her chin. When she addressed my students, I saw for myself her healing power. Luminous with her radiant smile, shining earrings, and blazing golden hair, dressed head to toe in what my wife later told me was Chanel, she wove her horrific and harrowing stories of surviving the Nazi death camps with humor, with an upbeat and feisty attitude, and with a presence and warmth I can only describe as pure light.

Dr. Eger's life has been full of darkness. She was imprisoned at Auschwitz when she was just a teenager. Despite torture, starvation, and the constant threat of annihilation, she preserved her mental and spiritual freedom. She was not broken by the horrors she experienced; she was emboldened and strengthened by them. In fact, her wisdom comes from deep within the most devastating episodes of her life.

She is able to help others heal because she has journeyed from trauma to triumph herself. She has discovered how to use her experience of human cruelty to empower so many— from military personnel like those aboard the USS *Nimitz* to couples struggling to rekindle intimacy, from those who were neglected or abused to those who are suffering from addiction or illness, from those who have lost loved ones to those who have lost hope. And for all of us who suffer from the everyday disappointments and challenges of life, her message inspires us to make our own choice to find freedom from suffering—to find our own inner light.

At the close of her lecture, every single one of my three hundred students leapt into a spontaneous standing ovation. Then, at least a hundred young men and women flooded the small stage, each waiting for a turn to thank and embrace this extraordinary woman. In all my decades of teaching I had never seen a group of students so inspired.

In the twenty years that Edie and I have worked and traveled together, this is the response I have come to expect from every audience she addresses around the world. From a Hero Round Table in Flint, Michigan, where we spoke to a group of young people in a city struggling with high poverty, 50 percent unemployment, and increasing racial conflict, to Budapest, Hungary, the city where many of Edie's relatives perished, where she spoke to hundreds of people trying to rebuild from a damaging past, I have seen it happen again and again: people are transformed in Edie's presence.

In this book, Dr. Eger weaves together the stories of her patients' transformations with her own unforgettable story of surviving Auschwitz. While her story of survival is as gripping and dramatic as any that has been told, it is not just her story that has made me passionate about sharing this book with the world. It is the fact that Edie has used her experiences to help so many to discover true freedom. In this way, her book is much more than another Shoah memoir, as important as such stories are for remembering the past. Her goal is nothing less than to help each of us to escape the prisons of our own minds. Each of us is in some way mentally imprisoned, and it is Edie's mission to help us realize that just as we can act as our own jailors, we can also be our own liberators.

When Edie is introduced to young audiences, she is often called "the Anne Frank who didn't die," because Edie and Anne were of a similar age and upbringing when they were deported to the camps. Both young women capture the innocence and compassion that allow a belief in the basic goodness of human beings, despite the cruelty and persecution they experienced. Of course, at the time Anne Frank was writing her diary, she had yet to experience the extremity of the camps, which makes Edie's insights as a survivor and as a clinician (and great-grandmother!) especially moving and compelling.

Like the most important books about the Holocaust, Dr. Eger's reveals both the darkest side of evil and the indomitable strength of the human spirit in the face of evil. But it does something else too. Perhaps the best comparison for Edie's book is to another Shoah memoir, Viktor Frankl's brilliant classic *Man's Search for Meaning*. Dr. Eger shares Frankl's profundity and deep knowledge of humanity, and adds the warmth and intimacy of a lifelong clinician. Viktor Frankl presented the psychology of the prisoners who were with him in Auschwitz. Dr. Eger offers us the psychology of freedom.

In my own work I have long studied the psychological foundations of negative forms of social influence. I've sought to understand the mechanisms by which we conform and obey and stand by in situations where peace and justice can be served only if we choose another path: if we act heroically. Edie has helped me to discover that heroism is not the province only of those who perform extraordinary deeds or take impulsive risks to protect themselves or others—though Edie has done both of these things. Heroism is rather a mind-set or an accumulation of our personal and social habits. It is a way of being. And it is a special way of viewing ourselves. To be a hero requires taking effective action at crucial junctures in our lives, to make an active attempt to address injustice or create positive change in the world. To be a hero requires great moral courage. And each of us has an inner hero waiting to be expressed. We are all "heroes in training." Our hero training is life, the daily circumstances that invite us to practice the habits of heroism: to commit daily deeds of kindness; to radiate compassion, starting with self-compassion; to bring out the best in others and ourselves; to sustain love, even in our most challenging relationships; to celebrate and exercise the power of our mental freedom. Edie is a hero—and doubly so, because she teaches each of us to grow and create meaningful and lasting change in ourselves, in our relationships, and in our world.

Two years ago Edie and I traveled together to Budapest, to the city where her sister was living when the Nazis began rounding up Hungarian Jews. We visited a Jewish synagogue, its courtyard a memorial to the Holocaust, its walls a canvas of photographs from before, during, and after the war. We visited the Shoes on the Danube Bank memorial that honors the people, including some of Edie's own family members, who were killed by the Arrow Cross militiamen during World War II, ordered to stand on the riverbank and take off their shoes, and then shot, their bodies falling into the water, carried away by the current. The past felt tangible.

Throughout the day, Edie grew more and more quiet. I wondered if she would find it difficult to speak to an audience of six hundred that night after an emotional journey that was almost certainly stirring up painful memories. But when she took the stage she didn't begin with a story of the fear or trauma or horror that our visit had likely made all too real for her again. She began with a story of kindness, an act of everyday heroism that, she reminded us, happened even in hell. "Isn't it amazing?" she said. "The worst brings out the best in us."

At the end of her speech, which she concluded with her trademark high ballet kick, Edie called out, "Okay, now everybody dance!" The audience rose as one. Hundreds of people ran onto the stage. There was no music. But we danced. We danced and sang and laughed and hugged in an incomparable celebration of life.

Dr. Eger is one of the dwindling number of survivors who can bear first-hand testimony to the horrors of the concentration camps. Her book recounts the hell and trauma that she and other survivors endured during and after the war. And it is a universal message of hope and possibility to all who are trying to free themselves from pain and suffering. Whether imprisoned by bad marriages, destructive families, or jobs they hate, or imprisoned within the barbed wire of self-limiting beliefs that trap them in their own minds, readers will learn from this book that they can choose to embrace joy and freedom regardless of their circumstances.

The Choice is an extraordinary chronicle of heroism and healing, resiliency and compassion, survival with dignity, mental toughness, and moral courage. All of us can learn from Dr. Eger's inspiring cases and riveting personal story to heal our own lives.

PART I

Prison

I Had My Secret,
and My Secret Had Me

I didn't know about the loaded gun hidden under his shirt, but the instant Captain Jason Fuller walked into my El Paso office on a summer day in 1980, my gut tightened and the back of my neck stung. War had taught me to sense danger even before I could explain why I was afraid.

Jason was tall, with the lean physique of an athlete, but his body was so rigid he appeared more wooden than human. His blue eyes looked distant, his jaw frozen, and he wouldn't—or couldn't—speak. I steered him to the white couch in my office. He sat stiffly, fists pressing into his knees. I had never met Jason and had no idea what had triggered his catatonic state. His body was close enough to touch, and his anguish practically palpable, but he was far away, lost. He did not even seem to notice my silver standard poodle, Tess, standing at attention near my desk, like a second living statue in the room.

I took a deep breath and searched for a way to begin. Sometimes I start a first session by introducing myself and sharing a little of my history and approach. Sometimes I jump right into identifying and investigating the feelings that have brought the patient to my office. With Jason, it felt critical not to overwhelm him with too much information or ask him to be too vulnerable too quickly. He was completely shut down. I had to find a way to give him the safety and permission he needed to risk showing me whatever he guarded so tightly inside. And I had to pay attention to my body's warning system without letting my sense of danger overwhelm my ability to help.

"How can I be useful to you?" I asked.

He didn't answer. He didn't even blink. He reminded me of a character in a myth or folktale who has been turned to stone. What magic spell could free him?

"Why now?" I asked. This was my secret weapon. The question I always ask my patients on a first visit. I need to know why they are motivated to change. Why today, of all days, do they want to start working with me? Why is today different from yesterday, or last week, or last year? Why is today different from tomorrow? Sometimes our pain pushes us, and sometimes our hope pulls us. Asking "Why now?" isn't just asking a question—it's asking everything.

One of his eyes briefly twitched closed. But he said nothing.

"Tell me why you're here," I invited again.

Still he said nothing.

My body tensed with a wave of uncertainty and an awareness of the tenuous and crucial crossroads where we sat: two humans face-to-face, both of us vulnerable, both of us taking a risk as we struggled to name an anguish and find its cure. Jason hadn't arrived with an official referral. It appeared that he had brought himself to my office by choice. But I knew from clinical and personal experience that even when someone chooses to heal, he or she can remain frozen for years.

Given the severity of the symptoms he exhibited, if I didn't succeed in reaching him my only alternative would be to recommend him to my colleague, the chief psychiatrist at the William Beaumont Army Medical Center, where I'd done my doctoral work. Dr. Harold Kolmer would diagnose Jason's catatonia, hospitalize him, and probably prescribe an antipsychotic drug like Haldol. I pictured Jason in a hospital gown, his eyes still glazed, his body, now so tense, racked with the muscle spasms that are often a side effect of the drugs prescribed to manage psychosis. I rely absolutely on the expertise of my psychiatrist colleagues, and I am grateful for the medications that save lives. But I don't like to jump to hospitalization if there's any chance of success with a therapeutic intervention. I feared that if I recommended Jason to be hospitalized and medicated without first exploring other options, he would trade one kind of numbness for another, frozen limbs for the involuntary movements of dyskinesia—an uncoordinated dance of repeating tics and motions, when the nervous system sends the signal for the body to move without the mind's permission. His pain, whatever its cause, might be muted by the drugs, but it wouldn't be resolved. He might feel better, or feel less—which we often mistake for feeling better—but he would not be healed.

What now? I wondered as the heavy minutes dragged past, as Jason sat frozen on my couch—there by choice, but still imprisoned. I had only one hour. One opportunity. Could I reach him? Could I help him to dissolve his potential for violence, which I could sense as clearly as the air conditioner's blast across my skin? Could I help him see that whatever his trouble and whatever his pain, he already held the key to his own freedom? I couldn't have known then that if I failed to reach Jason on that very day, a fate far worse than a hospital room awaited him—a life in an actual prison, probably on death row. I only knew then that I had to try.

As I studied Jason, I knew that to reach him I wouldn't use the language of feelings; I would use a language more comfortable and familiar to someone in the military. I would give orders. I sensed that the only hope for unlocking him was to get the blood moving through his body.

"We're going for a walk," I said. I didn't ask. I gave the command. "Captain, we will take Tess to the park—now."

Jason looked panicked for a moment. Here was a woman, a stranger, talking in a thick Hungarian accent, telling him what to do. I could see him looking around, wondering, "How can I get out of here?" But he was a good soldier. He stood up.

"Yes, ma'am," he said. "Yes, ma'am."

I would discover soon enough the origin of Jason's trauma, and he would discover that despite our obvious differences, there was much we shared. We both knew violence. And we both knew what it was like to become frozen. I also carried a wound within me, a sorrow so deep that for many years I hadn't been able to speak of it at all, to anyone.

My past still haunted me: an anxious, dizzy feeling every time I heard sirens, or heavy footsteps, or shouting men. This, I had learned, is trauma: a nearly constant feeling in my gut that something is wrong, or that something terrible is about to happen, the automatic fear responses in my body telling me to run away, to take cover, to hide myself from the danger that is everywhere. My trauma can still rise up out of mundane encounters. A sudden sight, a particular smell, can transport me back to the past. The day I met Captain Fuller, more than thirty years had passed since I'd been liberated from the concentration camps of the Holocaust. Today, more than seventy years have passed. What happened can never be forgotten and can never be changed. But over time I learned that I can choose how to respond to the past. I can be miserable, or I can be hopeful—I can be depressed, or I can be happy. We always have that choice, that opportunity for control. *I'm here, this is now*, I have learned to tell myself, over and over, until the panicky feeling begins to ease.

Conventional wisdom says that if something bothers you or causes you anxiety, then just don't look at it. Don't dwell on it. Don't go there. So we run from past traumas and hardships or from current discomfort or conflict. For much of my adulthood I had thought my survival in the present depended on keeping the past and its darkness locked away. In my early immigrant years in Baltimore in the 1950s, I didn't even know how to pronounce Auschwitz in English. Not that I would have wanted to tell you I was there even if I could have. I didn't want anyone's pity. I didn't want anyone to know.

I just wanted to be a Yankee doodle dandy. To speak English without an accent. To hide from the past. In my yearning to belong, in my fear of being swallowed up by the past, I worked very hard to keep my pain hidden. I hadn't yet discovered that my silence and my desire for acceptance, both founded in fear, were ways of running away from myself—that in choosing not to face the past and myself directly, decades after my literal imprisonment had ended, I was still choosing not to be free. I had my secret, and my secret had me.

The catatonic Army captain sitting immobile on my couch reminded me of what I had eventually discovered: that when we force our truths and stories into hiding, secrets can become their own trauma, their own prison. Far from diminishing pain, whatever we deny ourselves the opportunity to accept becomes as inescapable as brick walls and steel bars. When we don't allow ourselves to grieve our losses, wounds, and disappointments, we are doomed to keep reliving them.

Freedom lies in learning to embrace what happened. Freedom means we muster the courage to dismantle the prison, brick by brick.

* * *

Bad things, I am afraid, happen to everyone. This we can't change. If you look at your birth certificate, does it say life will be easy? It does not. But so many of us remain stuck in a trauma or grief, unable to experience our lives fully. This we can change.

At Kennedy International Airport recently, waiting for my flight home to San Diego, I sat and studied the faces of every passing stranger. What I saw deeply moved me. I saw boredom, fury, tension, worry, confusion, discouragement, disappointment, sadness, and, most troubling of all, emptiness. It made me very sad to see so little joy and laughter. Even the dullest moments of our lives are opportunities to experience hope, buoyancy, happiness. Mundane life is life too. As is painful life, and stressful life. Why do we so often struggle to feel alive, or distance ourselves from feeling life fully? Why is it such a challenge to bring life to life?

If you asked me for the most common diagnosis among the people I treat, I wouldn't say depression or post-traumatic stress disorder, although these conditions are all too common among those I've known, loved, and guided to freedom. No, I would say hunger. We are hungry. We are hungry for approval, attention, affection. We are hungry for the freedom to embrace life and to really know and be ourselves.

My own search for freedom and my years of experience as a licensed clinical psychologist have taught me that suffering is universal. But victimhood is optional. There is a difference between victimization and victimhood. We are all likely to be victimized in some way in the course of our lives. At some point we will suffer some kind of affliction or calamity or abuse, caused by circumstances or people or institutions over which we have little or no control. This is life. And this is victimization. It comes from the outside. It's the neighborhood bully, the boss who rages, the spouse who hits, the lover who cheats, the discriminatory law, the accident that lands you in the hospital.

In contrast, victimhood comes from the inside. No one can make you a victim but you. We become victims not because of what happens to us but when we choose to hold on to our victimization. We develop a victim's mind—a way of thinking and being that is rigid, blaming, pessimistic, stuck in the past, unforgiving, punitive, and without healthy limits or boundaries. We become our own jailors when we choose the confines of the victim's mind.

I want to make one thing very clear. When I talk about victims and survivors, I am not blaming victims—so many of whom never had a chance. I could never blame those who were sent

9

right to the gas chambers or who died in their cot, or even those who ran into the electric barbed wire fence. I grieve for all people everywhere who are sentenced to violence and destruction. I live to guide others to a position of empowerment in the face of all of life's hardships.

I also want to say that there is no hierarchy of suffering. There's nothing that makes my pain worse or better than yours, no graph on which we can plot the relative importance of one sorrow versus another. People say to me, "Things in my life are pretty hard right now, but I have no right to complain—it's not *Auschwitz*." This kind of comparison can lead us to minimize or diminish our own suffering. Being a survivor, being a "thriver" requires absolute acceptance of what was and what is. If we discount our pain, or punish ourselves for feeling lost or isolated or scared about the challenges in our lives, however insignificant these challenges may seem to someone else, then we're still choosing to be victims. We're not seeing our choices. We're judging ourselves. I don't want you to hear my story and say, "My own suffering is less significant." I want you to hear my story and say, "If she can do it, then so can I!"

One morning I saw two patients back to back, both mothers in their forties. The first woman had a daughter who was dying of hemophilia. She spent most of her visit crying, asking how God could take her child's life. I hurt so much for this woman— she was absolutely devoted to her daughter's care, and devastated by her impending loss. She was angry, she was grieving, and she wasn't at all sure that she could survive the hurt.

My next patient had just come from the country club, not the hospital. She, too, spent much of the hour crying. She was upset because her new Cadillac had just been delivered, and it was the wrong shade of yellow. On the surface, her problem seemed petty, especially compared to my previous patient's anguish over her dying child. But I knew enough about her to understand that her tears of disappointment over the color of her car were really tears of disappointment over the bigger things in her life that hadn't worked out the way she had hoped—a lonely marriage, a son who had been kicked out of yet another school, the aspirations for a career she had abandoned in order to be more available for her husband and child. Often, the little upsets in our lives are emblematic of the larger losses; the seemingly insignificant worries are representative of greater pain.

I realized that day how much my two patients, who appeared so different, had in common—with each other and with all people everywhere. Both women were responding to a situation they couldn't control in which their expectations had been upended. Both were struggling and hurting because something was not what they wanted or expected it to be; they were trying to reconcile what was with what ought to have been. Each woman's pain was real. Each woman was caught up in the human drama—that we find ourselves in situations we didn't see coming and that we don't feel prepared to handle. Both women deserved my compassion. Both had the potential to heal. Both women, like all of us, had choices in attitude and action that could move them from victim to survivor even if the circumstances they were dealing with didn't change. Survivors don't have time to ask, "Why me?" For survivors, the only relevant question is, "What now?"

Whether you're in the dawn or noon or late evening of your life, whether you've seen deep suffering or are only just beginning to encounter struggle, whether you're falling in love for the first time or losing your life partner to old age, whether you're healing from a life-altering event or in search of some little adjustments that could bring more joy to your life, I would love to help you discover how to escape the concentration camp of your own mind and become the person you were meant to be. I would love to help you experience freedom from the past, freedom from failures and fears, freedom from anger and mistakes, freedom from regret and unresolved grief—and the freedom to enjoy the full, rich feast of life. We cannot choose to have a life free of hurt. But we can choose to be free, to escape the past, no matter what befalls us, and to embrace the possible. I invite you to make the choice to be free.

Like the challah my mother used to make for our Friday night meal, this book has three strands: my story of survival, my story of healing myself, and the stories of the precious people I've had the privilege of guiding to freedom. I've conveyed my experience as I can best remember it. The stories about patients accurately reflect the core of their experiences, but I have changed all names and identifying details and in some instances created composites from patients working through similar challenges. What follows is the story of the choices, big and small, that can lead us from trauma to triumph, from darkness to light, from imprisonment to freedom.

CHAPTER 1

The Four Questions

If I could distill my entire life into one moment, into one still image, it is this: three women in dark wool coats wait, arms linked, in a barren yard. They are exhausted. They've got dust on their shoes. They stand in a long line.

The three women are my mother, my sister Magda, and me. This is our last moment together. We don't know that. We refuse to consider it. Or we are too weary even to speculate about what is ahead. It is a moment of severing—mother from daughters, life as it has been from all that will come after. And yet only hindsight can give it this meaning.

I see the three of us from behind, as though I am next in line. Why does memory give me the back of my mother's head but not her face? Her long hair is intricately braided and clipped on top of her head. Magda's light brown waves touch her shoulders. My dark hair is tucked under a scarf. My mother stands in the middle and Magda and I both lean inward. It is impossible to discern if we are the ones who keep our mother upright, or if it is the other way around, her strength the pillar that supports Magda and me.

This moment is a threshold into the major losses of my life. For seven decades I have returned again and again to this image of the three of us. I have studied it as though with enough scrutiny I can recover something precious. As though I can regain the life that precedes this moment, the life that precedes loss. As if there is such a thing.

I have returned so that I can rest a little longer in this time when our arms are joined and we belong to one another. I see our sloped shoulders. The dust holding to the bottoms of our coats. My mother. My sister. Me.

* * *

Our childhood memories are often fragments, brief moments or encounters, which together form the scrapbook of our life. They are all we have left to understand the story we have come to tell ourselves about who we are.

Even before the moment of our separation, my most intimate memory of my mother, though I treasure it, is full of sorrow and loss. We're alone in the kitchen, where she is wrapping up the leftover strudel that she made with dough I watched her cut by hand and drape like heavy linen over the dining room table. "Read to me," she says, and I fetch the worn copy of *Gone with the Wind* from her bedside table. We have read it through once before. Now we have begun again. I pause over the mysterious inscription, written in English, on the title page of the translated book. It's in a man's handwriting, but not my father's. All that my mother will say is that the book was a gift from a man she met when she worked at the Foreign Ministry before she knew my father.

We sit in straight-backed chairs near the woodstove. I read this grown-up novel fluently despite the fact that I am only nine. "I'm glad you have brains because you have no looks," she has told me more than once, a compliment and a criticism intertwined. She can be hard on me. But I savor this time. When we read together, I don't have to share her with anyone else. I sink into the words and the story and the feeling of being alone in a world with her. Scarlett returns to Tara at the end of the war to learn her mother is dead and her father is far gone in grief. "*As God is my witness*," Scarlett says, "*I'm never going to be hungry again.*" My mother has closed her eyes and leans her head against the back of the chair. I want to climb into her lap. I want to rest my head against her chest. I want her to touch her lips to my hair.

"Tara . . ." she says. "America, now that would be a place to see." I wish she would say my name with the same softness she reserves for a country where she's never been. All the smells of my mother's kitchen are mixed up for me with the drama of hunger and feast—always, even in the feast, that longing. I don't know if the longing is hers or mine or something we share.

We sit with the fire between us.

"When I was your age . . ." she begins.

Now that she is talking, I am afraid to move, afraid she won't continue if I do.

"When I was your age, the babies slept together and my mother and I shared a bed. One morning I woke up because my father was calling to me, 'Ilonka, wake up your mother, she hasn't made breakfast yet or laid out my clothes.' I turned to my mother next to me under the covers. But she wasn't moving. She was dead."

She has never told me this before. I want to know every detail about this moment when a daughter woke beside a mother she had already lost. I also want to look away. It is too terrifying to think about.

15

"When they buried her that afternoon, I thought they had put her in the ground alive. That night, Father told me to make the family supper. So that's what I did."

I wait for the rest of the story. I wait for the lesson at the end, or the reassurance.

"Bedtime," is all my mother says. She bends to sweep the ash under the stove.

Footsteps thump down the hall outside our door. I can smell my father's tobacco even before I hear the jangle of his keys.

"Ladies," he calls, "are you still awake?" He comes into the kitchen in his shiny shoes and dapper suit, his big grin, a little sack in his hand that he gives me with a loud kiss to the forehead. "I won again," he boasts. Whenever he plays cards or billiards with his friends, he shares the spoils with me. Tonight he's brought a petit four laced in pink icing. If I were my sister Magda, my mother, always concerned about Magda's weight, would snatch the treat away, but she nods at me, giving me permission to eat it.

She is standing now, on her way from the fire to the sink. My father intercepts her, lifts her hand so he can twirl her around the room, which she does, stiffly, without a smile. He pulls her in for an embrace, one hand on her back, one teasing at her breast. My mother shrugs him away.

"I'm a disappointment to your mother," my father half whispers to me as we leave the kitchen. Does he intend for her to overhear, or is this a secret meant only for me? Either way, it is something I store away to mull over later. Yet the bitterness in his voice scares me. "She wants to go to the opera every night, live some fancy cosmopolitan life. I'm just a tailor. A tailor and a billiards player."

My father's defeated tone confuses me. He is well known in our town, and well liked. Playful, smiling, he always seems comfortable and alive. He's fun to be around. He goes out with his many friends. He loves food (especially the ham he sometimes smuggles into our kosher household, eating it over the newspaper it was wrapped in, pushing bites of forbidden pork into my mouth, enduring my mother's accusations that he is a poor role model). His tailor shop has won two gold medals. He isn't just a maker of even seams and straight hems. He is a master of couture. That's how he met my mother—she came into his shop because she needed a dress and his work came so highly recommended. But he had wanted to be a doctor, not a tailor, a dream his father had discouraged, and every once in a while his disappointment in himself surfaces.

"You're not just a tailor, Papa," I reassure him. "You're the best tailor!"

"And you're going to be the best-dressed lady in Košice," he tells me, patting my head. "You have the perfect figure for couture."

He seems to have remembered himself. He's pushed his disappointment back into the shadows. We reach the door to the bedroom I share with Magda and our middle sister, Klara, where I can picture Magda pretending to do homework and Klara wiping rosin dust off her violin. My father and I stand in the doorway a moment longer, neither one of us quite ready to break away.

"I wanted you to be a boy, you know," my father says. "I slammed the door when you were born, I was that mad at having another girl. But now you're the only one I can talk to." He kisses my forehead.

I love my father's attention. Like my mother's, it is precious . . . and precarious. As though my worthiness of their love has less to do with me and more to do with their loneliness. As though my identity isn't about anything that I am or have and only a measure of what each of my parents is missing.

"Good night, Dicuka," my father says at last. He uses the pet name my mother invented for me. Ditzu-ka. These nonsense syllables are warmth to me. "Tell your sisters it's time for lights out."

As I come into the bedroom, Magda and Klara greet me with the song they have invented for me. They made it up when I was three and one of my eyes became crossed in a botched medical procedure. "You're so ugly, you're so puny," they sing. "You'll never find a husband." Since the accident I turn my head toward the ground when I walk so that I don't have to see anyone looking at my lopsided face. I haven't yet learned that the problem isn't that my sisters taunt me with a mean song; the problem is that I believe them. I am so convinced of my inferiority that I never introduce myself by name. I never tell people, "I am Edie." Klara is a violin prodigy. She mastered the Mendelssohn violin concerto when she was five. "I am Klara's sister," I say.

But tonight I have special knowledge. "Mama's mom died when she was exactly my age," I tell them. I am so certain of the privileged nature of this information that it doesn't occur to me that for my sisters this is old news, that I am the last and not the first to know.

"You're kidding," Magda says, her voice full of sarcasm so obvious that even I can recognize it. She is fifteen, busty, with sensual lips, wavy hair. She is the jokester in our family. When we were younger, she showed me how to drop grapes out of our bedroom window into the coffee cups of the patrons sitting on the patio below. Inspired by her, I will soon invent my own games; but by then, the stakes will have changed. My girlfriend and I will sashay up to boys at school or on the street. "Meet me at four o'clock by the clock on the square," we will trill, batting our eyelashes. They will come, they will always come, sometimes giddy, sometimes shy, sometimes swaggering with expectation. From the safety of my bedroom, my friend and I will stand at the window and watch the boys arrive.

"Don't tease so much," Klara snaps at Magda now. She is younger than Magda, but she jumps in to protect me. "You know that picture above the piano?" she says to me. "The one that Mama's always talking to? That's her mother." I know the picture she's talking about. I've looked at it every day of my life. "Help me, help me," our mother moans up at the portrait as she dusts the piano, sweeps the floor. I feel embarrassed that I have never asked my mother—or anyone—who was in that picture. And I'm disappointed that my information gives me no special status with my sisters.

I am used to being the silent sister, the invisible one. It doesn't occur to me that Magda might tire of being the clown, that Klara might resent being the prodigy. She can't stop being extraordinary, not for a second, or everything might be taken from her—the adoration she's accustomed to, her very sense of self. Magda and I have to work at getting something we are certain there will never be enough of; Klara has to worry that at any moment she might make a fatal mistake and lose it all. Klara has been playing violin all my life, since she was three. It's not until much later that I

19

realize the cost of her extraordinary talent: she gave up being a child. I never saw her play with dolls. Instead she stood in front of an open window to practice violin, not able to enjoy her creative genius unless she could summon an audience of passersby to witness it.

"Does Mama love Papa?" I ask my sisters now. The distance between our parents, the sad things they have each confessed to me, remind me that I have never seen them dressed up to go out together.

"What a question," Klara says. Though she denies my concern, I think I see a recognition in her eyes. We will never discuss it again, though I will try. It will take me years to learn what my sisters must already know, that what we call love is often something more conditional—the reward for a performance, what you settle for.

As we put on our nightgowns and get into bed, I erase my worry for my parents and think instead of my ballet master and his wife, of the feeling I get when I take the steps up to the studio two or three at a time and kick off my school clothes, pull on my leotard and tights. I have been studying ballet since I was five years old, since my mother intuited that I wasn't a musician, that I had other gifts. Just today we practiced the splits. Our ballet master reminded us that strength and flexibility are inseparable—for one muscle to flex, another must open; to achieve length and limberness, we have to hold our cores strong.

I hold his instructions in my mind like a prayer. Down I go, spine straight, abdominal muscles tight, legs stretching apart. I know to breathe, especially when I feel stuck. I picture my body expanding like the strings on my sister's violin, finding the exact place of tautness that makes the whole instrument ring. And I am down. I am here. In the full splits. "Brava!" My ballet master claps. "Stay right as you are." He lifts me off the ground and over his head. It's hard to keep my legs fully extended without the floor to push against, but for a moment I feel like an offering. I feel like pure light. "Editke," my teacher says, "all your ecstasy in life is going to come from the inside." It will take me years to really understand what he means. For now all I know is that I can breathe and spin and kick and bend. As my muscles stretch and strengthen, every movement, every pose seems to call out: *I am, I am, I am. I am me. I am somebody.*

* * *

Memory is sacred ground. But it's haunted too. It's the place where my rage and guilt and grief go circling like hungry birds scavenging the same old bones. It's the place where I go searching for the answer to the unanswerable question: *Why did I survive?*

I am seven years old, and my parents are hosting a dinner party. They send me out of the room to refill a pitcher of water. From the kitchen I hear them joke, "We could have saved that one." I think they mean that before I came along they were already a complete family. They had a daughter who played piano and a daughter who played violin. I am unnecessary, I am not good enough, there is no room for me, I think. This is the way we misinterpret the facts of our lives, the way we assume and don't check it out, the way we invent a story to tell ourselves, reinforcing the very thing in us we already believe.

One day when I am eight, I decide to run away. I will test the theory that I am dispensable, invisible. I will see if my parents even know that I am gone. Instead of going to school, I take the trolley to my grandparents' house. I trust my grandparents—my mother's father and stepmother—to cover for me. They engage in a continuous war with my mother on Magda's behalf, hiding cookies in my sister's dresser drawer. They are safety to me, and yet they sanction the forbidden. They hold hands, something my own parents never do. There's no performing for their love, no pretending for their approval. They are comfort—the smell of brisket and baked beans, of sweet bread, of *cholent*, a rich stew that my grandmother brings to the bakery to cook on Sabbath, when Orthodox practice does not permit her to use her own oven.

My grandparents are happy to see me. It is a wonderful morning. I sit in the kitchen, eating nut rolls. But then the doorbell rings. My grandfather goes to answer it. A moment later he rushes into the kitchen. He is hard of hearing, and he speaks his warning too loudly. "Hide, Dicuka!" he yells. "Your mother's here!" In trying to protect me, he gives me away.

What bothers me the most is the look on my mother's face when she sees me in my grandparents' kitchen. It's not just that she is surprised to see me here—it is as though the very fact of my existence has taken her by surprise. As though I am not who she wants or expects me to be.

I won't ever be beautiful—this my mother has made clear—but the year I turn ten she assures me that I won't have to hide my face anymore. Dr. Klein, in Budapest, will fix my crossed eye. On the train to Budapest I eat chocolate and enjoy my mother's exclusive attention. Dr. Klein is a celebrity, my mother says, the first to perform eye surgery without anesthetic. I am too caught up in the romance of the journey, the privilege of having my mother all to myself, to realize she is warning me. It has never occurred to me that the surgery will hurt. Not until the pain consumes me. My mother and her relatives, who have connected us to the celebrated Dr. Klein, hold my thrashing body against the table. Worse than the pain, which is huge and limitless, is the feeling of the people who love me restraining me so that I cannot move. Only later, long after the surgery has proved successful, can I see the scene from my mother's point of view, how she must have suffered at my suffering.

I am happiest when I am alone, when I can retreat into my inner world. One morning when I am thirteen, on the way to school, in a private gymnasium, I practice the steps to the "Blue Danube" routine my ballet class will perform at a festival on the river. Then invention takes hold, and I am off and away in a new dance of my own, one in which I imagine my parents meeting. I dance both of their parts. My father does a slapstick double take when he sees my mother walk into the room. My mother spins faster, leaps higher. I make my whole body arc into a joyful laugh. I have never seen my mother rejoice, never heard her laugh from the belly, but in my body I feel the untapped well of her happiness.

When I get to school, the tuition money my father gave me to cover an entire quarter of school is gone. Somehow, in the flurry of dancing, I have lost it. I check every pocket and crease of my clothing, but it is gone. All day the dread of telling my father burns like ice in my gut. At home he can't look at me as he raises his fists. This is the first time he has ever hit me, or any of us. He doesn't say a word to me when he is done. In bed that night I wish to die so that my father will suffer for what he did to me. And then I wish my father dead.

Do these memories give me an image of my strength? Or of my damage? Maybe every childhood is the terrain on which we try to pinpoint how much we matter and how much we don't, a map where we study the dimensions and the borders of our worth.

Maybe every life is a study of the things we don't have but wish we did, and the things we have but wish we didn't.

It took me many decades to discover that I could come at my life with a different question. Not: *Why did I live?* But: *What is mine to do with the life I've been given?*

My family's ordinary human dramas were complicated by borders, by wars. Before World War I, the Slovakian region where I was born and raised was part of Austro-Hungary, but in 1918, a decade before my birth, the Treaty of Versailles redrew the map of Europe and created a new state. Czechoslovakia was cobbled together from agrarian Slovakia, my family's region, which was ethnically Hungarian and Slovak; the more industrial regions of Moravia and Bohemia, which were ethnically Czech; and Subcarpathian Rus', a region that is now part of Ukraine. With the creation of Czechoslovakia, my hometown—Kassa, Hungary—became Košice, Czechoslovakia. And my family became double minorities. We were ethnic Hungarians living in a predominately Czech country, and we were Jewish.

Though Jews had lived in Slovakia since the eleventh century, it wasn't until 1840 that Jews were permitted to settle in Kassa. Even then, city officials, backed by Christian trade guilds, made it difficult for Jewish families who wanted to live there. Yet by the turn of the century, Kassa had become one of Europe's largest Jewish communities. Unlike in other Eastern European countries, such as Poland, Hungarian Jews weren't ghettoized (which is why my family spoke Hungarian exclusively and not Yiddish). We weren't segregated, and we enjoyed plenty of educational, professional, and cultural opportunities. But we still encountered prejudice, subtle and explicit. Anti-Semitism wasn't a Nazi invention. Growing up, I internalized a sense of inferiority and the belief that it was safer not to admit that I was Jewish, that it was safer to assimilate, to blend in, to never stand out. It was difficult to find a sense of identity and belonging. Then, in November 1938, Hungary annexed Košice again, and it felt like home had become home.

My mother stands on our balcony at Andrássy Palace, an old building that has been carved into single-family apartments. She has draped an Oriental rug across the railing. She's not cleaning; she's celebrating. Admiral Miklós Horthy, His Serene Highness the Regent of the Kingdom of Hungary, arrives today to formally welcome our town into Hungary. I understand my parents' excitement and pride. We belong! Today I, too, welcome Horthy. I perform a dance. I wear a Hungarian costume: bold floral embroidery on a bright wool vest and skirt, billowing white-sleeved blouse, ribbons, lace, red boots. When I do the high kick by the river, Horthy applauds. He embraces the dancers. He embraces me.

"Dicuka, I wish we were blond like Klara," Magda whispers at bedtime.

We are still years away from curfews and discriminatory laws, but Horthy's parade is the starting point of all that will come. Hungarian citizenship has brought belonging in one sense but exclusion in another. We are so happy to speak our native tongue, to be accepted as Hungarians—but that acceptance depends on our assimilation. Neighbors argue that only ethnic Hungarians *who are not Jewish* should be allowed to wear the traditional garments.

"It's best not to let on you're Jewish," my sister Magda warns me. "It will just make other people want to take away your beautiful things."

Magda is the firstborn; she reports the world to me. She brings me details, often troubling things, to study and ponder. In 1939, the year that Nazi Germany invades Poland, the Hungarian Nazis—the *nyilas*—occupy the apartment below ours in Andrássy Palace. They spit at Magda. They evict us. We move to a new apartment, at Kossuth Lajos Utca #6, on a side street instead of the main road, less convenient for my father's business. The apartment is available because its former occupants, another Jewish family, have left for South America. We know of other Jewish families leaving Hungary. My father's sister Matilda has been gone for years already. She lives in New York, in a place called the Bronx, in a Jewish immigrant neighborhood. Her life in America seems more circumscribed than ours. We don't talk about leaving.

Even in 1940, when I'm thirteen, and the *nyilas* begin to round up the Jewish men of Kassa and send them to a forced labor camp, the war feels far away from us. My father isn't taken. Not at first. We use denial as protection. If we don't pay attention, then we can continue our lives unnoticed. We can make the world safe in our minds. We can make ourselves invisible to harm.

But one day in June 1941, Magda is out on her bicycle when the sirens roar. She dashes three blocks to the safety of our grandparents' house, only to find half of it gone. They survived, thank God. But their landlady didn't. It was a singular attack, one neighborhood razed by one bombing. We're told the Russians are responsible for the rubble and death. No one believes it, and yet no one can refute it. We are lucky and vulnerable in the same instant. The only solid truth is the pile of smashed brick in the spot where a house used to be. Destruction and absence—these become facts. Hungary joins Germany in Operation Barbarossa. We invade Russia.

Around this time we are made to wear the yellow star. The trick is to hide the star, to let your coat cover it. But even with my star out of sight, I feel like I have done something bad, something punishable. What is my unpardonable sin? My mother is always near the radio. When we picnic by the river, my father tells stories about being a prisoner of war in Russia during World War I. I know that his POW experience—his trauma, though I don't know to call it that—has something to do with his eating pork, with his distance from religion. I know that war is at the root of his distress. But the war, this war, is still elsewhere. I can ignore it, and I do.

After school, I spend five hours at the ballet studio, and I begin to study gymnastics too. Though it begins as a complementary practice to the ballet, gymnastics soon grows to be an equal passion, an equal art. I join a book club, a group made up of girls from my private gymnasium and students from a nearby private boys' school. We read Stefan Zweig's *Marie Antoinette: The Portrait of an Average Woman*. We talk about Zweig's way of writing about history from the inside, from the mind of one person. In the book club, there's a boy named Eric, who notices me one day. I see him looking closely at me every time I speak. He's tall, with freckles and reddish hair. I imagine Versailles. I imagine Marie Antoinette's boudoir. I imagine meeting Eric there. I know nothing about sex, but I am romantic. I see him notice me, and I wonder, *What would our children look like? Would they have freckles too?* Eric approaches me after the discussion. He smells so good— like fresh air, like the grass on the banks of the Hornád River where we will soon take walks.

Our relationship holds weight and substance from the start. We talk about literature. We talk about Palestine (he is a devoted Zionist). This isn't a time of carefree dating, our bond isn't a casual crush, a puppy love. This is love in the face of war. A curfew has been imposed on Jews, but we sneak out one night without wearing our yellow stars. We stand in line at the cinema. We find our seats in the dark. It's an American film, starring Bette Davis. *Now, Voyager*, I later learn, is its American name, but in Hungary it's called *Utazás a múltból*, Journey to the Past. Bette Davis plays an unmarried daughter tyrannized by her controlling mother. She tries to find herself and her freedom but is constantly knocked down by her mother's criticisms. Eric sees it as a political metaphor about self-determination and self-worth. I see shades of my mother and Magda—my mother, who adores Eric but chastises Magda for her casual dating; who begs me to eat more but refuses to fill Magda's plate; who is often silent and introspective but rages at Magda; whose anger, though it is never directed at me, terrifies me all the same.

The battles in my family, the front with Russia closing in— we never know what is coming next. In the darkness and chaos

28

of uncertainty, Eric and I provide our own light. Each day, as our freedom and choices become more and more restricted, we plan our future. Our relationship is like a bridge we can cross from present worries to future joys. Plans, passion, promise. Maybe the turmoil around us gives us the opportunity for more commitment, less questioning. No one else knows what will come to pass, but we do. We have each other and the future, a life together we can see as clearly as we can see our hands when we join them. We go to the river one August day in 1943. He brings a camera and photographs me in my bathing suit, doing the splits in the grass. I imagine showing our children the picture one day. Telling them how we held our love and our commitment bright.

When I come home that day, my father is gone. He has been taken to the forced labor camp. He is a tailor, he is apolitical. How is he a threat to anyone? Why has he been targeted? Does he have an enemy? There are lots of things my mother won't tell me. Is it simply because she doesn't know? Or is she protecting me? Or herself? She doesn't talk openly about her worries, but in the long months that my father is away, I can feel how sad and scared she is. I see her trying to make several meals out of one chicken. She gets migraines. We take in a boarder to make up for the loss of income. He owns a store across the street from our apartment, and I sit long hours in his store just to be near his comforting presence.

Magda, who is essentially an adult now, who is no longer in school, finds out somehow where our father is and visits him. She watches him stagger under the weight of a table he has to heft from place to place. This is the only detail she tells me of her visit. I don't know what this image means. I don't know what work it is that my father is forced to do in his captivity, I don't know how long he will be a prisoner. I have two images of my father: one, as I have known him my entire life, cigarette hanging out of his mouth, tape measure around his neck, chalk in his hand for marking a pattern onto expensive cloth, his eyes twinkling, ready to burst into song, about to tell a joke. And this new one: lifting a table that is too heavy, in a no-name place, a no-man's-land.

On my sixteenth birthday, I stay home from school with a cold, and Eric comes to our apartment to deliver sixteen roses and my first sweet kiss. I am happy, but I am sad too. What can I hold on to? What lasts? I give the picture Eric took of me on the riverbank to a friend. I can't remember why. For safekeeping? I had no premonition that I would be gone soon, well before my next birthday. Yet somehow I must have known that I would need someone to preserve evidence of my life, that I would need to plant proof of my self around me like seeds.

Sometime in early spring, after seven or eight months at the work camp, my father returns. It is a grace—he has been released in time for Passover, which is just a week or two away. That's what we think. He takes up his tape measure and chalk again. He doesn't talk about where he has been.

I sit on the blue mat in the gymnastics studio one day, a few weeks after his return, warming up with a floor routine, pointing my toes, flexing my feet, lengthening my legs and arms and neck and back. I feel like myself again. I'm not the little cross-eyed runt afraid to speak her name. I'm not the daughter afraid for her family. I am an artist and an athlete, my body strong and limber. I don't have Magda's looks, or Klara's fame, but I have my lithe and expressive body, the budding existence of which is the only one true thing I need. My training, my skill—my life brims with possibility. The best of us in my gymnastics class have formed an Olympic training team. The 1944 Olympics have been canceled due to the war, but that just gives us more time to prepare to compete.

I close my eyes and stretch my arms and torso forward across my legs. My friend nudges me with her toe and I lift my head to see our coach walking straight toward me. We are half in love with her. It's not a sexual crush. It's hero worship. Sometimes we take the long way home so we can pass her house, where we go as slowly as possible along the sidewalk, hoping to catch a glimpse of her through the window. We are jealous of what we don't know of her life. With the promise of the Olympics when the war finally ends, much of my sense of purpose rests within the scope of my coach's support and faith in me. If I can manage to absorb all she has to teach me, and if I can fulfill her trust in me, then great things lie in store.

"Editke," she says as she approaches my mat, using my formal name, Edith, but adding a diminutive. "A word, please." Her fingers glide once over my back as she ushers me into the hall.

I look at her expectantly. Maybe she has noticed my improvements on the vault. Maybe she would like me to lead the team in more stretching exercises at the end of practice today. Maybe she wants to invite me over for supper. I'm ready to say yes before she has even asked.

"I don't know how to tell you this," she begins. She studies my face and then looks away toward the window where the dropping sun blazes in.

"Is it my sister?" I ask, before I even realize the terrible picture forming in my mind. Klara studies at the conservatory in Budapest now. Our mother has gone to Budapest to see Klara's concert and fetch her home for Passover, and as my coach stands awkwardly beside me in the hall, unable to meet my eyes, I worry that their train has derailed. It's too early in the week for them to be traveling home, but that is the only tragedy I can think of. Even in a time of war, the first disaster to cross my mind is a mechanical one, a tragedy of human error, not of human design, although I am aware that some of Klara's teachers, including some of the gentile ones, have already fled Europe because they fear what is to come.

"Your family is fine." Her tone doesn't reassure me. "Edith. This isn't my choice. But I must be the one to tell you that your place on the Olympic training team will go to someone else."

I think I might vomit. I feel foreign in my own skin. "What did I do?" I comb over the rigorous months of training for the thing I've done wrong. "I don't understand."

"My child," she says, and now she looks me full in the face, which is worse, because I can see that she is crying, and at this moment when my dreams are being shredded like newspaper at the butcher shop I do not want to feel pity for her. "The simple truth is that because of your background, you are no longer qualified."

I think of the kids who've spat at me and called me dirty Jew, of Jewish friends who have stopped going to school to avoid harassment and now get their courses over the radio. "If someone spits at you, spit back," my father has instructed me. "That's what you do." I consider spitting on my coach. But to fight back would be to accept her devastating news. I won't accept it.

"I'm not Jewish," I say.

"I'm sorry, Editke," she says. "I'm so sorry. I still want you at the studio. I would like to ask you to train the girl who will replace you on the team." Again, her fingers on my back. In another year, my back will be broken in exactly the spot she now caresses. Within weeks, my very life will be on the line. But here in the hallway of my cherished studio, my life feels like it is already over.

In the days that follow my expulsion from the Olympic training team, I plot my revenge. It won't be the revenge of hate; it will be the revenge of perfection. I will show my coach that I am the best. The most accomplished athlete. The best trainer. I will train my replacement so meticulously that I will prove what a mistake has been made by cutting me from the team. On the day that my mother and Klara are due back from Budapest, I cartwheel my way down the red-carpeted hall toward our apartment, imagining my replacement as my understudy, myself the headlining star.

My mother and Magda are in the kitchen. Magda's chopping apples for the *charoset*. Mother's mixing matzo meal. They glower over their work, barely registering my arrival. This is their relationship now. They fight all the time, and when they're not fighting they treat each other as though they are already in a face-off. Their arguments used to be about food, Mother always concerned about Magda's weight, but now the conflict has grown to a general and chronic hostility. "Where's Klarie?" I ask, swiping chopped walnuts from a bowl.

"Budapest," Magda says. My mother slams her bowl onto the counter. I want to ask why my sister isn't with us for the holiday. Has she really chosen music over us? Or was she not allowed to miss class for a holiday that none of her fellow students celebrates? But I don't ask. I am afraid my questions will bring my mother's obviously simmering anger to a boil. I retreat to the bedroom that we all share, my parents and Magda and me.

On any other evening, especially a holiday, we would gather around the piano, the instrument Magda had been playing and studying since she was young, where Magda and my father would take turns leading us in songs. Magda and I weren't prodigies like Klara, but we still had creative passions that our parents recognized and nurtured. After Magda played, it would be my turn to perform. "Dance, Dicuka!" my mother would say. And even though it was more a demand than an invitation, I'd savor my parents' attention and praise. Then Klara, the star attraction, would play her violin and my mother would look transformed. But there is no music in our house tonight. Before the meal, Magda tries to cheer me up by reminding me of seders past when I would stuff socks in my bra to impress Klara, wanting to show her that I'd become a woman while she was away. "Now you've got your own womanhood to flaunt around," Magda says. At the seder table she continues the antics, splashing her fingers around in the glass of wine we've set for Prophet Elijah, as is the custom. Elijah, who saves Jews from peril. On any other night our father might laugh, despite himself. On any other night our mother would end the silliness with a stern rebuke. But tonight our father is too distracted to notice, and our mother is too distraught by Klara's absence to chastise Magda. When we open the apartment door to let the prophet in, I feel a chill that has nothing to do with the cool evening. In some deep part of myself I know how badly we need protection now.

34

"You tried the consulate?" my father asks. He isn't even pretending to lead the seder anymore. No one but Magda can eat. "Ilona?"

"I tried the consulate," my mother says. It is as though she conducts her part in the conversation from another room.

"Tell me again what Klara said."

"Again?" my mother protests.

"Again."

She tells it blankly, her fingers fidgeting with her napkin. Klara had called her hotel at four that morning. Klara's professor had just told her that a former professor at the conservatory, Béla Bartók, now a famous composer, had called from America with a warning: The Germans in Czechoslovakia and Hungary were going to start closing their fist; Jews would be taken away come morning. Klara's professor forbade her to return home to Kassa. He wanted her to urge my mother to stay in Budapest as well and send for the rest of the family.

"Ilona, why did you come home?" my father moans.

My mother stabs her eyes at him. "What about all that we've worked for here? We should just leave it? And if you three couldn't make it to Budapest? You want me to live with that?"

I don't realize that they are terrified. I hear only the blame and disappointment that my parents routinely pass between them like the mindless shuttle on a loom. *Here's what you did. Here's what you didn't do. Here's what you did. Here's what you didn't do.* Later I'll learn that this isn't just their usual quarreling, that there's a history and a weight to the dispute they are having now. There are the tickets to America my father turned away. There is the Hungarian official who approached my mother with fake papers for the whole family, urging us to flee. Later we learn that they both had a chance to choose differently. Now they suffer with their regret, and they cover their regret in blame.

"Can we do the four questions?" I ask to disrupt my parents' gloom. That is my job in the family. To play peacemaker between my parents, between Magda and my mother. Whatever plans are being made outside our door I can't control. But inside our home, I have a role to fill. It is my job as the youngest child to ask the four questions. I don't even have to open my Haggadah. I know the text by heart. "Why is this night different from all other nights?" I begin.

At the end of the meal, my father circles the table, kissing each of us on the head. He's crying. *Why is this night different from all other nights?* Before dawn breaks, we'll know.

CHAPTER 2

What You Put in Your Mind

They come in the dark. They pound on the door, they yell. Does my father let them in, or do they force their way into our apartment? Are they German soldiers, or *nyilas*? I can't make sense out of the noises that startle me from sleep. My mouth still tastes of seder wine. The soldiers storm into the bedroom, announcing that we're being moved from our home and resettled somewhere else. We're allowed one suitcase for all four of us. I can't seem to find my legs to get off the cot where I sleep at the foot of my parents' bed, but my mother is instantly in motion. Before I know it she is dressed and reaching high into the closet for the little box that I know holds Klara's caul, the piece of amniotic sac that covered her head and face like a helmet when she was born. Midwives used to save cauls and sell them to sailors as protections against drowning. My mother doesn't trust the box to the suitcase—she tucks it deep into the pocket of her coat, a good luck totem. I don't know if my mother packs the caul to protect Klara, or all of us.

"Hurry, Dicu," she urges me. "Get up. Get dressed."

"Not that wearing clothes ever did your figure any good," Magda whispers. There's no reprieve from her teasing. How will I know when it's time to be really afraid?

My mother is in the kitchen now, packing leftover food, pots and pans. In fact, she will keep us alive for two weeks on the supplies she thinks to carry with us now—some flour, some chicken fat. My father paces the bedroom and living room, picking up books, candlesticks, clothing, putting things down. "Get blankets," my mother calls to him. I think that if he had one petit four that is the thing he would take along, if only for the joy of handing it to me later, of seeing a swift second of delight on my face. Thank goodness my mother is more practical. When she was still a child, she became a mother to her younger siblings, and she staved their hunger through many seasons of grief. *As God is my witness*, I imagine her thinking now, as she packs, *I'm never going to be hungry again.* And yet I want her to drop the dishes, the survival tools, and come back to the bedroom to help me dress. Or at least I want her to call to me. To tell me what to wear. To tell me not to worry. To tell me all is well.

The soldiers stomp their boots, knock chairs over with their guns. Hurry. Hurry. I feel a sudden anger with my mother. She would save Klara before she would save me. She'd rather cull the pantry than hold my hand in the dark. I'll have to find my own sweetness, my own luck. Despite the chill of the dark April morning, I put on a thin blue silk dress, the one I wore when Eric kissed me. I trace the pleats with my fingers. I fasten the narrow blue suede belt. I will wear this dress so that his arms can once again encircle me. This dress will keep me desirable, protected, ready to reclaim love. If I shiver, it will be a badge of hope, a signal of my trust in something deeper, better. I picture Eric and his family also dressing and scrambling in the dark. I can feel him thinking of me. A current of energy shoots down from my ears to my toes. I close my eyes and cup my elbows with my hands, allowing the afterglow of that flash of love and hope to keep me warm.

But the ugly present intrudes on my private world. "Where are the bathrooms?" one of the soldiers shouts at Magda. My bossy, sarcastic, flirtatious sister cowers under his glare. I've never known her to be afraid. She's never spared an opportunity to get a rise out of someone, to make people laugh. Authority figures have never held any power over her. In school she wouldn't stand up, as required, when a teacher entered the room. "Elefánt," her math teacher, a very short man, reprimanded her one day, calling her by our last name. My sister got up on tiptoes and peered at him. "Oh, are you there?" she said. "I didn't see you." But today the men hold guns. She gives no crude remark, no rebellious comeback. She points meekly down the hall toward the bathroom door. The soldier shoves her out of his way. He holds a gun. What other proof of his dominance does he need? This is when I start to see that it can always be so much worse. That every moment harbors a potential for violence. We never know when or how we will break. Doing what you're told might not save you.

"Out. Now. Time for you to take a little trip," the soldiers say. My mother closes the suitcase and my father lifts it. She fastens her gray coat and is the first to follow the commanding officer out into the street. I'm next, then Magda. Before we reach the wagon that sits ready for us at the curb, I turn to watch our father leave our home. He stands facing the door, suitcase in his hand, looking muddled, a midnight traveler patting down his pockets for his keys. A soldier yells a jagged insult and kicks our door back open with his heel.

"Go ahead," he says, "take a last look. Feast your eyes."

My father gazes at the dark space. For a moment he seems confused, as though he can't determine whether the soldier has been generous or unkind. Then the soldier kicks him in the knee and my father hobbles toward us, toward the wagon where the other families wait.

I'm caught between the urge to protect my parents and the sorrow that they can no longer protect me. *Eric*, I pray, *wherever we are going, help me find you. Don't forget our future. Don't forget our love.* Magda doesn't say a word as we sit side by side on the bare board seats. In my catalog of regrets, this one shines bright: that I didn't reach for my sister's hand.

Just as daylight breaks, the wagon pulls up alongside the Jakab brick factory at the edge of town, and we are herded inside. We are the lucky ones; early arrivers get quarters in the drying sheds. Most of the nearly twelve thousand Jews imprisoned here will sleep without a roof over their heads. All of us will sleep on the floor. We will cover ourselves with our coats and shiver through the spring chill. We will cover our ears when, for minor offenses, people are beaten with rubber truncheons at the center of the camp. There is no running water here. Buckets come, never enough of them, on horse-drawn carts. At first the rations, combined with the pancakes my mother makes from the scraps she brought from home, are enough to feed us, but after only a few days the hunger pains become a constant cramping throb. Magda sees her old gym teacher in the barracks next door, struggling to take care of a newborn baby in these starvation conditions. "What will I do when my milk is gone?" she moans to us. "My baby just cries and cries."

There are two sides to the camp, on either side of a street. Our side is occupied by the Jews from our section of town. We learn that all of Kassa's Jews are being held here at the brick factory. We find our neighbors, our shopkeepers, our teachers, our friends. But my grandparents, whose home was a thirty-minute walk from our apartment, are not on our side of the camp. Gates and guards separate us from the other side. We are not supposed to cross over. But I plead with a guard and he says I can go in search of my grandparents. I walk the wall-less barracks, quietly repeating their names. As I pace up and down the rows of huddled families, I say Eric's name too. I tell myself that it is only a matter of time and perseverance. I will find him, or he will find me.

I don't find my grandparents. I don't find Eric.

And then one afternoon when the water carts arrive and the crowds rush to scoop a little pail of it, he spies me sitting alone, guarding my family's coats. He kisses my forehead, my cheeks, my lips. I touch the suede belt of my silk dress, praising it for its good luck.

We manage to meet every day after that. Sometimes we speculate about what will befall us. Rumors spread that we will be sent to a place called Kenyérmező, an internment camp, where we will work and live out the war with our families. We don't know that the rumor was started by the Hungarian police and *nyilas* dishing out false hope. After the war, piles of letters from concerned relatives in faraway cities will sit in stacks in post offices, unopened; the address lines read: *Kenyérmező*. No such place exists.

The places that do exist, that await our coming trains, are beyond imagining. *After the war.* That is the time Eric and I allow ourselves to think about. We will go to the university. We will move to Palestine. We will continue the salons and book club we began at school. We will finish reading Freud's *Interpretation of Dreams.*

From inside the brick factory we can hear the streetcars trundle past. They are within reach. How easy it could be to jump aboard. But anyone who comes close to the outer fence is shot without warning. A girl only a little older than me tries to run. They hang her body in the middle of the camp as an example. My parents don't say a word to me or Magda about her death. "Try to get a little block of sugar," my father tells us. "Get a block of sugar and hold on to it. Always keep a little something sweet in your pocket." One day we hear that my grandparents have been sent away in one of the first transports to leave the factory. We'll see them in Kenyérmező, we think. I kiss Eric good night and trust that his lips are the sweetness I can count on.

One early morning, after we have been in the factory for about a month, our section of the camp is evacuated. I scramble to find someone who can pass a message to Eric. "Let it go, Dicu," my mother says. She and my father have written a goodbye letter to Klara, but there is no way to send it. I watch my mother throw it away, see her drop it onto the pavement like ash from a cigarette, see it disappear under three thousand pairs of feet. The silk of my dress brushes against my legs as we surge and stop and surge and stop, three thousand of us marched toward the factory gates, pressed into a long row of waiting trucks. Again we huddle in the dark. Just before the truck pulls away, I hear my name. It's Eric. He's calling through the slats of the truck. I shove my way toward his voice.

"I'm here!" I call as the engine starts. The slats are too narrow for me to see him or touch him.

"I'll never forget your eyes," he says. "I'll never forget your hands."

I repeat those sentences ceaselessly as we board a crowded car at the train station. I can't hear the shouting officers or crying children over the salve of his remembered voice. *If I survive today, then I can show him my eyes, I can show him my hands.* I breathe to the rhythm of this chant. *If I survive today . . . If I survive today, tomorrow I'll be free.*

The train car is like none I've ever been in. It's not a passenger train; it's for transporting livestock or freight. We are human cargo. There are a hundred of us in one car. Each hour feels like a week. The uncertainty makes the moments stretch. The uncertainty and the relentless noise of the wheels on the track. There is one loaf of bread for eight people to share. One bucket of water. One bucket for our bodily waste. It smells of sweat and excrement. People die on the way. We all sleep upright, leaning against our family members, shouldering aside the dead. I see a father give something to his daughter, a packet of pills. "If they try to do anything to you . . ." he says. Occasionally the train stops and a few people from each car are ordered to get out to fetch water. Magda takes the bucket once. "We're in Poland," she tells us when she returns. Later she explains how she knows. When she went for water, a man out in his field had yelled a greeting to her in Polish and in German, telling her the name of the town and gesturing frantically, drawing his finger across his neck. "Just trying to scare us," Magda says.

The train moves on and on. My parents slump on either side of me. They don't speak. I never see them touch. My father's beard is growing in gray. He looks older than his father, and it frightens me. I beg him to shave. I have no way of knowing that youthfulness could indeed save a life when we reach the end of this journey. It's just a gut feeling, just a girl missing the father she knows, longing for him to be the bon vivant again, the debonair flirt, the ladies' man. I don't want him to become like the father with the pills who mutters to his family, "This is worse than death."

But when I kiss my father's cheek and say, "Papa, please shave," he answers me with anger. "What for?" he says. "What for? What for?" I'm ashamed that I've said the wrong thing and made him annoyed with me. Why did I say the wrong thing? Why did I think it was my job to tell my father what to do? I remember his rage when I lost the tuition money for school. I lean against my mother for comfort. I wish my parents would reach for each other instead of sitting as strangers. My mother doesn't say much. But she doesn't moan either. She doesn't wish to be dead. She simply goes inside herself.

"Dicuka," she says into the dark one night, "listen. We don't know where we're going. We don't know what's going to happen. Just remember, no one can take away from you what you've put in your mind."

I fall into another dream of Eric. I wake again.

They open the cattle car doors and the bright May sun slashes in.
We are desperate to get out. We rush toward the air and the light.
We practically fall out of the car, tumbling against one another in
our hurry to descend. After several days of the ceaseless motion
of the train, it's hard to stand upright on firm ground. In every
way we are trying to get our bearings—piece out our location,
steady our nerves and our limbs. I see the crowded dark of
winter coats amassed on a narrow stretch of dirt. I see the flash
of white in someone's scarf or cloth bundle of belongings, the
yellow of the mandatory stars. I see the sign: ARBEIT MACHT FREI.
Music plays. My father is suddenly cheerful. "You see," he says,
"it can't be a terrible place." He looks as though he would dance
if the platform weren't so crowded. "We'll only work a little, till
the war's over," he says. The rumors we heard at the brick factory
must be true. We must be here to work. I search for the ripple
of nearby fields and imagine Eric's lean body across from me,
bending to tend a crop. Instead I see unbroken horizontal lines:
the boards on the cattle cars, the endless wire of a fence, low-
slung buildings. In the distance, a few trees and chimneys break
the flat plane of this barren place.

Men in uniform push among us. Nobody explains anything.
They just bark simple directions. *Go here. Go there.* The Nazis
point and shove. The men are herded into a separate line. I see
my father wave to us. Maybe they're being sent ahead to stake
out a place for their families. I wonder where we'll sleep tonight.
I wonder when we'll eat. My mother and Magda and I stand
together in a long line of women and children. We inch forward.
We approach the man who with a conductor's wave of a finger
will deliver us to our fates. I do not yet know that this man is Dr.

Josef Mengele, the infamous Angel of Death. As we advance toward him, I can't look away from his eyes, so domineering, so cold. When we've drawn nearer, I can see a boyish flash of gapped teeth when he grins. His voice is almost kind when he asks if anyone is sick, and sends those who say yes to the left.

"If you're over fourteen and under forty, stay in this line," another officer says. "Over forty, move left." A long line of the elderly and children and mothers holding babies branches off to the left. My mother has gray hair, all gray, early gray, but her face is as smooth and unlined as mine. Magda and I squeeze our mother between us.

It's our turn now. Dr. Mengele conducts. He points my mother to the left. I start to follow her. He grabs my shoulder. "You're going to see your mother very soon," he says. "She's just going to take a shower." He pushes Magda and me to the right.

We don't know the meaning of left versus right. "Where are we going now?" we ask each other. "What will happen to us?" We're marched to a different part of the sparse campus. Only women surround us, most young. Some look bright, almost giddy, glad to be breathing fresh air and enjoying the sun on their skin after the relentless stench and claustrophobic dark of the train. Others chew their lips. Fear circulates among us, but curiosity too.

We're stopped in front of more low buildings. Women in striped dresses stand around us. We soon learn that they are the inmates charged with governing the others, but we don't know yet that we're prisoners here. I've unbuttoned my coat in the steady sun and one of the girls in a striped dress eyes my blue silk. She walks toward me, cocking her head.

"Well, look at you," she says in Polish. She kicks dust on my low-heeled shoes. Before I realize what's happening, she reaches for the tiny coral earrings set in gold that, in keeping with Hungarian custom, have been in my ears since birth. She yanks and I feel a sharp sting. She pockets the earrings.

In spite of the physical hurt, I feel desperate for her to like me. As ever, I want to belong. Her humiliating sneer hurts more than my ripped earlobes. "Why did you do that?" I say. "I would have given you the earrings."

"I was rotting here while you were free, going to school, going to the theater," she says.

I wonder how long she's been here. She's thin, but sturdy. She stands tall. She could be a dancer. I wonder why she seems so angry that I have reminded her of normal life. "When will I see my mother?" I ask her. "I was told I'd see her soon."

She gives me a cold, sharp stare. There is no empathy in her eyes. There is nothing but rage. She points to the smoke rising up from one of the chimneys in the distance. "Your mother is burning in there," she says. "You better start talking about her in the past tense."

CHAPTER 3

Dancing in Hell

"All your ecstasy in life is going to come from the inside," my ballet master had told me. I never understood what he meant. Until Auschwitz.

Magda stares at the chimney on top of the building our mother entered. "The soul never dies," she says. My sister finds words of comfort. But I am in shock. I am numb. I can't think about the incomprehensible things that are happening, that have already happened. I can't picture my mother consumed by flames. I can't fully grasp that she is gone. And I can't ask why. I can't even grieve. Not now. It will take all of my attention to survive the next minute, the next breath. I will survive if my sister is there. I will survive by attaching myself to her as though I am her shadow.

We are herded through the silent yet echoing showers. We are robbed of our hair. We stand outside, shorn and naked, waiting for our uniforms. Taunts from the kapos and SS officers swarm us like arrows grazing our bare, wet skin. Worse than their words are their eyes. I'm sure the disgust with which they glare at us could tear my skin, split my ribs. Their hate is both possessive and dismissive, and it makes me ill. Once I thought that Eric would be the first man to see me naked. Now he will never see my flesh unscarred by their hatred. Have they already made me something less than human? Will I ever resemble the girl I was? *I will never forget your eyes, your hands.* I have to keep myself together, if not for myself then for Eric.

I turn to my sister, who has fallen into her own shocked silence, who has managed in each chaotic dash from place to place, in every crowded line, not to leave my side. She shivers as the sun falls. She holds in her hands her shorn locks, thick strands of her ruined hair. We have been standing naked for hours, and she grips her hair as though in holding it she can hold on to herself, her humanity. She is so near that we are almost touching, and yet I long for her. Magda. The confident, sexy girl with all the jokes. Where is she? She seems to be asking the same question. She searches for herself in her ragged clumps of hair.

The contradictions in this place unnerve me. Murder, we've just learned, is efficient here. Systematic. But there seems to be no system in place for distributing the uniforms for which we've been waiting most of the day. The guards are cruel and rigid, yet it seems that no one is in charge. The scrutiny they give our bodies doesn't signal our value, it signifies only the degree to which we have been forgotten by the world. Nothing makes sense. But this, too, the interminable waiting, the complete absence of reason, must be part of the design. How can I keep myself steady in a place where the only steadiness is in fences, in death, in humiliation, in the steadily churning smoke?

Magda finally speaks to me. "How do I look?" she asks. "Tell me the truth."

The truth? She looks like a mangy dog. A naked stranger. I can't tell her this, of course, but any lie would hurt too much and so I must find an impossible answer, a truth that doesn't wound. I gaze into the fierce blue of her eyes and think that even for her to ask the question, "How do I look?" is the bravest thing I've ever heard. There aren't mirrors here. She is asking me to help her find and face herself. And so I tell her the one true thing that's mine to say.

"Your eyes," I tell my sister, "they're so beautiful. I never noticed them when they were covered up by all that hair." It's the first time I see that we have a choice: to pay attention to what we've lost or to pay attention to what we still have.

"Thank you," she whispers.

The other things I want to ask her, tell her, seem better left wordless. Words can't give shape to this new reality. To the gray coat of my mama's shoulder as I lean on her and the train goes on and on. To my papa's face overgrown with shadow. To what I wouldn't give to have those dark and hungry hours back again. To the transformation of my parents into smoke. Both of my parents. I must assume my father is dead too. I am about to muster a voice to ask Magda if we dare hope that we haven't been totally orphaned in the space of a day, but I see that Magda has let her hair fall out of her fingers and onto the dusty ground.

They bring the uniforms—gray, ill-fitting dresses made of scratchy cotton and wool. The sky is going dark. They herd us to the gloomy, primitive barracks where we will sleep on tiered shelves, six to a board. It is a relief to go into the ugly room, to lose sight of the endlessly smoking chimney. The kapo, the young woman who stole my earrings, assigns us bunks and explains the rules. No one is allowed outside at night. There is the bucket—our nighttime bathroom. With our bunkmates, Magda and I try lying on our board on the top tier. We discover there's more room if we alternate heads and feet. Still, no one person can roll over or adjust her position without displacing someone else. We work out a system for rolling together, coordinating our turns. The kapo distributes a bowl to each new inmate. "Don't lose it," she warns. "If you don't have a bowl, you don't eat." In the darkening barracks, we stand waiting for the next command. Will we be fed a meal? Will we be sent to sleep? We hear music. I think I must be imagining the sound of woodwinds and strings, but another inmate explains there is a camp orchestra here, led by a world-class violinist. *Klara!* I think. But the violinist she mentions is Viennese.

We hear clipped voices speaking German outside the barracks. The kapo pulls herself straight as the door rattles open. There on the threshold I recognize the uniformed officer from the selection line. I know it's him, the way he smiles with his lips parted, the gap between his front teeth. Dr. Mengele, we learn. He is a refined killer and a lover of the arts. He trawls among the barracks in the evenings, searching for talented inmates to entertain him. He walks in tonight with his entourage of assistants and casts his gaze like a net over the new arrivals with our baggy dresses and our hastily shorn hair. We stand still, backs to the wooden bunks that edge the room. He examines us. Magda ever so subtly grazes my hand with hers. Dr. Mengele barks out a question, and before I know what is happening, the girls standing nearest me, who know I trained as a ballerina and gymnast back in Kassa, push me forward, closer to the Angel of Death.

He studies me. I don't know where to put my eyes. I stare straight ahead at the open door. The orchestra is assembled just outside. They are silent, awaiting orders. I feel like Eurydice in the underworld, waiting for Orpheus to strike a chord on his lyre that can melt the heart of Hades and set me free. Or I am Salome, made to dance for her stepfather, Herod, lifting veil after veil to expose her flesh. Does the dance give her power, or does the dance strip it away?

"Little dancer," Dr. Mengele says, "dance for me." He directs the musicians to begin playing. The familiar opening strain of "The Blue Danube" waltz filters into the dark, close room. Mengele's eyes bulge at me. I'm lucky. I know a routine to "The Blue Danube" that I can dance in my sleep. But my limbs are heavy, as in a nightmare when there's danger and you can't run away. "Dance!" he commands again, and I feel my body start to move.

First the high kick. Then the pirouette and turn. The splits. And up. As I step and bend and twirl, I can hear Mengele talking to his assistant. He never takes his eyes off me, but he attends to his duties as he watches. I can hear his voice over the music. He discusses with the other officer which ones of the hundred girls present will be killed next. If I miss a step, if I do anything to displease him, it could be me. I dance. I dance. I am dancing in hell. I can't bear to see the executioner as he decides our fates. I close my eyes.

I focus on my routine, on my years of training—each line and curve of my body like a syllable in verse, my body telling a story: A girl arrives at a dance. She spins in excitement and anticipation. Then she pauses to reflect and observe. What will happen in the hours ahead? Whom will she meet? She turns toward a fountain, arms sweeping up and around to embrace the scene. She bends to pick up flowers and tosses them one at a time to her admirers and fellow revelers, throwing flowers to the people, handing out tokens of love. I can hear the violins swell. My heart races. In the private darkness within, I hear my mother's words come back to me, as though she is there in the barren room, whispering below the music. *Just remember, no one can take away from you what you've put in your own mind.* Dr. Mengele, my fellow starved-to-the-bone inmates, the defiant who will survive and the soon to be dead, even my beloved sister disappear, and the only world that exists is the one inside my head. "The Blue Danube" fades, and now I can hear Tchaikovsky's *Romeo and Juliet*. The barracks's floor becomes a stage at the Budapest opera house. I dance for my fans in the audience. I dance within the glow of hot lights. I dance for my lover, Romeo, as he lifts me high above the stage. I dance for love. I dance for life.

As I dance, I discover a piece of wisdom that I have never forgotten. I will never know what miracle of grace allows me this insight. It will save my life many times, even after the horror is over. I can see that Dr. Mengele, the seasoned killer who just this morning murdered my mother, is more pitiful than me. I am free in my mind, which he can never be. He will always have to live with what he's done. He is more a prisoner than I am. As I close my routine with a final, graceful split, I pray, but it isn't myself I pray for. I pray for him. I pray, for his sake, that he won't have the need to kill me.

He must be impressed by my performance, because he tosses me a loaf of bread—a gesture, as it turns out, that will later save my life. As evening turns to night, I share the bread with Magda and our bunkmates. I am grateful to have bread. I am grateful to be alive.

In my first weeks at Auschwitz I learn the rules of survival. If you can steal a piece of bread from the guards, you are a hero, but if you steal from an inmate, you are disgraced, you die; competition and domination get you nowhere, cooperation is the name of the game; to survive is to transcend your own needs and commit yourself to someone or something outside yourself. For me, that someone is Magda, that something is the hope that I will see Eric again tomorrow, when I am free. To survive, we conjure an inner world, a haven, even when our eyes are open. I remember a fellow inmate who managed to save a picture of herself from before internment, a picture in which she had long hair. She was able to remind herself who she was, that that person still existed. This awareness became a refuge that preserved her will to live.

I remember that some months later, in winter, we were issued old coats. They just tossed us the coats, willy-nilly, with no attention to size. It was up to us to find the one with the best fit and fight for it. Magda was lucky. They threw her a thick warm coat, long and heavy, with buttons all the way up to the neck. It was so warm, so coveted. But she traded it instantly. The coat she chose in its place was a flimsy little thing, barely to the knees, showing off plenty of chest. For Magda, wearing something sexy was a better survival tool than staying warm. Feeling attractive gave her something inside, a sense of dignity, more valuable to her than physical comfort.

I remember that even when we were starving, we would feast. We cooked all the time at Auschwitz. In our heads, we were having celebrations at every hour, fighting over how much paprika you put in Hungarian chicken paprikash, or how to make the best seven-layer chocolate cake. We'd wake at 4:00 A.M. for the *Appell*, the roll call, stand in the freezing dark to be counted, and recounted, and we'd smell the rich, full aroma of cooking meat. Marching to our daily labor—to a warehouse called Canada, where we were ordered to sort the belongings of the newly arrived inmates; to the barracks that we had to clean and clean and clean; or to the crematoriums, where the unluckiest were forced to harvest gold teeth and hair and skin from the corpses waiting to be burned—we talked as though we were heading to market, planning our weekly menu, how we would test each fruit and vegetable for ripeness. We'd give one another cooking lessons. Here's how to make *palacsinta*, Hungarian crêpes. How thin the pancake must be. How much sugar to use. How many nuts. Do you put caraway in your *székely gulyás*? Do you use two onions? No, three. No, just one and a half. We'd salivate over our imaginary dishes, and as we ate our one actual meal of the day—watery soup, a stale piece of bread—I would talk about the goose my mother kept in the attic and fed with corn each day, its liver bulging, more and more, until it was time to slaughter the goose and blend its liver into pâté. And when we fell onto our bunks at night and finally slept, we dreamt of food then too. The village clock chimes 10:00 A.M., and my father slips into our apartment with a package from the butcher across the street. Today, a cut of pork hidden in newspaper. "Dicuka, come taste," he beckons. "What a role model you are," my mother gripes, "feeding a Jewish girl pork." But she is almost smiling. She's making strudel, stretching the phyllo dough over the dining room table, working it with her hands and blowing underneath it till it's paper thin.

The tang of peppers and cherries in my mother's strudel; her deviled eggs; the pasta she cut by hand, so fast I feared she'd lose a finger; especially the challah, our Friday night bread. For my mother, food was as much about the artistry of creating it as it was about enjoying the finished meal. Food fantasies sustained us at Auschwitz. Just as athletes and musicians can become better at their craft through mental practice, we were barracks artists, always in the thick of creating. What we made in our minds provided its own kind of sustenance.

One night we enact a beauty pageant in the barracks before bed. We model in our gray, shapeless dresses, our dingy underwear. There's a Hungarian saying that beauty is all in the shoulders. Nobody can strike a pose like Magda. She wins the pageant. But no one is ready for sleep.

"Here's a better competition," Magda says. "Who's got the best boobs?"

We strip in the dark and parade around with our chests sticking out. Mere months ago I was working out for more than five hours a day in the studio. I would ask my father to beat my stomach to feel how strong I was. I could even pick him up and carry him. I feel that pride in my body now, topless and freezing in the barracks. I used to envy my mother's round, inviting bosom and feel embarrassed by my tiny breasts. But this is how we prized them in Europe. I strut around in the dark like a model. And I win the contest!

"My famous sister," Magda says as we drift off to sleep.

We can choose what the horror teaches us. To become bitter in our grief and fear. Hostile. Paralyzed. Or to hold on to the childlike part of us, the lively and curious part, the part that is innocent.

Another night I learn that the young woman in the bunk next to mine was married before the war. I pump her for information. "What is it like?" I ask. "To belong to a man?" I'm not asking about sex, not entirely. Of course passion interests me. More so, the idea of daily belonging. In her sigh I hear the echo of something beautiful, unharmed by loss. For a few minutes, as she talks, I see marriage not as my parents lived it but as something luminous. It's brighter even than the peaceful comfort of my grandparents' affection. It sounds like love, whole love.

When my mother said to me, "I'm glad you have brains because you have no looks," those words stoked my fear that I was inadequate, worthless. But at Auschwitz, my mother's voice rang in my ears with a different significance. *I've got brains. I'm smart. I'm going to figure things out.* The words I heard inside my head made a tremendous difference in my ability to maintain hope. This was true for other inmates as well. We were able to discover an inner strength we could draw on—a way to talk to ourselves that helped us feel free inside, that kept us grounded in our own morality, that gave us foundation and assurance even when the external forces sought to control and obliterate us. *I'm good,* we learned to say. *I'm innocent. Somehow, something good will come of this.*

I knew a girl at Auschwitz who was very ill and wasting away. Every morning I expected to find her dead on her bunk, and I feared at every selection line that she'd be sent toward death. But she surprised me. She managed to gather strength each morning to work another day and kept a lively spark in her eyes each time she faced Mengele's pointing finger in a selection line. At night she would collapse onto her bunk, breathing in rasps. I asked her how she was managing to go on. "I heard we're going to be liberated by Christmas," she said. She kept a meticulous calendar in her head, counting down the days and then the hours until our liberation, determined to live to be free.

Then Christmas came, but our liberators did not. And she died the next day. I believe that her inner voice of hope kept her alive, but when she lost hope she wasn't able to keep living. While nearly everyone around me—SS officers, kapos, fellow inmates—told me every moment of every day, from *Appell* to the end of the workday, from selection lines to meal lines, that I would never get out of the death camp alive, I worked to develop an inner voice that offered an alternative story. *This is temporary*, I'd tell myself. *If I survive today, tomorrow I will be free.*

We were sent to the showers every day at Auschwitz, and every shower was fraught with uncertainty. We never knew whether water or gas would stream out of the tap. One day when I feel the water falling down on us, I let out my breath. I spread greasy soap over my body. I'm not skin and bones yet. Here in the quiet after the fear, I can recognize myself. My arms and thighs and stomach are still taut with my dancer muscles. I slip into a fantasy of Eric. We are university students now, living in Budapest. We take our books to study at a café. His eyes leave the page and travel over my face. I feel him pausing over my eyes and lips. Just as I imagine lifting my face to receive his kiss, I realize how quiet the shower room has become. I feel a chill in my gut. The man I fear above all others stands at the door. The Angel of Death is gazing right at me. I stare at the floor, waiting for the others to begin breathing again so that I know he is gone. But he doesn't leave.

"You!" he calls. "My little dancer."

I try to hear Eric's voice more loudly than Mengele's. *I'll never forget your eyes. I'll never forget your hands.*

"Come," he orders.

I follow. What else can I do? I walk toward the buttons on his coat, avoiding the eyes of my fellow inmates, because I can't stand the thought of seeing my fear mirrored there. *Breathe, breathe,* I tell myself. He leads me, naked and wet, down a hall and into an office with a desk, a chair. Water runs from my body onto the cold floor. He leans against the desk and looks me over, taking his time. I am too terrified to think, but little currents of impulse move through my body like reflexes. Kick him. A high kick to the face. Drop to the floor in a little ball and hold myself tight. I hope that whatever he plans to do to me will be over quickly.

"Come closer," he says.

I face him as I inch forward, but I don't see him. I focus only on the living part of me, the *yes I can, yes I can.* I feel his body as I near him. A menthol smell. The taste of tin can on my tongue. As long as I'm shaking, I know I'm alive. His fingers work over his buttons. *Yes I can, yes I can.* I think of my mama and her long, long hair. The way she'd wind it up on top of her head and let it down like a curtain at night. I'm naked with her murderer, but he can't ever take her away. Just as I am close enough for him to touch me, with fingers that I determine not to feel, a phone rings in another room. He flinches. He rebuttons his coat.

"Don't move," he orders as he opens the door.

I hear him pick up the phone in the next room, his voice neutral and curt. I don't make a decision. I run. The next thing I know I'm sitting beside my sister as we devour the daily ladle of soup, the little pieces of potato skin in the weak broth bobbing up at us like scabs. The fear that he will find me again and punish me, that he will finish what he started, that he will select me for death never leaves me. It never goes away. I don't know what will happen next. But in the meantime I can keep myself alive inside. *I survived today*, I chant in my head. *I survived today. Tomorrow I will be free.*

CHAPTER 4

A Cartwheel

At some point in the summer of 1944, Magda and I realize that no more Hungarian Jews are arriving at the camp. Later we will learn that in July, Prime Minister Horthy, tired of bowing to German authority, put the deportations on hold. He was too late. Hundreds of thousands of us had already been sent to the camps, four hundred thousand of us killed in two short months. By October, Horthy's government fell to the Nazis. The two hundred thousand Jews still remaining in Hungary—mostly in Budapest—weren't sent to Auschwitz. They were force-marched two hundred miles to Austria. But we didn't know any of this then, we didn't know anything of life or the war outside.

One winter morning, we stand in yet another line. The cold bites. We are to be tattooed. I wait my turn. I roll up my sleeve. I present my arm. I am responding automatically, making the motions required of me, so cold and hungry, so cold and hungry that I am almost numb. *Does anyone know I'm here?* I used to wonder that all the time, and now the question comes at me sluggishly, as if through a dense and constant fog. I can't remember how I used to think. I have to remind myself to picture Eric, but if I think about him too consciously, I can't re-create his face. I have to trick myself into memory, catch myself unawares. *Where's*

Magda? That's the first thing I ask when I wake, when we march to work, before we crash into sleep. I dart my eyes around to confirm that she's still behind me. Even if our eyes don't meet, I know that she is also keeping watch for me. I've begun saving my bread at the evening meal so we can share it in the morning.

The officer with the needle and ink is right in front of me now. He grabs my wrist and starts to prick, but then shoves me aside. "I'm not going to waste the ink on you," he says. He pushes me into a different line.

"This line is death," the girl nearest me says. "This is the end." She is completely gray, as though she's covered in dust. Someone ahead of us in the line is praying. In a place where the threat of death is constant, this moment still pierces me. I think suddenly about the difference between deadly and deadening. Auschwitz is both. The chimneys smoke and smoke. Any moment could be the last one. So why care? Why invest? And yet, if this moment, this very one, is my last on Earth, do I have to waste it in resignation and defeat? Must I spend it as if I'm already dead?

"We never know what the lines mean," I tell the girl nearest me. What if the unknown could make us curious instead of gut us with fear? And then I see Magda. She's been selected for a different line. If I'm sent to die, if I'm sent to work, if they evacuate me to a different camp as they've begun to do to others . . . nothing matters except that I stay with my sister, that she stay with me. We are of the few, the lucky inmates who have not yet been completely cut off from our families. It is no exaggeration to say that I live for my sister. It is no exaggeration to say that my sister lives for me. There is chaos in the yard. I don't know what the lines mean. The only thing I know is that

I must pass to whatever lies ahead *with Magda*. Even if what lies ahead is death. I eye the gap of crusted-over snow that separates us. Guards ring us. I don't have a plan. Time is slow and time is fast. Magda and I share a glance. I see her blue eyes. And then I am in motion. I am doing cartwheels, hands to earth, feet to sky, around, around. A guard stares at me. He's right side up. He's upside down. I expect a bullet any second. And I don't want to die, but I can't keep myself from turning around again and again. He doesn't raise his gun. Is he too surprised to shoot me? Am I too dizzy to see? He winks at me. I swear I see him wink. *Okay*, he seems to say, *this time, you win*.

In the few seconds that I hold his complete attention, Magda runs across the yard into my line to join me. We melt back into the crowd of girls waiting for whatever will happen next.

We're herded across the icy yard toward the train platform where we arrived six months before, where we parted from our father, where we walked with our mother between us in the final moments of her life. Music played then; it's silent now. If wind is silence. The constant rush of burdensome cold, the wide-open sighing mouth of death and winter no longer sound like noise to me. My head teems with questions and dread, but these thoughts are so enduring they don't feel like thoughts anymore. It is always almost the end.

We're just going to a place to work until the end of the war, we have been told. If we could hear even two minutes of news, we would know that the war itself might be the next casualty. As we stand there waiting to climb the narrow ramp into the cattle car, the Russians are approaching Poland from one side, the Americans

from the other. The Nazis are evacuating Auschwitz bit by bit.
The inmates we are leaving behind, those who can survive one
more month at Auschwitz, will soon be free. We sit in the dark,
waiting for the train to pull away. A soldier—Wehrmacht, not
SS—puts his head in the door and speaks to us in Hungarian.
"You have to eat," he says. "No matter what they do, remember
to eat, because you might get free, maybe soon." Is this hope
he's offering us? Or false promise? A lie? This soldier is like the
nyilas at the brick factory, spreading rumors, a voice of authority
to silence our inner knowing. Who reminds a starving person
to eat?

But even in the dark of the cattle car, his face backlit by miles
of fence, miles of snow, I can tell that his eyes are kind. How
strange that kindness now seems like a trick of the light.

I lose track of the time we are in motion. I sleep on Magda's
shoulder, she on mine. Once I wake to my sister's voice. She is
talking to someone I can't make out in the dark. "My teacher,"
she explains. The one from the brick factory, the one whose
baby had cried and cried. At Auschwitz, all the women with
small children were gassed from the start. The fact that she is
still alive can mean only one thing: her baby died. Which is worse,
I wonder, to be a child who has lost her mother or a mother who
has lost her child? When the door opens, we're in Germany.

There are no more than a hundred of us. We're housed in what
must be a children's summer camp, with bunk beds and a kitchen
where, with scant provisions, we prepare our own meals.

In the morning, we are sent to work in a thread factory. We
wear leather gloves. We stop the spinning machine wheels to

keep the threads from running together. Even with the gloves on, the wheels slice our hands. Magda's former teacher sits at a wheel next to Magda. She is crying loudly. I think it's because her hands are bleeding and sore. But she is weeping for Magda. "You need your hands," she moans. "You play piano. What will you do without your hands?"

The German forewoman who oversees our work silences her. "You're lucky to be working now," she says. "Soon you will be killed."

In the kitchen that night we prepare our evening meal supervised by guards. "We've escaped the gas chamber," Magda says, "but we'll die making thread." It's funny because we *are* alive. We might not survive the war, but we have survived Auschwitz. I peel potatoes for our supper. Too accustomed to starvation rations, I am unable to waste any scrap of food. I hide the potato skins in my underwear. When the guards are in another room, I toast the peels in the oven. When we lift them eagerly to our mouths with our aching hands, the skins are still too hot to eat.

"We've escaped the gas chamber, but we'll die eating potato peels," someone says, and we laugh from a deep place in us that we didn't know still existed. We laugh, as I did every week at Auschwitz when we were forced to donate our blood for transfusions for wounded German soldiers. I would sit with the needle in my arm and humor myself. *Good luck winning a war with my pacifist dancer's blood!* I'd think. I couldn't yank my arm away, or I'd have been shot. I couldn't defy my oppressors with a gun or a fist. But I could find a way to my own power. And there's power in our laughter now. Our camaraderie, our lightheartedness reminds me of the night at Auschwitz when I won the boob contest. Our talk is sustenance.

"Who's from the best country?" a girl named Hava asks. We debate, singing the praises of home. "Nowhere is as beautiful as Yugoslavia," Hava insists. But this is an unwinnable competition. Home isn't a place anymore, not a country. It's a feeling, as universal as it is specific. If we talk too much about it, we risk it vanishing.

After a few weeks at the thread factory, the SS come for us one morning with striped dresses to replace our gray ones. We board yet another train. But this time we are forced on top of the cars in our striped uniforms, human decoys to discourage the British from bombing the train. It carries ammunition.

"From thread to bullets," someone says.

"Ladies, we've been handed a promotion," Magda says.

The wind on top of the boxcar is punishing, obliterating. But at least I can't feel hunger when I'm this cold. Would I rather die by cold or by fire? Gas or gun? It happens all of a sudden. Even with human prisoners on top of the trains, the British send the hiss and crash of bombs at us. Smoke. Shouts. The train stops and I jump. I'm the first one down. I run straight up the snowy hillside that hugs the tracks toward a stand of thin trees, where I stop to scan the snow for my sister, catch my breath. Magda isn't there among the trees. I don't see her running from the train. Bombs hiss and erupt on the tracks. I can see a heap of bodies by the side of the train. Magda.

I have to choose. I can run. Escape into the forest. Scavenge a life. Freedom is that close, a matter of footsteps. But if Magda's alive and I abandon her, who will give her bread? And if she's dead? It's a second like a shutter's flap. *Click*: forest. *Click*: tracks. I run back down the hill.

Magda sits in the ditch, a dead girl in her lap. It's Hava. Blood streams from Magda's chin. In a nearby train car, men are eating. They're prisoners, too, but not like us. They're dressed in civilian clothes, not in uniforms. And they have food. German political prisoners, we guess. In any case, they are more privileged than we are. They're eating. Hava is dead and my sister lives and all I can think of is food. Magda, the beautiful one, is bleeding.

"Now that there's a chance to ask for some food, you look like this," I scold her. "You're too cut up to flirt." As long as I can be angry with her, I am spared from feeling fear, or the inverted, inside-out pain of what almost was. Instead of rejoicing, giving thanks that we are both alive, that we have survived another fatal moment, I am furious at my sister. I am furious at God, at fate, but I direct my confusion and hurt onto my sister's bleeding face.

Magda doesn't respond to my insult. She doesn't wipe away the blood. The guards circle in, shouting at us, prodding bodies with their guns to make sure that those who aren't moving are really dead. We leave Hava in the dirty snow and stand with the other survivors.

"You could have run," Magda says. She says it like I'm an idiot.

Within an hour, the ammunition has been reloaded into new train cars and we're on top again in our striped uniforms, the blood dried on Magda's chin.

We are prisoners and refugees. We have long since lost track of the date, of time. Magda is my guiding star. As long as she is near,

I have everything I need. We are pulled from the ammunition trains one morning, and we march many days in a row. The snow begins to melt, giving way to dead grass. Maybe we march for weeks. Bombs fall, sometimes close by. We can see cities burning. We stop in small towns throughout Germany, moving south sometimes, moving east, forced to work in factories along the way.

Counting inmates is the SS preoccupation. I don't count how many of us remain. Maybe I don't count because I know that each day the number is smaller. It's not a death camp. But there are dozens of ways to die. The roadside ditches run red with blood from those shot in the back or the chest—those who tried to run, those who couldn't keep up. Some girls' legs freeze, completely freeze, and they keel over like felled trees. Exhaustion. Exposure. Fever. Hunger. If the guards don't pull a trigger, the body does.

For days we have gone without food. We come to the crest of a hill and see a farm, outbuildings, a pen for livestock.

"One minute," Magda says. She runs toward the farm, weaving between trees, hoping not to be spotted by the SS who have stopped to smoke.

I watch Magda zigzag toward the garden fence. It's too early for spring vegetables, but I would eat cow feed, I would eat dried-up stalk. If a rat scurries into the room where we sleep, girls pounce on it. I try not to call attention to Magda with my gaze. I look away, and when I glance back I can't see her. A gun fires. And again. Someone has spotted my sister. The guards yell at us, count us, guns drawn. A few more shots crack. There's no sight of Magda. *Help me, help me.* I realize that I'm praying to my mother. I'm talking to her the way she used to pray to her mother's portrait over the piano. Even in labor she did this,

Magda has told me. The night I was born, Magda heard our mother screaming, "Mother, help me!" Then Magda heard the baby cry—me—and our mother said, "You helped me." Calling on the dead is my birthright. *Mother, help us*, I pray. I see a flash of gray between the trees. She's alive. She escaped the bullets. And somehow, now, she escapes detection. I don't breathe until Magda stands with me again.

"There were potatoes," she says. "If those bastards hadn't started shooting we'd be eating potatoes."

I imagine biting into one like an apple. I wouldn't even take the time to rub it clean. I would eat the dirt along with the starch, the skin.

We go to work in an ammunition factory near the Czech border. It is March, we learn. One morning I can't get off the bench in the shed-like dorms where we sleep. I'm burning with fever, shaking and weak.

"Get up, Dicuka," Magda orders me. "You can't call in sick." At Auschwitz, the ones who couldn't work were told they'd be taken to a hospital, but then they disappeared. Why would it be any different now? There's no infrastructure for killing here, no pipes laid, bricks mortared for the purpose. But a single bullet makes you just as dead. Still, I can't get up. I hear my own voice rambling about our grandparents. They'll let us skip school and take us to the bakery. Our mother can't take away the sweets. Somewhere in my head I know I am delirious, but I can't regain my senses. Magda tells me to shut up and covers me with a coat—to keep me warm if the fever breaks, she says, but more so to keep me hidden. "Don't move even a finger," she says.

The factory is nearby, across a little bridge over a fast stream. I lie under the coat, pretending not to exist, anticipating the moment when I will be discovered missing and a guard will come into the shed to shoot me. Will Magda be able to hear the gunshot over the noise of the machines? I am no use to anyone now.

I swirl into delirious sleep. I dream of fire. It's a familiar dream—I have dreamt for nearly a year of being warm. Yet I wake from the dream, and this time the smell of smoke chokes me. Is the shed on fire? I am afraid to go to the door, afraid I won't make it on my weak legs, afraid that if I do I'll give myself away. Then I hear the bombs. The whistle and blast. How did I sleep through the beginning of the attack? I pull myself off the bench. Where is the safest place? Even if I could run, where would I go? I hear shouts. "Factory's on fire! Factory's on fire!" someone yells.

I am aware again of the space between me and my sister: I have become an expert at measuring the space. How many hands between us? How many legs? Cartwheels? Now there's a bridge. Water and wood. And fire. I see it from the shed door where I finally stand and lean against the frame. The bridge to the factory is ablaze, the factory swallowed in smoke. For anyone who has lived through the bombing, the chaos is a respite. An opportunity to run. I picture Magda pushing out a window and dashing for the trees. Looking up through the branches toward the sky. Ready to run even as far as that to be free. If she makes a run for it, then I'm off the hook. I can slide back down to the floor and never get up. What a relief it will be. To exist is such an obligation. I let my legs fold up like scarves. I relax into the fall. And there is Magda in a halo of flame. Already dead. Beating me to it. I'll catch up. I feel the heat from the fire. Now I'll join her. Now. "I'm coming!" I call. "Wait for me!"

I don't catch the moment when she stops being a phantom and becomes flesh again. Somehow she makes me understand: She has crossed the burning bridge to return to me.

"You idiot," I say, "you could have run."

It's April now. Grass bursts green on the hills. Light stretches each day. Children spit at us as we pass through the outskirts of a town. How sad, I think, that these children have been brainwashed to hate me.

"You know how I'm going to get revenge?" Magda says. "I'm going to kill a German mother. A German kills my mother; I'm going to kill a German mother."

I have a different wish. I wish for the boy who spits at us to one day see that he doesn't have to hate. In my revenge fantasy, the boy who yells at us now—"Dirty Jew! Vermin!"—holds out a bouquet of roses. "Now I know," he says, "there's no reason to hate you. No reason at all." We embrace in mutual absolution. I don't tell Magda my fantasy.

One day as dusk comes, the SS shove us into a community hall where we'll sleep for the night. There's no food again.

"Anyone who leaves the premises will be shot immediately," the guard warns.

"Dicuka," Magda moans as we sink onto the wooden boards that will be our bed, "soon it's going to be the end for me."

"Shut up," I say. She is scaring me. Her despondence is more terrifying to me than a raised gun. She doesn't talk like this. She doesn't give up. Maybe I've been a burden to her. Maybe keeping me strong through my illness has depleted her. "You're not going to die," I tell her. "We're going to eat tonight."

"Oh, Dicuka," she says, and rolls toward the wall.

I'll show her. I'll show her there's hope. I'll get a little food. I'll revive her. The SS have gathered near the door, near the last evening light, to eat their rations. Sometimes they'll throw a scrap of food at us just for the pleasure of seeing us grovel. I go to them on my knees. "Please, please," I beg. They laugh. One soldier holds a wedge of canned meat toward me and I lunge for it, but he puts it in his mouth and they all laugh harder. They play with me like this until I am worn out. Magda is asleep. I refuse to let it go, let her down. The SS break up their picnic to relieve themselves or to smoke, and I slip out a side door.

I can smell manure and apple blossoms and German tobacco. The grass is damp and cool. On the other side of a stucco fence I see a garden: small lettuce heads, vines of beans, the feathery green plumes of carrot tops. I can taste the carrots as if I've already picked them, crisp and earthy. Climbing the wall isn't hard. I skin my knees a little as I shimmy over the top and the bright spots of blood feel like fresh air on my skin, like a good thing deep down surfacing. I'm giddy. I grab the carrot tops and pull, the sound like a seam ripping as the earth releases the roots. They're heavy in my hands. Clumps of dirt dangle from the roots. Even the dirt smells like a feast—like seeds—every possible thing contained there. I scale the wall again, dirt raining onto my knees. I picture Magda's face as she bites into the first fresh vegetable we've eaten in a year. I have done a daring thing and it has borne fruit. This is what I want Magda to see, more than a meal, more than nutrients dissolving into her blood: simply, hope. I jump to earth again.

But I'm not alone. A man stares down at me. He clutches a gun. He's a soldier—Wehrmacht, not SS. Worse than the gun are his eyes, punitive eyes. *How dare you?* his eyes say. *I'll teach you to obey.* He pushes me down to my knees. He cocks the gun and points it at my chest. *Please, please, please, please.* I pray like I did with Mengele. *Please help him to not kill me.* I'm shivering. The carrots knock against my leg. He puts the gun down for a brief second, then raises it again. *Click. Click.* Worse than the fear of death is the feeling of being locked in and powerless, of not knowing what will happen in the next breath. He yanks me to my feet and turns me toward the building where Magda sleeps. He uses the butt of his gun to shove me inside.

"Pissing," he says to the guard inside, and they chuckle crassly. I hold the carrots folded in my dress.

Magda won't wake up at first. I have to put the carrot in her palm before she'll open her eyes. She eats so quickly that she bites the inside of her cheek. When she thanks me, she cries.

The SS shout us awake in the morning. Time to march again. I am starving and hollow and I think I must have dreamt the carrots, but Magda shows me a handful of greens she has tucked in a pocket for later. They have wilted. They're scraps that in a former life we would have thrown away or fed to the goose in the attic, but now they appear enchanted, like a pot in a fairy tale that magically fills with gold. The drooping, browning carrot tops are proof of a secret power. I shouldn't have risked picking them, but I did. I shouldn't have survived, but I did. The "shoulds" aren't important. They aren't the only kind of governance. There's a different principle, a different authority at work. We are skeletal. We are so sick and undernourished that we can barely walk, much less march, much less work. And yet the carrots make me feel strong. *If I survive today, tomorrow I will be free.* I sing the chant in my head.

We line up in rows for the count. I'm still singing to myself. Just as we're about to head out into the chilly morning for another day of horrors, there's a commotion at the door. The SS guard shouts in German, and another man shouts back, pushing his way into the room. My breath catches and I grab Magda's elbow so that I don't fall over. It's the man from the garden. He's looking sternly around the room.

"Where is the girl who dared to break the rules?" he demands.

I shake. I can't calm my body. He's back for revenge. He wants to mete out punishment publicly. Or he feels he must. Someone has learned of his inexplicable kindness to me, and now he must pay for *his* risk. He must pay for his risk by making me pay for mine. I quake, almost unable to breathe I'm so afraid. I am trapped. I know how close I am to death.

"Where is the little criminal?" he asks again.

He will spot me any second. Or he will spy the carrot tops poking out of Magda's coat. I can't bear the suspense of waiting for him to recognize me. I drop to the ground and crawl toward him. Magda hisses at me, but it's too late. I crouch at his feet. I see the mud on his boots, the grain of the wood on the floor.

"You," he says. He sounds disgusted. I close my eyes. I wait for him to kick me. I wait for him to shoot.

Something heavy drops near my feet. A stone? Will he stone me to death, the slow way?

No. It's bread. A small loaf of dark rye bread.

"You must have been very hungry to do what you did," he says. I wish I could meet that man now. He's proof that twelve years of Hitler's Reich isn't enough hate to take the good out of people. His eyes are my father's eyes. Green. And full of relief.

CHAPTER 5

The Stairs of Death

We march for days or weeks again. Since Auschwitz, we have been kept in Germany, but one day we come to the Austrian border, where we wait to cross. The guards gossip as we stand in the interminable lines that have become for me the illusion of order, the illusion that one thing naturally follows another. It is a relief to stand still. I listen to the conversation between the guards. President Roosevelt has died, they are saying. Truman is left to carry out the rest of the war. How strange to hear that in the world outside our purgatory, things change. A new course is determined. These events occur so far from our daily existence that it is a shock to realize that now, even right now, someone is making a choice about me. Not about me specifically. I have no name. But someone with authority is making a decision that will determine what happens to me. North, south, east, or west? Germany or Austria? What should be done with the surviving Jews before the war is over?

"When the war ends . . ." a guard says. He doesn't finish the thought. This is the kind of future talk that Eric and I once entertained. *After the war* . . . If I concentrate in just the right way, can I figure out if he still lives? I pretend that I'm waiting outside a train station where I will buy a ticket, but I have only one chance to figure out the city where I am to meet him. Prague? Vienna? Düsseldorf? Prešov? Paris? I reach into my pocket, feeling reflexively for my passport. *Eric, my sweet love, I am on my way.* A female border guard shouts at me and Magda in German and points us to a different line. I start to move. Magda stays still. The guard shouts again. Magda won't move, won't respond. Is she delirious? Why won't she follow me? The guard yells in Magda's face and Magda shakes her head.

"I don't understand," Magda says to the guard in Hungarian. Of course she understands. We're both fluent in German.

"Yes, you do!" the guard shouts.

"I don't understand," Magda repeats. Her voice is completely neutral. Her shoulders are straight and tall. Am I missing something? Why is she pretending not to understand? There is nothing to be gained from defiance. Has she lost her mind? The two continue to argue. Except Magda isn't arguing. She is only repeating, flatly, calmly, that she doesn't understand, she doesn't understand. The guard loses control. She smacks Magda's face with the butt of her gun. She beats her again across the shoulders. She hits and hits until Magda topples over and the guard gestures to me and another girl to drag her away with us.

Magda is bruised and coughing, but her eyes shine. "I said, 'No!'" she says. "I said, 'No.'" For her, it is a marvelous beating. It is proof of her power. She held her ground while the guard lost control. Magda's civil disobedience makes her feel like the author of choice, not the victim of fate.

But the power Magda feels is short-lived. Soon we are marching again, toward a place worse than any we have yet seen.

* * *

We arrive at Mauthausen. It's an all-male concentration camp at a quarry where prisoners are made to hack and carry granite that will be used to build Hitler's fantasy city, a new capital for Germany, a new Berlin. I see nothing but stairs and bodies. The stairs are white stone and stretch up and up ahead of us, as though we could walk them to the sky. The bodies are everywhere, in heaps. Bodies crooked and splayed like pieces of broken fence. Bodies so skeletal and disfigured and tangled that they barely have a human shape. We stand in a line on the white stairs. The Stairs of Death, they are called. We are waiting on the stairs for another selection, we presume, that will point us to death or more work. Rumors shudder down the line. The inmates at Mauthausen, we learn, have to carry 110-pound blocks of stone from the quarry below up the 186 stairs, running in line. I picture my ancestors, the pharaoh's slaves in Egypt, bent under the weight of stones. Here on the Stairs of Death, we're told, when you're carrying a stone, running up the stairs, and someone in front of you trips or collapses, you are the next to fall, and on, and on, until the whole line buckles into a heap. If you survive, it's worse, we hear. You have to stand along a wall at the edge of a cliff. *Fallschirmspringerwand*, it's called—the Parachutist's Wall. At gunpoint, you choose: Will you be shot to death, or will you push the inmate beside you off the cliff?

"Just push me," Magda says. "If it comes to that."

"Me too," I say. I would rather fall a thousand times than see my sister shot. We are too weak and starved to say this out of politeness. We say this out of love, but also out of self-preservation. Don't give me another heavy thing to carry. Let me fall among the stones.

I weigh less, much less, than the rocks the inmates lift up the Stairs of Death. I am so light I could drift like a leaf or a feather. Down, down. I could fall now. I could just fall backward instead of taking the next step up. I think I am empty now. There is no heaviness to hold me to the earth. I am about to indulge this fantasy of weightlessness, of releasing the burden of being alive, when someone ahead of me in line breaks the spell.

"There's the crematorium," she says.

I look up. We have been away from the death camps for so many months that I have forgotten how matter-of-factly the chimneys rise. In a way, they are reassuring. To feel death's proximity, death's imminence, in the straight stack of brick—to see the chimney that is a bridge, that will house your passage from flesh to air—to consider yourself already dead—makes a certain kind of sense.

And yet, as long as that chimney produces smoke, I have something to fight against. I have a purpose. "We die in the morning," the rumors announce. I can feel resignation tugging at me like gravity, an inevitable and constant force.

Night falls and we sleep on the stairs. Why have they waited so long to begin the selection? My courage wavers. *We die in the morning. In the morning we die.* Did my mother know what was about to happen when she joined the line of children and the elderly? When she saw Magda and me pointed a different way? Did she fight death? Did she accept it? Did she remain oblivious until the end? Does it matter, when you go, if you are aware that you are dying? *We die in the morning. In the morning we die.* I hear the rumor, the certainty, repeat as though it is echoing off the quarry rock. Have we really been marched these many hundreds of miles only to vanish?

I want to organize my mind. I don't want my last thoughts to be cliché ones, or despondent ones. *What's the point? What has it all meant?* I don't want my last thoughts to be a replaying of the horrors we've seen. I want to feel alive. I want to savor what aliveness is. I think of Eric's voice and his lips. I try to conjure thoughts that might still have the power to make me tingle. *I'll never forget your eyes. I'll never forget your hands.* That's what I want to remember—warmth in my chest, a flush across my skin—though "remember" isn't the right word. I want to enjoy my body while I still have one. An eternity ago, in Kassa, my mother forbade me to read Émile Zola's *Nana*, but I snuck it into the bathroom and read it in secret. If I die tomorrow, I will die a virgin. Why have I had a body at all, never to know it completely? So much of my life has been a mystery. I remember the day I got my first period. I rode my bike home after school, and when I got there I saw blood streaks all over my white skirt. I was frightened. I ran to my mother, crying, asking her to help me locate the wound. She slapped me. I didn't know it was a Hungarian tradition for a girl to be slapped upon her first period. I didn't know about menstruation at all. No one, not my mother or sisters or teachers or coaches or friends, had ever explained anything about my anatomy. I knew there was something men had that women didn't. I'd never seen my father naked, but I'd felt that part of Eric pressing against me when he held me. He had never asked me to touch it, had never acknowledged his body. I had liked the feeling that his body—and my own—were mysteries waiting to be uncovered, something that caused an energy to shoot between us when we touched.

Now it was a mystery I would never solve. I had experienced little stars of desire but would now never feel their fulfillment, the whole promised galaxy of light. I cry about it now, on the Stairs of Death. It is terrible to lose, to have lost, all the known things: mother, father, sister, boyfriend, country, home. Why do I have to lose the things I don't know too? Why do I have to lose the future? My potential? The children I'll never mother? The wedding dress my father will never make? *I'm going to die a virgin*. I don't want this to be my last thought. I should think about God.

I try to picture an immovable power. Magda has lost her faith. She and many others. "I can't believe in a God who would let this happen," they say. I understand what they mean. And yet I've never found it difficult to see that it isn't God who is killing us in gas chambers, in ditches, on cliff sides, on 186 white stairs. God doesn't run the death camps. People do. But here is the horror again and I don't want to indulge it. I picture God as being like a dancing child. Sprightly and innocent and *curious*. I must be also if I am to be close to God now. I want to keep alive the part of me that feels wonder, that *wonders*, until the very end. I wonder if anyone knows that I am here, knows what's going on, that there is such a place as an Auschwitz, a Mauthausen? I wonder if my parents can see me now. I wonder if Eric can. I wonder what a man looks like naked. There are men all around me. Men no longer living. It wouldn't hurt their pride anymore for me to look. The worse transgression would be to relinquish my curiosity, I convince myself.

I leave Magda sleeping on the stairs and crawl to the muddy hillside where the corpses are piled. I won't undress anyone still in clothes. I won't tamper with the dead. But if a man has fallen, I will look.

I see a man, his legs askew. They don't seem to belong to the same body, but I can make out the place where the legs are joined. I see hair like mine, dark, coarse, and a little appendage. It's like a little mushroom, a tender thing that pushes out of the dirt. How strange that women's parts are all tucked away and men's are exposed, so vulnerable. I feel satisfied. I won't die ignorant of the biology that made me.

At daybreak, the line starts to move. We don't talk much. Some wail. Some pray. Mostly we are private in our dread or regret or resignation or relief. I don't tell Magda what I saw the night before. This line is moving quickly. There won't be much time. I try to remember the constellations I used to recognize in the night sky. I try to remember the taste of my mother's bread.

"Dicuka," Magda says, but it takes me a few hollow breaths to recognize my name. We've reached the top of the stairs. The selection officer is just ahead. Everyone is being sent in the same direction. This isn't a selection line. It's an ushering. It really is the end. They've waited until morning to send us all to death. Should we make a promise to each other? An apology? What is there that must be said? Five girls ahead of us now. What should I say to my sister? Two girls.

And then the line stops. We're led toward a crowd of SS guards by a gate.

"If you try to run, you'll be shot!" they shout at us. "If you fall behind, you'll be shot."

We have been saved again. Inexplicably.

We march.

This is the Death March, from Mauthausen to Gunskirchen. It is the shortest distance we have been forced to walk, but we are so weakened by then that only one hundred out of the two thousand of us will survive. Magda and I cling to each other, determined to stay together, to stay upright. Each hour, hundreds of girls fall into the ditches on either side of the road. Too weak or too ill to keep moving, they're killed on the spot. We are like the head of a dandelion gone to seed and blown by the wind, only a few white tufts remaining. Hunger is my only name.

Every part of me is in pain; every part of me is numb. I can't walk another step. I ache so badly I can't feel myself move. I am just a circuitry of pain, a signal that feeds back on itself. I don't know that I have stumbled until I feel the arms of Magda and the other girls lifting me. They have laced their fingers together to form a human chair.

"You shared your bread," one of them says.

The words don't mean anything to me. When have I ever tasted bread? But then a memory rises up. Our first night at Auschwitz. Mengele ordering the music and Mengele ordering me to dance. This body danced. This mind dreamt of the opera house. This body ate that bread. I am the one who had the thought that night and who thinks it again now: Mengele killed my mother; Mengele let me live. Now a girl who shared a crust with me nearly a year ago has recognized me. She uses her last strength to interlace her fingers with Magda's and those of the other girls and lift me up into the air. In a way, Mengele allowed this moment to happen. He didn't kill any of us that night or any night after. He gave us bread.

CHAPTER 6

To Choose a Blade of Grass

There is always a worse hell. That is our reward for living. When we stop marching, we are at Gunskirchen Lager. It's a subcamp of Mauthausen, a few wooden buildings in a marshy forest near a village, a camp built to house a few hundred slave laborers, where eighteen thousand are crowded now. It is not a death camp. There are no gas chambers here, no crematoria. But there is no doubt that we have been sent here to die.

It is already hard to tell who is living and who is dead. Disease passes into and between our bodies. Typhus. Dysentery. White lice. Open sores. Flesh upon flesh. Living and rotting. A horse's carcass half gnawed. Eat it raw. Who needs a knife to cut the flesh? Just gnaw it away from the bone. You sleep three deep, in the crowded wooden structures or on the bare ground. If someone below you dies, keep sleeping. No strength to haul the dead away. There's a girl doubled over in hunger. There's a foot, black, rotted through. We have been herded into the dank, thick woods to be killed in a giant blaze, all of us lit on fire. The whole place is rigged with dynamite. We wait for the explosion that will consume us in its flame. Until the big blast there are the other hazards: starvation, fever, disease. There is only one twenty-hole latrine for the entire camp. If you can't wait your turn to defecate, they shoot you right there, where your waste has pooled. Trash fires smolder. The earth is a mud pit, and if you can find the strength to walk, your feet spin in a pulp that is part mud, part shit. It is five or six months since we left Auschwitz.

Magda flirts. That is her answer to death's beckoning. She meets a Frenchman, a guy from Paris, who lived before the war on Rue de something, an address I tell myself I won't ever forget. Even in the depths of this horror there is chemistry, person to person, that gallop in the throat, that brightening. I watch them talk as though they are seated at a summer café, little plates clinking between them. This is what the living do. We use our sacred pulse as a flint against fear. Don't ruin your spirit. Send it up like a torch. Tell the Frenchman your name and tuck his address away, savor it, chew it slowly like bread.

In just a few days at Gunskirchen I become a person who cannot walk. Although I don't know it yet, I have a broken back (even now I don't know when the injury occurred, or how). I only sense that I have reached the end of my reserves. I lie out in the heavy air, my body entwined with strangers' bodies, all of us in a heap, some already dead, some long dead, some, like me, barely alive. I see things I know aren't real. I see them all mixed in with the things that *are* real but shouldn't be. My mother reads to me. Scarlett cries, "*I've loved something that doesn't really exist.*" My father throws me a petit four. Klara starts the Mendelssohn violin concerto. She plays by the window so that a passerby will notice her, lift a face toward her, so she can beckon for the attention she craves but can't ask for outright. This is what the living do. We set strings vibrating with our needs.

Here in hell, I watch a man eat human flesh. Could I do it? For the sake of my own life, could I put my mouth around the skin left hanging on a dead person's bones and chew? I have seen flesh defiled in unforgivable cruelty. A boy tied to a tree while the SS officers shot his foot, his hand, his arms, an ear—an innocent child used as target practice. Or the pregnant woman who somehow made it to Auschwitz without being killed outright. When she went into labor, the SS tied her legs together. I've never seen agony like hers. But it's watching a starving person eat a dead person's flesh that makes the bile rise in me, that makes my vision black. I cannot do it. And yet I must eat. I must eat or I will die. Out of the trampled mud grows grass. I stare at the blades, I see their different lengths and shades. I will eat grass. I will choose this blade of grass over that one. I will occupy my mind with the choice. This is what it means to choose. To eat or not eat. To eat grass or to eat flesh. To eat this blade or that one. Mostly we sleep. There is nothing to drink. I lose all sense of time. I am often asleep. Even when I am awake I struggle to remain conscious.

Once I see Magda crawling back to me with a can in her hand, a can that glints in the sun. A can of sardines. The Red Cross, in its neutrality, has been allowed to deliver aid to prisoners, and Magda has huddled in a line and been handed a can of sardines. But there's no way to open it. It's just a new flavor of cruelty. Even a good intention, a good deed, becomes futility. My sister is dying slowly of starvation; my sister holds food in her hand. She clutches the tin the way she clutched her hair once, trying to hold on to herself. An unopenable can of fish is the most human part of her now. We are the dead and the near dead. I can't tell which I am.

* * *

I am aware at the corners of my consciousness of day trading places with night. When I open my eyes, I don't know if I have slept or fainted, or for how long. I don't have the capacity to ask, How long? Sometimes I can feel that I am breathing. Sometimes I try to move my head to look for Magda. Sometimes I can't think of her name.

Cries break me out of a sleep that resembles death. The cries must be death's herald. I wait for the promised explosion, for the promised heat. I keep my eyes closed and wait to burn. But there's no explosion. There's no flame. I open my eyes, and I can see jeeps rolling slowly in through the pine forest that obscures the camp from the road and from the sky. "The Americans have arrived! The Americans are here!" This is what the feeble are shouting. The jeeps look wavy and blurry, as if I am watching them through water or in an intense heat. Could this be a collective hallucination? Someone is singing "When the Saints Go Marching In." For more than seventy years these sensory impressions have stayed with me, indelible. But as they happen, I have no idea what they mean. I see men in fatigues. I see flags with stars and stripes—American flags, I realize. I see flags emblazoned with the number 71. I see an American handing cigarettes to inmates, who are so hungry they eat them, paper and all. I watch from a tangle of bodies. I can't tell which legs are my legs. "Are there any living here?" the Americans call in German. "Raise your hand if you are alive." I try to move my fingers to signal that I am alive. A soldier walks so near to me that I can see the streaks of mud on his pants. I can smell his sweat. *Here I am*, I want to call. *I'm here.* I have no voice. He scours the bodies. His eyes pass over me without recognition.

He holds a piece of dirty cloth to his face. "Raise your hand if you can hear me," he says. He barely moves the cloth away from his mouth when he speaks. I work to find my fingers. *You'll never get out of here alive*, they've said: the kapo who ripped out my earrings, the SS officer with the tattoo gun who didn't want to waste the ink, the forewoman in the thread factory, the SS who shot us down on the long, long march. This is how it feels for them to be right.

The soldier shouts something in English. Someone outside my field of vision yells back. They're leaving.

And then a patch of light explodes on the ground. Here's the fire. At last. I am surprised that it makes no noise. The soldiers turn. My numb body suddenly flushes hot—from flame, I think, or fever. But no. There is no fire. The gleam of light isn't fire at all. It is the sun colliding with Magda's sardine can! Whether on purpose or by accident, she has arrested the soldiers' attention with a tin of fish. They are returning. We have one more chance. If I can dance in my mind, I can make my body seen. I close my eyes and concentrate, raising my hands above my head in an imaginary arabesque. I hear the soldiers yell again, one to the other. One is very close to me. I keep my eyes locked shut and continue my dance. I imagine that I am dancing with him. That he lifts me over his head like Romeo did in the barracks with Mengele. That there is love and it springs out of war. That there is death and always, always its opposite.

And now I can feel my hand. I know it is my hand because the soldier is touching it. I open my eyes. I see that his wide, dark hand circles my fingers. He presses something into my hand. Beads. Colorful beads. Red, brown, green, yellow.

"Food," the soldier says. He looks into my eyes. His skin is the darkest I have ever seen, his lips thick, his eyes deep brown. He helps me lift my hand to my mouth. He helps me release the beads onto my dry tongue. Saliva gathers and I taste something sweet. I taste chocolate. I remember the name of this flavor. *Always keep a little something sweet in your pocket*, my father said. Here is the sweetness.

But Magda? Has she been discovered too? I don't have words yet, or a voice. I can't stammer a thank you. I can't form the syllables of my sister's name. I can barely swallow the little candies that the soldier has given me. I can barely think of anything other than the desire for more food. Or a drink of water. His attention is occupied now in getting me out of the pile of bodies. He has to pull the dead away from me. They are slack in the face, slack in their limbs. As skeletal as they are, they are heavy, and he grimaces and strains as he lifts them. Sweat streaks his face. He coughs at the stench. He adjusts the cloth over his mouth. Who knows how long the dead have been dead? Maybe only a breath or two separates them from me. I don't know how to speak my thankfulness. But I feel it prickling all across my skin.

He lifts me now and deposits me on the ground, on my back, at a slight distance from the dead bodies. I can see the sky in pieces between the treetops. I feel the humid air on my face, the damp of the muddy grass beneath me. I let my mind rest in sensation. I picture my mother's long coiled hair, my father's top hat and mustache. Everything I feel and have ever felt stems from them, from the union that made me. They rocked me in their arms. They made me a child of the earth. I remember Magda's story about my birth. "You helped me," my mother cried to her mother. "You helped me."

And now Magda is beside me in the grass. She holds her can of sardines. We have survived the final selection. We are alive. We are together. We are free.

PART II

Escape

CHAPTER 7

My Liberator, My Assailant

When I permitted myself to imagine a moment like this—the end of my imprisonment, the end of the war—I imagined a joy blooming in my chest. I imagined yelling in my fullest voice, "I AM FREE! I AM FREE!" But now I have no voice. We are a silent river, a current of the freed that flows from the Gunskirchen graveyard toward the nearest town. I ride on a makeshift cart. The wheels squeak. I can barely stay conscious. There is no joy or relief in this freedom. It's a slow walk out of a forest. It's a dazed face. It's being barely alive and returning to sleep. It's the danger of gorging on sustenance. The danger of the wrong kind of sustenance. Freedom is sores and lice and typhus and carved-out bellies and listless eyes.

I am aware of Magda walking beside me. Of pain throughout my body as the cart jolts. For more than a year I have not had the luxury of thinking about what hurts or doesn't hurt. I have been able to think only about how to keep up with the others, how to stay one step ahead, to get a little food here, to walk fast enough, to never stop, to stay alive, to not be left behind. Now that the danger is gone, the pain within and the suffering around me turn awareness into hallucination. A silent movie. A march of skeletons. Most of us are too physically ruined to walk. We lie on carts, we lean on sticks. Our uniforms are filthy and worn, so ragged and tattered that they hardly cover our skin. Our skin hardly covers our bones. We are an anatomy lesson. Elbows, knees, ankles, cheeks, knuckles, ribs jut out like questions. What are we now? Our bones look obscene, our eyes are caverns, blank, dark, empty. Hollow faces. Blue-black fingernails. We are trauma in motion. We are a slow-moving parade of ghouls. We stagger as we walk, our carts roll over the cobblestones. Row on row, we fill the square in Wels, Austria. Townspeople stare at us from windows. We are frightening. No one speaks. We choke the square with our silence. Townspeople run into their homes. Children cover their eyes. We have lived through hell only to become someone else's nightmare.

The important thing is to eat and drink. But not too much, not too fast. It is possible to overdose on food. Some of us can't help it. Restraint has dissolved along with our muscle mass, our flesh. We have starved for so long. Later I will learn that a girl from my hometown, the sister of my sister Klara's friend, was liberated from Auschwitz only to die from eating too much. It's deadly both to sustain and to end a hunger. A blessing, then, that the strength I need to chew returns to me only intermittently. A blessing that the GIs have little food to offer, mostly candy, those little beads of color, M&M's, we learn.

No one wants to house us. Hitler has been dead for less than a week, Germany is still days away from official surrender. The violence is waning across Europe, but it is still wartime. Food and hope are scarce for everyone. And we survivors, we former captives, are still the enemy to some. Parasites. Vermin. The war does not end anti-Semitism. The GIs bring Magda and me to a house where a German family lives, a mother, father, grandmother, three children. This is where we will live until we are strong enough to travel. Be careful, the Americans warn us in broken German. There's no peace yet. Anything could happen.

The parents move all of the family's possessions into a bedroom, and the father makes a show of locking the door. The children take turns staring at us and then run to hide their faces behind their mother's skirt. We are containers for their fascination and their fear. I am used to the blank-eyed, automatic cruelty of the SS, or their incongruous cheer—their delight in power. I am used to the way they lift themselves up, to feel big, to heighten their sense of purpose and control. The way the children look at us is worse. We are an offense to innocence. That's the way the children look at us—as though we are the transgressors. Their shock is more bitter than hate.

The soldiers bring us to the room where we will sleep. It's the nursery. We are the orphans of war. They lift me into a wooden crib. I am that small; I weigh seventy pounds. I can't walk on my own. I am a baby. I barely think in language. I think in terms of pain, of need. I would cry to be held, but there's no one to hold me. Magda curls into a ball on the little bed.

A noise outside our door splinters my sleep. Even rest is fragile. I am afraid all the time. I am afraid of what has already happened. And of what could happen. Sounds in the dark bring back the image of my mother tucking Klara's caul into her coat, my father gazing back at our apartment on the early morning of our eviction. As the past replays, I lose my home and my parents all over again. I stare at the wooden slats of the crib and try to soothe myself back to sleep, or at least into calm. But the noises persist. Crashes and stomps. And then the door flies open. Two GIs careen into the room. They stumble over each other, over a little shelf. Lamplight strains into the dark room. One of the men points at me and laughs and grabs his crotch. Magda isn't there. I don't know where she is, if she is close enough to hear me if I scream, if she is cowering somewhere, as afraid as I am. I hear my mother's voice. *Don't you dare lose your virginity before you're married*, she would lecture us, before I even knew what virginity was. I didn't have to. I understood the threat. Don't ruin yourself. Don't disappoint. Now rough handling could do more than tarnish me, it could kill me. I am that brittle. But it's not just dying or more pain that I fear. I'm afraid of losing my mother's respect. The soldier shoves his friend back to the door to keep watch. He comes at me, cooing absurdly, his voice grainy, dislocated. His sweat and the alcohol on his breath smell sharp, like mold. I have to keep him away from me. There is nothing to throw. I can't even sit. I try to scream, but my voice is just a warble. The soldier at the door is laughing. But then he isn't. He speaks harshly. I can't understand English, but I know he says something about a baby. The other soldier leans against the crib rail. His hand gropes toward his waist. He will use me. Crush me. He pulls out his gun. He waves it crazily like a torch. I wait for his hands to clamp down on me. But he moves away instead. He moves toward the door, toward his friend. The door clicks shut. I'm alone in the dark.

I can't sleep. I'm sure the soldier will return. And where is Magda? Has some other soldier taken her? She is emaciated, but her body is in much better shape than mine, and there is still a hint of her feminine figure. To settle my mind, I try to organize what I know of men, of the human palette: Eric, tender and optimistic; my father, disappointed in himself and circumstance, sometimes defeated, sometimes making the best of it, finding the little joys; Dr. Mengele, lascivious and controlled; the Wehrmacht who caught me with the carrots fresh from the ground, punitive but merciful, then kind; the GI who pulled me from the heap of bodies at Gunskirchen, determined and brave; and now this new flavor, this new shade. A liberator, but an assailant, his presence heavy but also void. A big dark blank, as though his humanity has vacated his body. I will never learn where Magda was that night. Even now, she doesn't remember. But I will carry something vital away from that terrifying night, something I hope I never forget. The man who nearly raped me, who might have come back to do what he started to do, saw horror too. Like me, he probably spent the rest of his life trying to chase it away, to push it to the margins. That night, I believe he was so lost in the darkness that he almost became it. But he didn't. He made a choice not to.

He comes back in the morning. I know it is him because he still reeks of booze, because fear has made me memorize the map of his face even though I saw it in semi-darkness. I hug my knees and whimper. I sound like an animal. I can't stop. It's a keening, droning noise, part insect. He kneels by the crib. He is weeping. He repeats two words. I don't know what they mean, but I remember how they sound. *Forgive me. Forgive me.* He hands me a cloth sack. It's too heavy for me to lift so he empties it for me, spilling the contents—small tins of army rations—onto the mattress. He shows me the pictures on the cans. He points and talks, a crazy maître d' explaining the menu, inviting me to choose my next meal. I can't understand a word he says. I study the pictures. He pries open a can and feeds me with a spoon. It's ham with something sweet, raisins. If my father hadn't shared his secret packages of pork, I might not know the taste of it— though Hungarians would never pair ham with anything sweet. I keep opening my mouth, receiving another bite. Of course I forgive him. I am starving, and he brings me food to eat.

He comes back every day. Magda is well enough to flirt again, and I believe at the time that he makes a point of visiting this house because he enjoys her attention. But day after day, he barely notices her. He comes for me. I am what he needs to resolve. Maybe he's doing penance for his near assault. Or maybe he needs to prove to himself that hope and innocence can be resurrected, his, mine, the world's—that a broken girl can walk again. The GI—in the six weeks he cares for me I am too weak and shattered to ever learn to say or spell his name—lifts me out of the crib and holds my hands and coaxes me a step at a time around the room. The pain in my upper back feels like a burning coal when I try to move. I concentrate on shifting my weight from one foot to the other, trying to feel the exact moment when the weight transfers. My hands reach overhead, holding on to his fingers. I pretend he is my father, my father who wished I'd been a boy and then loved me anyway. *You'll be the best-dressed girl in town*, he told me over and over again. When I think of my father, the heat pulls out of my back and glows in my chest. There is pain and there is love. A baby knows these two shades of the world, and I am relearning them too.

Magda is physically better off than I am, and she tries to put our lives in order. One day when the German family is out of the house, Magda opens closets until she finds dresses for us to wear. She sends letters—to Klara, to our mother's brother in Budapest, to our mother's sister in Miskolc, letters that won't ever be read—to discover who might still be living, to discover where to build a life when it's time to leave Wels. I can't remember how to write my own name. Much less an address. A sentence. *Are you there?*

One day the GI brings paper and pencils. We start with the alphabet. He writes a capital *A*. A lowercase *a*. Capital *B*. Lowercase *b*. He gives me the pencil and nods. Can I make any letters? He wants me to try. He wants to see how far I've regressed, how much I remember. I can write *C* and *c*. *D* and *d*. I remember! He encourages me. He cheers me on. *E* and *e*. *F* and *f*. But then I falter. I know that *G* comes next, but I can't picture it, can't think how to form it on the page.

One day he brings a radio. He plays the happiest music I have ever heard. It's buoyant. It propels you. I hear horns. They insist that you move. Their shimmer isn't seduction—it's deeper than that, it's invitation, impossible to refuse. The GI and his friends show Magda and me the dances that go along with the sound—jitterbug, boogie-woogie. The men pair up like ballroom dancers. Even the way they hold their arms is new to me—it's ballroom style but loose, pliable. It's informal but not sloppy. How do they keep themselves so taut with energy and yet so flexible? So *ready*? Their bodies live out whatever the music sets in motion. I want to dance like that. I want to let my muscles remember.

Magda goes to take a bath one morning and returns to the room shaking. Her hair is wet, her clothes half off. She rocks on the bed with her eyes closed. I've been sleeping on the bed while she bathed—I'm too big for the crib now—and I don't know whether or not she knows I am awake.

It's been more than a month since liberation. Magda and I have spent almost every hour of the last forty days together in this room. We have regained the use of our bodies, we have regained the ability to talk and to write and even to try to dance. We can talk about Klara, about our hope that somewhere she is alive and trying to find us. But we can't talk about what we have endured.

Maybe in our silence we are trying to create a sphere that is free from our trauma. Wels is a limbo life, but presumably a new life beckons. Maybe we are trying to give each other and ourselves a blank room in which to build the future. We don't want to sully the room with images of violence and loss. We want to be able to see something besides death. And so we tacitly agree not to talk about anything that will rupture the bubble of survival.

Now my sister is trembling and hurting. If I tell her I am awake, if I ask her what is wrong, if I become witness to her breakdown, she won't have to be all alone with whatever is making her shake. But if I pretend I am asleep, I can preserve for her a mirror that doesn't reflect back this new pain; I can be a selective mirror, I can shine back at her the things she wants to cultivate and leave everything else invisible.

In the end, I don't have to decide what to do. She begins to speak.

"Before I leave this house, I will get my revenge," she vows.

We rarely see the family whose house we occupy, but her quiet, bitter anger compels me to imagine the worst. I picture the father coming into the bathroom while she undressed. "Did he . . ." I stammer.

"No." Her breath is jagged. "I tried to use the soap. The room started spinning."

"Are you ill?"

"No. Yes. I don't know."

"Do you have a fever?"

"No. It's the soap, Dicu. I couldn't touch it. A sort of panic came over me."

"No one hurt you?"

"No. It was the soap. You know what they say. They say it's made from people. From the ones they killed." I don't know if it's true. But this close to Gunskirchen? Maybe.

"I still want to kill a German mother," Magda says. I remember all the miles we walked in winter when this was her fantasy, her refrain. "I could do it, you know."

There are different ways to keep yourself going. I will have to find my own way to live with what has happened. I don't know what it is yet. We're free *from* the death camps, but we also must be free *to*—free to create, to make a life, to choose. And until we find our *freedom to*, we're just spinning around in the same endless darkness.

Later there will be doctors to help us repair our physical health. But no one will explain the psychological dimension of recovery. It will be many years before I begin to understand that.

*   *   *

One day the GI and his friends come to tell us we'll be leaving Wels, that the Russians are helping transport the survivors home. They come to say goodbye. They bring the radio. Glenn Miller's "In the Mood" comes on, and we let loose. With my broken back, I can barely manage the steps, but in my mind, in my spirit, we are spinning tops. Slow, slow, fast-fast, slow. Slow, slow, fast-fast, slow. I can do it too—keep my arms and legs loose but not limp. Glenn Miller. Duke Ellington. I repeat the big names in big band over and over. The GI leads me in a careful turn, a tiny dip, a breakaway. I am still so weak, but I can feel the potential in my body, all the things it will be possible to say with it when I have healed. Many years later I'll work with an amputee, and he'll explain the disorientation of feeling his phantom limb. When I dance to Glenn Miller six weeks after liberation, with my sister who is alive and the GI who almost raped me but didn't, I have reverse phantom limbs. It's sensation not in something that is lost but in a part of me that is returning, that is coming into its own. I can feel all the potential of the limbs and the life I can grow into again.

* * *

During the several hours' train ride from Wels to Vienna, through Russian-occupied Austria, I scratch at the rash, from lice or rubella, that still covers my body. Home. We are going home. In two more days we will be home! And yet it is impossible to feel the joy of our homecoming uncoupled from the devastation of loss. I know my mother and grandparents are dead, and surely my father too. They have been dead for more than a year. To go home without them is to lose them again. *Maybe Klara*, I allow myself to hope. *Maybe Eric*.

In the seat next to ours, two brothers sit. They are survivors too. Orphans. From Kassa, like us! Lester and Imre, they are called. Later we will learn that their father was shot in the back as he walked between them on the Death March. Soon we will understand that out of more than fifteen thousand deportees from our hometown, we are among the only seventy who have survived the war.

"We have one another," they say now. "We are lucky, lucky."

Lester and Imre, Magda and me. We are the anomalies. The Nazis didn't just murder millions of people. They murdered families. And now, beside the incomprehensible roster of the missing and the dead, our lives go on. Later we will hear stories from the displaced persons camps all over Europe. Reunions. Weddings. Births. We will hear of the special rations tickets issued to couples to obtain wedding clothes. We, too, will scour the United Nations Relief and Rehabilitation Administration newspapers and hold our breath, hoping to see familiar names among the list of survivors scattered over the Continent. But for now we do nothing but stare out the windows of the train, looking at empty fields, broken bridges, and, in some places, the fragile beginnings of crops. The Allied occupation of Austria will last another ten years. The mood in the towns we pass through isn't of relief or celebration—it's a teeth-clenched atmosphere of uncertainty and hunger. The war is over, but it's not over.

"Do I have ugly lips?" Magda asks as we near the outskirts of Vienna. She is studying her reflection in the window glass, superimposed over the landscape.

"Why, are you planning to use them?" I joke with her, I try to coax out that relentlessly teasing part of her. I try to tamp my own impossible fantasies, that Eric is alive somewhere, that soon I will be a postwar bride under a makeshift veil. That I will be together with my beloved forever, never alone.

"I'm serious," she says. "Tell me the truth."

Her anxiety reminds me of our first day at Auschwitz when she stood naked with her shaved head, gripping strands of her hair. Maybe she condenses the huge global fears about what will happen next into more specific and personal fears—the fear that she is not attractive enough to find a man, the fear that her lips are ugly. Or maybe her questions are tangled up in deeper uncertainty—about her essential worth.

"What's wrong with your lips?" I ask.

"Mama hated them. Someone on the street complimented my eyes once and she said, 'Yes, she's got beautiful eyes, but look at her thick lips.'"

Survival is black and white, no "buts" can intrude when you are fighting for your life. Now the "buts" come rushing in. We have bread to eat. *Yes, but we are penniless.* You are gaining weight. *Yes, but my heart is heavy.* You are alive. *Yes, but my mother is dead.*

Lester and Imre decide to stay on in Vienna for a few days; they promise to look for us at home. Magda and I board another train that will carry us eight hours northwest to Prague. A man blocks the entrance to the train car. "*Nasa lude,*" he sneers. *Our people.* He is Slovak. The Jews must ride on top of the train car.

"The Nazis lost," Magda mutters, "but it's the same as before."

There is no other way to get home. We climb to the top of the train car, joining ranks with the other displaced persons. We hold hands. Magda sits beside a young man named Laci Gladstein. He caresses Magda's fingers with his own, his fingers barely more than bones. We do not ask one another where we have been. Our bodies and our haunted eyes say everything there is to know. Magda leans against Laci's thin chest, searching for warmth. I am jealous of the solace they seem to find in each other, the attraction, the belonging. I am too committed to my love for Eric, to my hope that I will find him again, to seek a man's arms to hold me now. Even if I didn't carry Eric's voice with me still, I think I would be too afraid to look for comfort, for intimacy. I am skin and bones. I am covered in bugs and sores. Who would want me? Better not to risk connection and be denied, better not to have my damage confirmed. And besides, who would provide the best shelter now? Someone who knows what I have endured, a fellow survivor? Or someone who doesn't, who can help me forget? Someone who knew me before I went through hell, who can help me back to my former self? Or someone who can look at me now without always seeing what's been destroyed? *I'll never forget your eyes*, Eric told me. *I'll never forget your hands.* For more than a year I have held on to these words like a map that could lead me to freedom. But what if Eric can't face what I have become? What if we find each other and build a life, only to find that our children are the children of ghosts?

I huddle against Magda. She and Laci talk about the future.

"I'm going to be a doctor," he says.

It's noble, a young man who, like me, was little more than dead only a month or two ago. He has lived, he will heal, he will heal others. His ambition reassures me. And it startles. He has come out of the death camps with dreams. It seems an unnecessary risk. Even now that I have known starvation and atrocity, I remember the pain of lesser hurts, of a dream ruined by prejudice, of the way my coach spoke to me when she cut me from the Olympic training team. I remember my grandfather, how he retired from the Singer Sewing Machine Company and waited for his pension check. How he waited and waited, how he talked of little else. Finally he received his first check. A week later we were evacuated to the brick factory. A few weeks later, he was dead. I don't want to dream the wrong thing.

"I have an uncle in America," Laci continues. "In Texas. I'll go there, work, save up for school."

"Maybe we'll go to America too," Magda says. She must be thinking of Aunt Matilda, in the Bronx. All around us on the top of the train car there is talk of America, of Palestine. Why keep living in the ashes of our loss? Why keep scratching for survival in a place where we're not wanted? Soon we will learn of the restrictive immigration limits in America and Palestine. There is no haven free of limitation, of prejudice. Wherever we go, life might always be like this. Trying to ignore the fear that any minute we'll be bombed, shot, tossed in a ditch. Or at best forced to ride on top of the train. Holding hands against the wind.

* * *

In Prague we are to change trains again. We say goodbye to Laci. Magda gives him our old address, Kossuth Lajos Utca #6. He promises to keep in touch. There's time before the next departure, time to stretch our legs, sit in the sun and the quiet to eat our bread. I want to find a park. I want to see green growth, flowers. I close my eyes every few steps and take in the smells of a city, the streets and sidewalks and civilian bustle. Bakeries, car exhaust, perfume. It's hard to believe that all of this existed while we were in our hell. I gaze in shop windows. It doesn't matter that I am penniless. It will matter, of course. In Košice food won't be given out for free. But at this moment I feel completely full just seeing that there are dresses and stockings to buy, jewelry, pipes, stationery. Life and commerce go on. A woman fingers the weight of a summer dress. A man admires a necklace. Things aren't important, but beauty is. Here is a city full of people who have not lost the capacity to imagine, make, and admire beautiful things. I will be a resident again—a resident of somewhere. I will run errands and buy gifts. I will stand in line at the post office. I will eat bread that I have baked. I will wear fine couture in honor of my father. I will go to the opera in honor of my mother, of how she would sit at the edge of her chair listening to Wagner, how she would weep. I will go to the symphony. And for Klara, I'll seek out every performance of Mendelssohn's violin concerto. That longing and wistfulness. The urgency as the line climbs, and then the rippling cadenza, the crashing, rising chords. And then the more sinister theme in the strings, threatening the solo violin's rising dreams. Standing on the sidewalk, I've closed my eyes so I can hear the echo of my sister's violin. Magda startles me.

"Wake up, Dicu!"

And when I open my eyes, right here in the thick of the city, near the entrance to the park, there's a concert poster advertising a performance with a solo violinist.

The picture on the poster is my sister's.

There on the paper my Klarie sits, holding her violin.

CHAPTER 8

In Through a Window

We step off the train in Košice. Our hometown is no longer in Hungary. It is part of Czechoslovakia again. We blink into the June sun. We have no money for a taxi, no money for anything, no idea if our family's old apartment is occupied, no idea how we will find a way to live. But we are home. We are ready to search for Klara. Klara, who gave a concert in Prague only weeks ago. Klara who, somewhere, is alive.

We walk through Mestský Park, toward the center of town. People sit at outdoor tables, on benches. Children gather around the fountains. There's the clock where we watched the boys gather to meet Magda. There's the balcony of our father's shop, the gold medals blazing from the railing. *He's here!* I am so certain of it that I smell his tobacco, feel his mustache on my cheek. But the windows of the shop are dark. We walk toward our apartment at Kossuth Lajos Utca #6, and here on the sidewalk near the place where the wagon parked before it carried us to the brick factory, a miracle occurs. Klara materializes, walking out the front door. Her hair is braided and coiled like our mother's. She carries her violin. When she sees me, she drops the violin case on the sidewalk and runs to me. She's moaning. "Dicuka, Dicuka!" she cries. She picks me up like a baby, her arms a cradle.

"Don't hug us!" Magda shrieks. "We're covered in bugs and sores!"

I think what she means is, *Dear sister, we're scarred.* She means, *Don't let what we've seen hurt you. Don't make it worse. Don't ask us what happened. Don't vanish into thin air.*

Klara rocks me and rocks me. "This is my little one!" she calls to a passing stranger. From this moment on she becomes my mother. She has already seen in our faces that the position is empty and must be filled.

It has been at least a year and a half since we have seen her. She is on her way to the radio station to give a concert. We are desperate not to have her out of sight, out of touch. "Stay, stay," we beg. But she is already late. "If I don't play, we don't eat," she says. "Hurry, follow me inside." Maybe it is a blessing that there is no time to talk now. We wouldn't know how to begin. Though it must shock Klara to see us so physically ravaged, maybe that is a blessing too. There is something concrete Klara can do to express her love and relief, to point us in the direction of healing. It will take more than rest. Perhaps we will never recover. But there is something she can do right now. She brings us inside and strips off our dirty clothes. She helps us stretch out on the white sheets in the bed where our parents used to sleep. She rubs calamine lotion into the rash that covers our bodies. The rash that makes us itch and itch, that passes instantly from our bodies to hers so she can barely play her concert for the burning all over her skin. Our reunion is physical.

Magda and I spend at least a week in bed, naked, bodies doused in calamine. Klara doesn't ask us questions. She doesn't ask us where our mother and father are. She talks so that we don't have to. She talks so that she doesn't have to hear. Everything she tells us is phrased like a miracle. And it is miraculous. Here we are together. We are the lucky ones. There are few reunions like ours. Our aunt and uncle—our mother's siblings—were thrown off a bridge and drowned in the Danube, Klara tells us, blunt, matter-of-fact, but when the last remaining Jews in Hungary were rounded up, she escaped detection. She lived in her professor's house, disguised as a gentile. "One day my professor said, 'You have to learn the Bible tomorrow, you are going to start teaching it, you are going to live in a nunnery.' It seemed like the best way to keep me hidden. The convent was nearly two hundred miles from Budapest. I wore a habit. But one day a girl from the academy recognized me, and I snuck away on a train back to Budapest."

Sometime in the summer, she got a letter from our parents. It was the letter they had written while we were in the brick factory, telling Klara where we were imprisoned, that we were together, safe, that we thought we would be transferred to a work camp called Kenyérmező. I remember seeing my mother drop the letter onto the street during our evacuation from the brick factory, since there was no way to mail it. At the time I thought she had dropped it in resignation. But listening to Klara tell her story of survival, I see things differently. In releasing the letter, my mother wasn't relinquishing hope—she was kindling it. Either way, whether she dropped the letter in defeat or in hope, she took a risk. The letter pointed a finger at my sister, a blond-haired Jew hiding in Budapest. It gave her address. While we trundled in the dark toward Auschwitz, someone, a stranger, held that letter in his hand. He could have opened it, he could have turned Klara in to the *nyilas*. He could have thrown the letter away in the trash, or left it in the street. But this stranger put a stamp on it and mailed it to Klara in Budapest. This is as unbelievable to me as my sister's reappearance, it's a magic trick, evidence of a lifeline that runs between us, evidence, too, that kindness still existed in the world even then. Through the dirt kicked up by three thousand pairs of feet, many of them headed straight for a chimney in Poland, our mother's letter flew. A blond-haired girl set her violin down to rip open the seal.

Klara tells another story with a happy ending. With the knowledge that we'd been evacuated to the brick factory, that we expected any day to get shipped away, to Kenyérmező or who knows where, she went to the German consulate in Budapest to demand to be sent to wherever we were. At the consulate, the doorman told her, "Little girl, go away. Don't come in here." She wasn't going to be told no. She tried to sneak back in the building. The doorman saw her and beat her up, punching her shoulders, her arms, her stomach, her face. "Get out of here," he said again.

"He beat me up and saved my life," she tells us.

Near the end of the war when the Russians surrounded Budapest, the Nazis became even more determined to rid the city of Jews. "We had to carry identification cards with our name, religion, picture. They were checking these cards all the time on the streets, and if they saw you were a Jew they might kill you. I did not want to carry my card, but I was afraid I would need something to prove who I was after the war. So I decided to give mine to a girlfriend to keep for me. She lived across the harbor, so I had to cross the bridge to get there, and when I got to the bridge the soldiers were checking identification. They said, 'Please show me who you are.' I said I had nothing, and somehow, I don't know how, they let me go across. My blond hair and blue eyes must have convinced them. I never went back to my friend's house to retrieve the card."

When you can't go in through a door, go in through a window, our mother used to say. There is no door for survival. Or recovery either. It's all windows. Latches you can't reach easily, panes too small, spaces where a body shouldn't fit. But you can't stand where you are. You must find a way.

After the German surrender, while Magda and I were recovering in Wels, Klara went to a consulate again, this time the Russian consulate, because Budapest had been liberated from Nazi control by the Red Army, and tried to learn what had become of us. They had no information about our family, but in exchange for a free concert, they offered to help her get home to Košice. "When I played, two hundred Russians attended, and then I was brought home on top of a train. They watched over me when we stopped and slept." When she opened the door to our old apartment, everything was in disarray, our furniture and possessions looted. The rooms had been used as a stable and the floors were covered in horse manure. While we were learning to eat, walk, write our names in Wels, Klara began playing concerts for money and scrubbing the floors.

And now we've come. When our rashes are healed, we take turns leaving the apartment. There is only one good pair of shoes among the three of us. When it's my turn to wear the shoes, I walk slowly on the sidewalk, back and forth, still too weak to go far. A neighbor recognizes me. "I'm surprised to see you made it," he says. "You were always such a skinny little kid." I could feel triumph. Against all odds, a happy ending! But I feel guilt. Why me? Why did I make it? There is no explanation. It's a fluke. Or a mistake.

People can be sorted two ways: survived; didn't. The latter are not here to tell their tale. The portrait of our mother's mother still hangs on the wall. Her dark hair is parted down the middle and pulled back in a tight bun. A few curly strands feather across her smooth forehead. She doesn't smile in the picture, but her eyes are more sincere than severe. She watches us, knowing and no-nonsense. Magda talks to her portrait as our mother used to do. Sometimes she asks for help. Sometimes she mutters and rants. "Those Nazi bastards . . . The fucking *nyilas* . . ." The piano that lived against the wall under her portrait is gone. The piano was so present in our daily lives that it was almost invisible, like breath. Now its absence dominates the room. Magda rages at the empty space. With the piano gone, something in her is missing too. A piece of her identity. An outlet for her self-expression. In its absence, she finds anger. Vibrant, full voiced, willful. I admire her for it. My anger turns inward and congeals in my lungs.

Magda grows stronger as the days pass, but I am still weak. My upper back continues to ache, making it difficult to walk, and my chest is heavy with congestion. I rarely leave the house. Even if I weren't sick, there is nowhere I want to go. When death is the answer to every question, why go walking? Why talk when any interaction with the living serves to prove that you move through the world in the company of an ever-growing congregation of ghosts? Why miss anyone in particular when everyone has so many to mourn?

I rely on my sisters: Klara, my devoted nurse; Magda, my source of news, my connection to the greater world. One day she comes home breathless. "The piano!" she says. "I found it. It's in the coffeehouse. *Our* piano. We've got to get it back."

The coffeehouse owner won't believe that it's ours. Klara and Magda take turns pleading. They describe the family chamber music concerts in our parlor, how János Starker, Klara's cellist friend, another child prodigy from the conservatory, played a concert with Klara in our house the year of his professional debut. None of their words holds sway. Finally, Magda seeks out the piano tuner. He comes with her to the café and talks to the owner and then looks inside the piano lid to read the serial number. "Yes," he says, nodding, "this is the Elefánt piano." He gets together a crew of men to bring it back to our apartment.

Is there something inside me that can verify *my* identity, that can restore myself to myself? If such a thing existed, who would I seek out to lift the lid, read the code?

One day a package arrives from Aunt Matilda. *Valentine Avenue, the Bronx*, the return address reads. She sends tea, Crisco. We have never seen Crisco before and so have no idea that it's a butter substitute to be used for cooking and baking. We eat it plain, we spread it on bread. We reuse the tea bags again and again. How many cups can we brew with the same leaves?

Occasionally, our doorbell rings, and I jolt up in bed. These are the best moments. Someone is waiting outside the door, and in the seconds before we open it, that person could be anyone. Sometimes I imagine it is our father. He survived the first selection after all. He found a way to work, to appear young throughout the rest of the war, and here he is, smoking a cigarette, holding a piece of chalk, a long measuring tape slung around his neck like a scarf. Sometimes it is Eric I imagine on the stoop. He holds a bouquet of roses.

My father never comes. That is how we know for sure that he is dead.

One day Lester Korda, one of the two brothers who rode with us on the train from Wels to Vienna, rings the bell. He has come to see how we are making out. "Call me Csicsi," he says. He is like fresh air rushing into our stale rooms. We are in an ongoing limbo, my sisters and I, between looking back and moving on. So much of our energy is used just to restore things—our health, our belongings, what we can of life before loss and imprisonment. Csicsi's warmth and interest in our welfare remind me that there is more to live for than that.

Klara is in the other room, practicing violin. Csicsi's eyes light up when he hears the music. "May I meet the musician?" he asks, and Klara obliges. She plays a Hungarian czardas. Csicsi dances. Maybe it is time to build our lives—not back to what they were, but anew.

Throughout the summer of 1945, Csicsi becomes a regular visitor. When Klara has to travel to Prague for another concert, Csicsi offers to go with her.

"Shall I bake a wedding cake now?" Magda asks.

"Stop it," Klara says. "He has a girlfriend. He's just being polite."

"Are you sure you're not falling in love?" I ask.

"He remembers our parents," she says, "and I remember his."

When I have been home a few weeks, although I am barely strong enough, I make the journey on foot to Eric's old apartment. No one from his family has returned. The apartment is empty. I vow to go back as often as I can. The pain of staying away is greater than the disappointment of vigilance. To mourn him is to mourn more than a person. In the camps I could long for his physical presence and hold on to the promise of our future. *If I survive today, tomorrow I will be free.* The irony of freedom is that it is harder to find hope and purpose. Now I must come to terms with the fact that anyone I marry won't know my parents. If I ever have children, they won't know their grandparents. It isn't just my own loss that hurts. It's the way it ripples out into the future. The way it perpetuates. My mother used to tell me to look for a man with a wide forehead because that means he's intelligent. "Watch how he uses his handkerchief," she would say. "Make sure he always carries a clean one. Make sure his shoes are polished." She won't be at my wedding. She won't ever know who I become, whom I choose.

Klara is my mother now. She does it out of love and a natural competence. She also does it out of guilt. She wasn't there to protect us at Auschwitz. She will protect us now. She does all the cooking. She feeds me with a spoon, like I'm a baby. I love her, I love her attention, I love being held and made to feel safe. But it is suffocating too. Her kindness leaves me no breathing room. And she seems to need something from me in return. Not gratitude or appreciation. Something deeper. I can feel that she relies on me for her own sense of purpose. For her reason for being. In taking care of me, she finds the reason why she was spared. My role is to be healthy enough to stay alive yet helpless enough to need her. That is my reason for having survived.

By the end of June, my back still isn't healed. There is a constant crunching, piercing feeling between my shoulder blades. And my chest still hurts, even to breathe. Then I break out in a fever. Klara takes me to the hospital. She insists that I be given a private room, the very best care. I worry about the expense, but she says she will just play more concerts, she will find a way to cover it. When the doctor comes in to examine me, I recognize him. He's the older brother of my former schoolmate. His name is Gaby. I remember that his sister called him the Angel Gabriel. She is dead now, I learn. She died at Auschwitz. He asks me if I ever saw her there. I wish I had a last image for him to remember her by, and I consider lying, telling him a story in which I witnessed her do something brave, speak of him lovingly. But I don't lie. I would rather face the unknown void of my father and Eric's last minutes than to be told something that, however comforting, isn't true. The Angel Gabriel gives me my first medical attention since liberation. He diagnoses me with typhoid fever, pneumonia, pleurisy, a broken back. He makes a removable cast for me that covers my whole torso. I place it on the bed at night so that I can climb inside it, my plaster shell.

Gaby's visits become more than just physically therapeutic. He doesn't charge me for his medical care. We sit and reminisce. I can't grieve with my sisters, not explicitly. It's too raw, too present. And to grieve with them seems like a defilement of the miracle of our togetherness. We never hold one another and cry. But with Gaby I can allow myself to grieve. One day I ask Gaby about Eric. He remembers him but doesn't know what became of him. Gaby has colleagues working at a repatriation center in the Tatra Mountains. He says he will ask them to see what they can learn about Eric.

One afternoon Gaby examines my back. He waits until I am lying down on my stomach to tell me what he has learned. "Eric was sent to Auschwitz," he says. "He died in January. The day before liberation."

I erupt in a wail. I think my chest will break. The blast of sorrow is so severe that tears won't come—only a jagged moaning in my throat. I am not yet capable of clear thoughts or questions about my beloved's last days, about his suffering, about the state of his mind and his spirit when his body gave out. I am consumed by the grief and injustice of losing him. If he could have held on for a few more hours, maybe even just a few more breaths, we could be together now. I moan into the table until my voice goes hoarse.

As the shock dissolves, I understand that in a strange way the pain of knowing is merciful. I have no such certainty about my own father's death. To know for sure that Eric is gone is like receiving a diagnosis after a long ache. I can pinpoint the reason for the hurt. I can clarify what has to heal.

But a diagnosis is not a cure. I don't know what to do with Eric's voice now, the remembered syllables, the hope.

By the end of July my fever is gone, but Gaby still isn't satisfied with my progress. My lungs, compressed too long by my broken back, are full of fluid. He worries that I might have contracted tuberculosis and recommends that I go to a TB hospital in the Tatra Mountains, near the repatriation center where he learned of Eric's death. Klara will accompany me on the train to the nearest village in the mountains. Magda will stay at the apartment. After the effort of reclaiming it, on the off-chance of an unexpected visitor, we can't risk leaving it empty, even for a day. Klara tends me on the journey as if I am a child. "Look at my little one!" she exclaims to fellow passengers. I beam at them like a precocious toddler. I practically look like one. My hair has fallen out again from the typhoid and is just starting to grow back, baby soft. Klara helps me cover my head with a scarf. As we gain elevation, the dry alpine air feels clean in my chest, but it's still hard to breathe. There is a constant sludge in my lungs. It's as though all the tears I can't allow myself to shed on the outside are draining into a pool inside. I can't ignore the grief, but I can't seem to expel it either.

Klara is due back in Košice for another radio performance—her concerts are our only source of income—and can't accompany me to the TB hospital where I am to stay until I am well, but she refuses to let me go alone. We ask around at the repatriation center to see if anyone knows of someone going to the hospital, and I'm told that a young man staying in the nearby hotel is also going there to be treated. When I approach him in the lobby of the hotel, he is kissing a girl.

"Meet me at the train," he growls.

When I approach him on the train platform he is still kissing the girl. He is gray haired, at least ten years older than I am. I will turn eighteen in September, but with my skinny limbs and flat chest and bald head I look more like twelve. I stand beside them awkwardly as they embrace, not sure how to get his attention. I'm annoyed. *This* is the man to whom I'm to be entrusted?

"Could you help me, sir?" I finally ask. "You are supposed to escort me to the hospital."

"I'm busy," he says. He barely breaks his kiss to respond to me. He is like an older sibling shaking away an annoying sister. "Meet me on the train."

After Klara's constant fawning and attention, his dismissiveness cuts. I don't know why it bothers me so much. Is it that his girlfriend is alive while my boyfriend is dead? Or is it that I am already so diminished that without another person's attention or approval I feel I am in danger of disappearing entirely?

He buys me a sandwich on the train and a newspaper for himself. We don't talk, other than to exchange names and formalities. Béla is his name. To me he is just a rude person on a train, a person I must grudgingly ask for help, a person who only grudgingly gives it.

When we arrive at the station, we learn we have to walk to the TB hospital, and now there is no newspaper to distract him.

"What did you do before the war?" he asks. I notice what I didn't hear before—he speaks with a stutter. When I tell him that I was a gymnast and I danced ballet, he says, "That reminds me of a joke."

I look at him expectantly, ready for a dose of Hungarian humor, ready for the relief I felt at Auschwitz when Magda and I hosted the boob contest with our bunkmates, the lift of laughter in terrible times.

"There was a bird," he says, "and the bird was about to die. A cow came and warmed him up a little—from his rear end, if you know what I mean—and the bird started to perk up. Then a truck came and finished off the bird. A wise old horse came by and saw the dead bird on the road. The horse said, 'Didn't I tell you if you have shit on your head, don't dance?'" Béla laughs at his own joke.

But I feel insulted. He means to be funny, but I think he is trying to tell me, you have shit on your head. I think he means, you're a real mess. I think he's saying, you shouldn't call yourself a dancer if you look like this. For a moment, before his insult, it had been such a relief to have his attention, such a relief to be asked who I was before the war. Such a relief to acknowledge the me who existed—who thrived—before the war. His joke reinforces how irreparably the war has changed and damaged me. It hurts for a stranger to cut me down. It hurts because he's right. I am a mess. Still, I won't let an insensitive man or his Hungarian sarcasm get the last word. I will show him that the buoyant dancer still lives in me, no matter how short my hair is, how thin my face, how thick the grief in my chest. I bound ahead of him and do the splits in the middle of the road.

I don't have TB, as it turns out. They keep me for three weeks in the hospital all the same to treat the fluid building up in my lungs. I am so afraid of contracting TB that I open doors with my feet instead of my hands, even though I know the disease can't be spread through touch, germs on doorknobs. It is a good thing that I don't have TB, but I am still not well. I don't have the vocabulary to explain the flooded feeling in my chest, the dark throb in my forehead. It's like grit smeared across my vision. Later, this feeling will have a name. Later, I will know to call it depression. Now all I know is that it takes effort to get out of bed. There's the effort of breath. And, worse, the existential effort. Why get up? What is there to get up for? I wasn't suicidal at Auschwitz, when things were hopeless. Every day I was surrounded by people who said, "The only way you'll get out of here is as a corpse." But the dire prophecies gave me something to fight against. Now that I am recuperating, now that I am facing the irrevocable fact that my parents are never coming back, that Eric is never coming back, the only demons are within. I think of taking my own life. I want a way out of pain. Why not choose not to be?

Béla has been assigned the room right above mine. One day he stops by my room to check on me. "I'll make you laugh," he says, "and that will make you better. You'll see." He waggles his tongue, pulls on his ears, makes animal noises, the way you might entertain a baby. It's absurd, maybe insulting, yet I can't help myself. The laugh rises out of me like a tide. "Don't laugh," the doctors had warned me, as though laughter was a constant temptation, as though I was in danger of laughing to death. "If you laugh, you will have more pain." They were right. It does hurt, but it also feels good.

I lie awake that night thinking of him in the bed just above mine, thinking up things to impress him, things I studied in school. The next day, when he visits my room, I tell him everything I have been able to remember in the night about Greek myths, calling up the most obscure gods and goddesses. I tell him about Freud's *Interpretation of Dreams*, the last book Eric and I read together. I perform for him, the way I used to perform for my parents' dinner guests, my turn in the spotlight before Klara, the headlining act, took the stage. He looks at me the way a teacher looks at a star pupil. He tells me very little about himself, but I do learn that he studied violin when he was young and still loved to play chamber music recordings and conduct in the air.

Béla is twenty-seven years old. I am only a child. He has other women in his life. The woman he was kissing on the train platform when I interrupted him. And, he tells me, another patient here at the TB hospital, his cousin Marianna's best friend, a girl he dated in high school, before the war. She is very ill. She isn't going to make it. He calls himself her fiancé, a gesture of hope for her on her deathbed, a gesture of hope for her mother. Months later, I will learn that Béla also has a wife—a near stranger, a woman with whom he was never intimate, a gentile, with whom he made an arrangement on paper in the early days of the war in an effort to protect his family and his fortune.

It isn't love. It's that I am hungry, so very hungry, and I amuse him. And he looks at me the way Eric did that long-ago day in the book club, as though I am intelligent, as though I have worthwhile things to say. For now, that's enough.

On my last night in the TB hospital, I lie in my snug little room and a voice comes to me, from the bottom of the mountains, from the very center of the Earth. Up through the floor and thin mattress, it envelops me, charges me. *If you live*, the voice says, *you've got to stand for something.*

"I'll write to you," Béla says in the morning, when we say goodbye. It's not love. I don't hold him to it.

* * *

When I return to Košice, Magda meets me at the train station. Klara has been so possessive of me since our reunion that I have forgotten what it is like to be alone with Magda. Her hair has grown. Waves frame her face. Her eyes are bright again. She looks well. She is bursting with gossip from the three weeks that I've been away. Csicsi has broken things off with his girlfriend and is now unabashedly courting Klara. The Košice survivors have formed an entertainment club, and she has already promised that I will perform. And Laci, the man from the top of the train, has written to tell us that he has received an affidavit of support from his relatives in Texas. Soon he will join them in a place called El Paso, she tells me, where he will work in their furniture store and save money for medical school.

"Klara better not humiliate me by marrying first," Magda says.

This is how we will heal. Yesterday, cannibalism and murder. Yesterday, choosing blades of grass. Today, the antiquated customs and proprieties, the rules and roles that make us feel normal. We will minimize the loss and horror, the terrible interruption of life, by living as though none of it happened. We will not be a lost generation.

"Here," my sister says. "I have something for you." She hands me an envelope, my name written on it in the cursive script we were taught to write in school. "Your old friend came by."

For a moment, I think she means Eric. He is alive. Inside the envelope is my future. He has waited for me. Or he has already moved on.

But the envelope isn't from Eric. And it doesn't contain my future. It holds my past. It holds a picture of me, perhaps the last picture taken of me before Auschwitz, the picture of me doing the splits by the river, the picture Eric took, the picture I gave to my friend Rebeka. She has kept it safe for me. In my fingers I hold the me who has yet to lose her parents, who doesn't know how soon she will lose her love.

Magda takes me to the entertainment club that night. Klara and Csicsi are there, and Rebeka, and Csicsi's brother Imre. Gaby, my doctor, is there too, and perhaps that is why, weak as I am, I agree to dance. I want to show him I am getting well. I want to show him that the time he has devoted to my care has made a difference, that he hasn't wasted his effort. I ask Klara and the other musicians to play "The Blue Danube," and I begin my routine, the same dance that a little more than a year ago I performed my first night at Auschwitz, the dance that Josef Mengele rewarded with a loaf of bread. The steps have not changed, but my body has. I have none of the lean, limber muscle, none of the strength in my limbs or my core. I am a wheezing husk, a broken-backed girl with no hair. I close my eyes as I did in the barracks. That long-ago night I held my lids shut so that I wouldn't have to look at Mengele's terrifying and murderous eyes, so that I could keep from crumbling to the ground under the force of his stare. Now I close my eyes so that I can feel my body, not escape the room, so that I can feel the heat of appreciation from my audience. As I find my way back to the movements, to the familiar steps, the high kick, the splits, I grow more confident and comfortable in the moment. And I find my way back in time, to the days when we could imagine no worse encroachment on our freedom than curfews or yellow stars. I dance toward my innocence. Toward the girl who bounded up the stairs to the ballet studio. Toward the wise and loving mother who first brought her there. *Help me*, I call to her. *Help me. Help me to live again.*

A few days later, a thick letter arrives, addressed to me. It's from Béla. It is the first of many long letters he will write, first from the TB hospital, and then from his home in Prešov, where he was born and raised—the third-largest city in Slovakia, just twenty miles north of Košice. As I learn more about Béla, begin to assemble the facts he gives me in these letters into a life, the gray-haired man with a stutter and sarcastic sense of humor becomes a person with contours.

Béla's earliest memory, he writes, is of going for a walk with his grandfather, one of the wealthiest men in the country, and being denied a cookie from the patisserie. When he leaves the hospital, he will take over this same grandfather's business, wholesaling produce from the region's farmers, grinding coffee and grinding wheat for all of Slovakia. Béla is a full pantry, a country of plenty, he is a feast.

Like my mother, Béla lost one of his parents when he was very young. His father, who had been the mayor of Prešov, and before that, a renowned lawyer for the poor, went to a conference in Prague the winter Béla was four. He stepped off the train and fell into an avalanche of snow. Or that is what the police told Béla's mother. Béla suspects that his father, a controversial figure because he rebelled against the Prešov elite by serving as an advocate for the poor and disenfranchised, was murdered, but the official word was that he'd suffocated under all that snow. Ever since his father's death, Béla has spoken with a stutter.

His mother never recovered from his father's death. Her father-in-law, Béla's grandfather, kept her locked up in the house to keep her from meeting other men. During the war, Béla's aunt and uncle invited her to join them in Hungary, where they were living in hiding using false identification papers. One day Béla's mother was at the market when she saw a group of SS soldiers. She panicked. She ran up to them and shouted a confession. "I am Jewish!" she said. They shipped her off to Auschwitz, where she died in the gas chamber. The rest of the family, exposed by Béla's mother's confession, managed to flee to the mountains.

Béla's brother George has lived in America since before the war. Before he immigrated, he was walking down the street in Bratislava, the capital of Slovakia, when he was attacked by gentiles, his glasses broken. He left the brewing anti-Semitism in Europe to live with their great-uncle in Chicago. Their cousin Marianna escaped to England. Béla, though he had studied in England as a boy and spoke English fluently, refused to leave Slovakia. He wanted to protect everyone in his family. That was not to be. His grandfather died of stomach cancer. And his aunt and uncle, coaxed out of the mountains by Germans who promised that all Jews who returned would be treated kindly, were lined up in the street and shot.

Béla escaped the Nazis by hiding in the mountains. He could barely hold a screwdriver, he writes, he was afraid of weapons, he didn't want to fight, he was clumsy, but he became a partisan. He took up a gun and joined ranks with the Russians who were fighting the Nazis. While with the partisans, he contracted TB. He hadn't had to survive the camps. Instead he had survived the mountain forests. For this I am grateful. I will never see the imprint of the smokestacks mirrored in his eyes.

Prešov is only an hour's drive from Košice. One weekend Béla visits me, pulling Swiss cheese and salami from a bag. Food. This is what I fall in love with first. If I can keep him interested in me, he will feed me and my sisters—this is what I think. I don't pine for him the way I did for Eric. I don't fantasize about kissing him or long to have him near. I don't even flirt—not in a romantic way. We are like two shipwrecked people staring at the sea for signs of life. And in each other we see a glimmer. I find that I am stepping into life again. I feel that I am going to belong to someone. I know Béla is not the love of my life, not the way Eric was. I'm not trying to replace Eric. But Béla tells me jokes and writes me twenty-page letters, and I have a choice to make.

When I tell Klara that I am going to marry Béla, she doesn't congratulate me. She turns to Magda. "Ah, two cripples getting hitched," she says. "How's that going to work?" Later, at the table, she speaks to me directly. "You're a baby, Dicuka," she says. "You can't make decisions like this. You're not whole. And he isn't either. He has TB. He stutters. You can't marry him." Now I have a new motivation for this marriage to work. I have to prove my sister wrong.

Klara's objection isn't the only impediment. There is the fact that Béla is still legally married to the gentile woman who protected his family fortune from the Nazis, and she refuses to divorce him. They have never lived together, never had a relationship of any kind other than that of convenience—for her, his money; for him, her gentile status—but she won't grant him the divorce, not at first, not until he agrees to pay her a large sum of money.

And then there is his fiancée in the Tatra Mountains, dying of TB. He begs her friend Marianna, his cousin who had escaped to England but returned after the war, to deliver the news that he isn't going to marry her. Marianna is justifiably furious. "You're horrible!" she yells. "You can't do this to her. I won't in a million years tell her you're breaking your promise." Béla asks me to come with him back to the hospital so he can tell her himself. She is gracious and kind to me, and very, very ill. It rattles me to see someone so physically devastated. It is too much like the recent past. I am afraid to stand so close to death's door. She tells me she is happy that Béla will marry someone like me, someone with so much energy and life. I am glad to have her blessing. And yet how easily I could have been the one in bed, propped up on scratchy pillows, coughing between words, filling a handkerchief with blood.

That night Béla and I stay in a hotel together, the hotel where we met. In all of his visits to Košice we have slept in separate rooms. We have never shared a bed. We have never seen each other without clothes. But tonight is different. I try to remember the forbidden words in Zola's *Nana*. What else can prepare me to give him pleasure, to pursue pleasure myself? No one has instructed me on the choreography of intimacy. Nakedness has been degrading, humiliating, terrifying. I have to learn again how to inhabit my skin.

"You're shivering," Béla says. "Are you cold?" He goes to his suitcase and takes out a package wrapped with a shining bow. Inside the box, nestled in tissue paper, is a beautiful silk negligee. It is an extravagant gift. But that isn't what moves me. He somehow knew that I would need a second skin. It isn't that I want to shield myself from him, my husband-to-be. It's not cover I'm after. It's a way to heighten myself, extend, a way to step into the chapter that hasn't been written yet. I tremble as he slips it over my head, as the fabric falls against my legs. The right costume can augment the dance. I twirl for him.

"*Izléses*," he says. Classy.

I am so happy that someone is looking at me. His gaze is more than a compliment. Just as my mother's words once taught me to value my intelligence, through Béla's eyes I find a new appreciation of my body—of my life.

CHAPTER 9

Next Year in Jerusalem

I marry Béla Eger on November 12, 1946, at the city hall in Košice. We could have celebrated with a lavish affair at the Eger mansion, we could have chosen a Jewish ceremony. But I am a girl, I am only nineteen, I have never had the chance to finish high school, I am falling from one thing to another. And my parents are dead. One of my father's old friends, a gentile, has been checking in on my sisters and me. He is a judge, and it turns out that he knew Béla's brother when George was in law school. He is a link between Béla's family and my own, he is a link to my father, and so he is the one we choose to marry us.

In the fifteen months since Béla and I met, my hair has grown from meager fuzz to full waves all the way to my shoulders. I wear it down, a white barrette clipped at my temple. I am married in a borrowed dress—knee-length black rayon, with puffed shoulders and a white collar and tapered sleeves. I hold a small bouquet of lilies and roses tied with a wide satin ribbon. I smile for photographs on the balcony of my father's shop. There are only eight people at the wedding—me, Béla, Magda, Klara, Csicsi, Imre, and two of my father's old friends, one of them a bank president, the other the judge who marries us. Béla stutters when he says his vows, and Klara gives me a look, an admonition. The

133

reception is in our apartment. Klara has cooked all of the food. Roasted chicken. Hungarian couscous. Potatoes with butter and parsley. And *dobos torte*—seven-layer chocolate cake. We try to put a happy spin on the day, but all of the absences tug at us. Orphans marry orphans. Later I will hear that we marry our parents. But I say we marry our unfinished business. For Béla and me, our unfinished business is grief.

We honeymoon in Bratislava, on the Danube. I dance with my husband to waltzes we knew before the war. We visit Maximilian's fountain and Coronation Hill. Béla pretends to be the new monarch, pointing his sword north, south, east, west, promising to defend me. We see the old city wall, double fortified against the Turks. We think the storm has passed.

That night at the hotel we wake to pounding on our door. Police officers push their way into our room. The police are constantly checking up on civilians, our lives a labyrinth of bureaucratic necessities, official permission needed for even the minutiae of daily life. They can whisk you off to jail with barely a pretext. And because my husband is wealthy, he is an important person, so it shouldn't surprise me that we've been followed. But I am surprised. And afraid (I am always afraid). And also embarrassed. And angry. This is my honeymoon. Why are they bothering us?

"We were just married," Béla reassures them in Slovak. (I grew up speaking only Hungarian, but Béla is also fluent in Czech and Slovak and other languages necessary for his wholesaling business.) He shows them our passports, our marriage license, our rings, everything that can confirm our identities and our reason for being in the hotel. "Please don't bother us."

The police give no explanation for their invasion of our privacy, for their suspicion of us. Are they following Béla for some reason? Had they mistaken him for someone else? I try not to register the intrusion as an omen. I focus on the smoothness of my husband's voice beneath his stutter. We have nothing to hide. But high alert is my constant state. And I can't lose the feeling that I am guilty of something. That I will be found out.

My transgression is life. And the beginnings of a cautious joy.

On the train home we have a private room. I prefer its spare elegance to the hotel. I can imagine myself into a story. We are explorers, settlers. The motion of the train unspools the apprehension and turmoil of my brain and helps me focus on Béla's body. Or maybe it's just the smallness of the bed. My body surprises me. Pleasure is an elixir. A salve. We reach for each other again and again as the train moves through the night.

I have to run for the bathroom when we return to Košice to visit my sisters. I vomit over and over. It is good news, but I don't know it yet. All I know is that after more than a year of slow recovery, I am sick again.

"What have you done to my baby?" Klara screams.

Béla runs his handkerchief in cool water and wipes my face.

While my sisters continue life in Košice, I begin an unexpected life of luxury. I move into the Eger mansion in Prešov, a five-hundred-year-old monastery, wide and long, a block of a house, horses and carriages lined up along the drive. Béla's business is downstairs and we live upstairs. Renters occupy other parts of the enormous house. A woman does our laundry, boiling the sheets, ironing, everything white. We eat off of china made for the family, their name—my new name—in gold. In the dining room there is a button I can push that Mariska, the housekeeper, hears in the kitchen. I can't eat enough of her rye bread. I push the button and request more bread.

"You're eating like pigs," she mutters to me.

She doesn't disguise her unhappiness that I have joined the family. I am a threat to her way of life, to the way she manages the house. It pains me to see Béla hand her the money for groceries. I am his wife. I feel useless.

"Please teach me to cook," I ask Mariska one day.

"I don't ever want you in this kitchen," she says.

To launch me on my new life, Béla introduces me to the Prešov elite, the lawyers and doctors and businessmen and their wives, beside whom I feel gangly and young and inexperienced. I meet two women about my age. Ava Hartmann is a fashionable woman married to a wealthy, older man. She wears her dark hair in a side part. Marta Vadasz is married to Béla's best friend, Bandi. She has reddish hair and a kind, patient face. I watch Ava and Marta intently, trying to see how I should behave and what I should say. Ava and Marta and the other women drink cognac. I drink cognac. Ava and Marta and the other women all smoke. One night after a dinner party at Ava's house—she made the best chopped liver I have ever tasted, with green pepper in addition to onions—I remark to Béla that I'm the only one who doesn't smoke, and the next day he brings me a silver cigarette case and silver cigarette holder. I don't know how to use it—how to insert the cigarette into one end, how to inhale, how to blow the smoke out through my lips. I try to mirror the other women. I feel like an elegant parrot, nothing but an echo dolled up in nice clothes that my father did not make for me.

Do they know where I've been? Sitting in parlors and around ornate dining tables, I gaze at our friends and acquaintances and wonder. Have they lost the same things Béla and I have lost? We don't talk about it. Denial is our shield. We don't yet know the damage we perpetuate by cutting ourselves off from the past, by maintaining our conspiracy of silence. We are convinced that the more securely we lock the past away, the safer and happier we will be.

I try to relax into my new privilege and wealth. There will be no more loud knocks on the door disrupting sleep, I tell myself. Only the comfort of eiderdowns and clean white sheets. No more starvation. I eat and eat—Mariska's rye bread, spaetzle dumplings, one batch made with sauerkraut, another with bryndza, a Slovakian sheep's milk cheese. I am gaining weight. The memories and loss occupy only a little sliver of me. I will push and push against them so they know their place. I watch my hand lift the silver cigarette holder up to my face and away. I pretend it's a new dance. I can learn every gesture.

The weight I'm putting on is not just due to rich food. In early spring I discover that I'm pregnant. At Auschwitz we didn't get our periods. Perhaps the constant distress and starvation were enough to stop our cycles, or maybe the extreme weight loss. But now my body, the body that was starved and emaciated and left for dead, houses a new life. I count the weeks since I last bled and calculate that Béla and I must have conceived on our honeymoon, maybe on the train. Ava and Marta tell me that they are pregnant too.

I expect my doctor, the Eger family doctor, the same man who attended at Béla's birth, to congratulate me. But he lectures me instead. "You're not strong enough," he tells me. He urges me to schedule an abortion, and soon. I refuse. I run home in tears. He follows me. Mariska lets him into the parlor. "Mrs. Eger, you will die if you have this child," he says. "You are too skinny, too weak."

I look him in the eye. "Doctor, I am going to give life," I say. "Good night."

Béla follows him to the door. I can hear my husband apologizing to the doctor for my lack of respect. "She's a tailor's daughter, she doesn't know better," he explains. The words he speaks to protect me create another small hole in my still fragile ego.

But as my womb expands, so do my self-confidence and determination. I don't hide in the corners. I gain fifty pounds, and when I walk in the streets I push out my stomach and watch reflections of this new version of me glide by in shop windows. I don't immediately recognize this feeling. Then I remember. This is what it feels like to be happy.

Klara and Csicsi marry in the spring of 1947, and Béla and I drive to Košice in his green Opel Adam for the ceremony. It's another momentous occasion that our parents miss, another happy day made less so by their absence. But I am pregnant and my life is full and I will not let sorrow pull me down. Magda plays the family piano. She sings the tunes our father used to sing. Béla struggles with competing notions: to sweep me up in a dance or to make me sit and rest my feet. My sisters lay their hands on my belly. This new life inside me belongs to all of us. It's our new beginning. A piece of our parents, and grandparents, that will continue on and out into the future.

That is the topic of conversation as we take a break from the music, as the men light up cigars. The future. Csicsi's brother Imre will leave soon for Sydney. Our family group is already so small. I don't like the thought of us dispersing. Prešov already feels so far away from my sisters. Before the night is through, before Béla and I drive home, Klara pulls me and Magda into the bedroom.

"I have to tell you something, little one," she says.

I can tell from Magda's frown that she already knows what Klara is about to say.

"If Imre goes to Sydney," Klara says, "we will go there too."

Australia. Among our friends in Prešov, because of the Communist takeover under way in Czechoslovakia, there is also talk of immigrating, maybe to Israel, maybe to America, but the immigration policies are looser in Australia. Ava and her husband have mentioned Sydney too. But it is so far away. "What about your career?" I ask Klara.

"There are orchestras in Sydney."

"You don't speak English." I am throwing every excuse at her. As if these are objections she hasn't already thought of herself.

"Csicsi made a promise," she says. "Just before he died, Csicsi's father told him to take care of his brother. If Imre goes, we go."

"So you're both abandoning me," Magda says. "After all that work to survive, I thought we'd stick together."

I remember the April night, only two years ago, when I worried that Magda might die, when I risked a beating or worse to scale a wall and pick her fresh carrots. We survived a haunting ordeal— we each survived because we had the other for protection, and because we each held the other as something to live for. I have my sister to thank for my very life.

"You'll be married soon," I reassure her. "You'll see. No one is sexier than you."

I don't yet understand that my sister's pain has less to do with loneliness and more to do with the belief that she is undeserving of love. But where she sees pain, hell, deficit, damage, I see something else. I see her courage. I see her triumph and her strength. It is like our first day at Auschwitz, when the absence of her hair revealed to me with new clarity the beauty of her eyes.

"Are you interested in anyone?" I ask her. I want to gossip as we did when we were girls. Magda always offers scintillating information, or funny impersonations—she can make even heavy things feel light. I want her to dream.

Magda shakes her head. "I'm not thinking about a person," she says. "I'm thinking about a place." She points to a postcard she has tucked in the frame of the mirror on her dresser. The picture shows a barren desert, a bridge. *El Paso*, the script across the image reads. It's from Laci. "He got away," Magda says. "So can I."

To me, El Paso looks like the end of the Earth. "Has Laci asked you to join him?"

"Dicuka, my life is no fairy tale. I'm not counting on a man to rescue me." She drums her fingers in her lap as though she is playing piano. There is more she wants to say. "Do you remember what Mama had in her pocket the day she died?"

"Klarie's caul."

"And a dollar bill. A dollar Aunt Matilda had sent sometime, from America."

Why don't I know this? There were so many little things our mother did to signal hope. Not just the dollar bill, which I don't remember, and the caul, which I do, but the schmaltz, the chicken fat she packed along for cooking in the brick factory, the letter to Klara. Magda seems to mirror our mother's practicality, and also her hope.

"Laci's not going to marry me," she says. "But somehow, I'm getting to America." She has written to Aunt Matilda, asking her to send an affidavit of support sponsoring her immigration.

Australia. America. While the next generation stirs inside me, my sisters threaten to float out of reach. I was the first to choose a new life after the war. Now they are choosing. I am glad for them. Yet I think of the day during the war when I was too sick to work, when Magda went to the ammunition factory without me and it was bombed, when Magda could have run free but chose to return to the barracks to rescue me. I have found a good and lucky life. There is no need for her to see to my survival now. But if there is one small piece of hell I miss, it is the part that made me understand that survival is a matter of interdependence, that survival isn't possible alone. In choosing different directions, my sisters and I, are we in danger of breaking the spell?

Béla is out of town when I feel the first contractions early one September morning. They cinch and cinch, strong enough to snap me. I call Klara. By the time she arrives two hours later, the doctor still isn't there. I labor in the same room that Béla was born in, the same bed. When I buckle against the pain, I feel a connection to his mother, a woman I never had the chance to meet. This baby I'm working to get into the world will have no grandparents. The doctor still hasn't come. Klara hovers near me, offering me water, wiping my face. "Get away!" I yell at her. "I can't stand your smell." I can't be the baby and birth a baby. I have to inhabit myself and she is distracting me. Out of the razor-sharp haziness of labor comes the memory of the pregnant woman in Auschwitz who labored in agony with her tied-together legs. I can't stop her face, her voice from coming into the room with me now. She haunts me. She inspires me. Every impulse in her body, her heart, pointing to life, while she and her baby were both consigned to an unspeakably cruel death. The sorrow breaks across me. I am a landslide. I will break myself open on the sharp edge of her torment. I will accept this pain because she didn't have a choice. I will accept my pain so that it might erase hers, might erase every memory, because if this pain doesn't destroy me, memory might. The doctor finally comes. My waters burst and I feel the baby shoot out of me. "It's a little girl!" Klara yells. For a moment I feel complete. I am here. My baby girl is here. All is well and right.

I want to name her Anna-Marie, a romantic name, a French-sounding name, but the Communists keep a roster of the permissible names, and Anna-Marie isn't allowed. So we choose the inversion: Marianne, a tribute to Béla's cousin Marianna, the one who still calls me a dumb goose for having broken up the engagement between Béla and her friend, the friend who is now dead. Béla hands out cigars. He won't bow to the tradition of passing out cigars only for sons. His daughter will be celebrated by every ritual, every act of pride. He brings me a jeweler's box. Inside is a gold bracelet of linked squares the size of postage stamps, made of two kinds of gold. It looks heavy, but it's light.

"To the future," Béla says, and clasps it around my wrist.

He says it and I know the direction of my life. This is what I will stand for: this child. My commitment to her will be as complete and unified as the gold circle around my wrist. I can see my purpose. I will live to ensure that she will never experience what I did. The continuity, from me to her, will grow out of our shared roots, making a new branch, a limb that climbs toward hope and joy.

Still, we take precautions. We christen her. For safety's sake. The same reason our friends Marta and Bandi use a Hungarian last name, Vadasz, meaning "hunter," instead of their Jewish name.

But what control do we really have? Marta's baby is born dead.

Marianne weighs ten pounds at birth. She takes up the whole carriage.

"Do I breast-feed?" I ask the German pediatrician.

"What do you think your tits are for?" she says.

My milk is an abundance. I have more than enough to feed Marianne and also my friend Ava's baby girl. I can feed every hunger. I stand for plenty. I lean down into her when I nurse so that she never has to strain for my body, her source. I give her every drop. When she empties me, I feel the most full.

* * *

Marianne is so protected and cuddled and cared for and bundled up that when, in November 1948, she is fourteen months old and falls ill, I don't believe it at first. I know how to read her fussiness. She's hungry, I think. She's tired. But when I go to her again in the night, a fever rages. She is coal-hot. Her eyes are glassy. Her body complains; cries come out. But she is too sick to register my presence. Or I make no difference. She doesn't want to nurse. My arms are no comfort. Every few minutes a deep throttling cough seizes up her chest. I wake the household. Béla calls the doctor, the doctor who delivered him, who delivered Marianne, and paces the room where he was born.

The doctor is stern with me. She has pneumonia. "This is life or death," he says. He sounds angry, as if the illness is my fault, as if he can't let me forget that from the very beginning Marianne's life has been founded on risk, on my foolish audacity. Now see what has come to pass. But maybe what sounds like anger is just weariness. He lives to heal. How often his labor must end in loss.

"What do we do?" Béla asks. "Tell us what to do."

"You've heard of penicillin?"

"Yes, of course."

"Get your baby penicillin. And fast."

Béla stares at him, dumbfounded, as the doctor buttons his coat. "You're the doctor. Where's the penicillin?" he demands.

"Mr. Eger, there is no penicillin in this country. None that you can buy legally. Good night. Good luck."

"I'll pay any price!"

"Yes," the doctor says. "You must make your own arrangements."

"The Communists?" I suggest when the doctor has left. They liberated Slovakia from Nazi occupation. They have been courting Béla, courting his wealth and influence. They have offered him a position as minister of agriculture if he will join the party.

Béla shakes his head. "Black market sellers will have more direct access," he says.

Marianne has fallen back into a fitful sleep. I must keep her hydrated, but she won't accept water or milk. "Get me the cash," I say, "and tell me where to go."

Black market dealers run business alongside the legal sellers at the market in the center of town. Béla will be recognized, but I can preserve my anonymity. I am to visit the butcher and say a coded message, and then go to the baker and say another code, and then someone will seek me out. The dealer intercepts me near the flower vendor.

"Penicillin," I say. "Enough for a sick child."

He laughs at the impossibility of my request. "There's no penicillin here," he says. "I'll have to fly to London. I can leave today. Return tomorrow. It'll cost." The price he names is twice the amount Béla has wrapped in newspaper and put in my purse.

I don't waver. I say what I will pay him. I say the exact amount I carry. "It must be done. If you don't go, I'll find someone else." I think of the guard the day we left Auschwitz, my cartwheel, his wink. I have to speak to the part of this man that will cooperate with me. "You see this bracelet?" I pull up my sleeve to reveal the gold bracelet that I have worn every day since Marianne's birth.

He nods. Maybe he imagines how it will look on his wife or girlfriend's wrist. Maybe he is mentally calculating the price he can get for it.

"My husband gave this to me when our daughter was born. Now I am giving you the opportunity to save our daughter's life."

I see his eyes flicker with something bigger than greed. "Give me the money," he says. "Keep the bracelet."

The doctor comes again the next night to help administer the first dose of penicillin. He stays until Marianne's fever breaks and she accepts my breast.

"I knew you'd find a way," he says.

By morning, Marianne is well enough to smile. She falls asleep suckling. Béla kisses her forehead, kisses my cheeks.

Marianne is better, but other threats simmer. Béla passes up the minister of agriculture post—"Yesterday's Nazis become today's Communists," he says—and his Opel Adam convertible is driven off the road one day. Béla isn't hurt, but the driver suffers some minor injuries. Béla goes to his house to bring supplies and good wishes for his recovery. The driver cracks the door but won't open it all the way. His wife calls from another room. "Don't let him in," she says. Béla forces the door open and sees one of his mother's finest tablecloths on their table.

He comes home and checks the cabinet where the good linens are stored. Many items are missing. I expect him to be angry, to fire the driver, maybe other employees. He shrugs. "Always use your beautiful things," he tells me. "You never know when they'll be gone."

I think of my family's apartment caked in manure, our piano sitting in the coffeehouse down the road, the way the big political moments—power changing hands, borders rewritten—are always personal too. Košice becomes Kassa and then Košice again.

"I can't do it anymore," I tell Béla. "I can't live with a target on my back. My daughter is not going to lose her parents."

"No," he agrees.

I think of Aunt Matilda. Magda has received her affidavit and is waiting for a visa. I am on the cusp of suggesting to Béla that we try to follow Magda to America, but then I remember that Magda has been warned that it could take years to get the visa, because even with sponsorship, immigration is subject to quota restrictions. We can't rely on a years-long process to protect us from the Communists. We need a swifter exit.

On December 31, 1948, Marta and Bandi come to our house to welcome the New Year. They are ardent Zionists. They toast the health of the new state of Israel, drink after drink.

"We could go there," Béla says. "We could start a business."

It's not the first time I have pictured myself in Palestine. In high school, I was a Zionist, and Eric and I had imagined living in Palestine together after the war. In the midst of prejudice and uncertainty, we couldn't stop our classmates from spitting on us, or the Nazis from overtaking our streets, but we could advocate for a future home, we could build a place of safety.

I can't tell if I should greet Béla's suggestion as the fulfillment of my old deferred dream or worry that we are relying on an illusion, an expectation that will lead to disappointment. Israel is such a new state that it has yet to hold its first elections, and it is already at war with its Arab neighbors. Furthermore, there is not yet a Law of Return, the legislation that several years later will grant any Jew, from any country, the ability to immigrate and settle in Israel. We will have to get there illegally, relying on Bricha, the underground organization that helped Jews flee Europe during the war, to arrange our passage on a ship. Bricha is still underground, and still helping people—refugees, the dispossessed, the homeless and stateless—to a new life. But even if we can secure seats on a boat, our plan isn't a sure bet. Only a year ago, the *Exodus*, carrying forty-five hundred Jewish immigrants seeking asylum and resettlement in Israel, was sent back to Europe.

But it is New Year's Eve. We are hopeful. We feel brave. In the final hours of 1948, our plan for the future takes shape. We will use the Eger fortune to buy all the equipment we need to start a business in Israel. In the following weeks, after much research, Béla will decide that a macaroni factory is the wisest investment, and we will pack a boxcar with all of our belongings, with enough to sustain us through the first years in our new home.

We Hungarians can't end a night of drinking without eating sauerkraut soup. Mariska brings steaming bowls of it.

"Next year in Jerusalem," we say.

In the coming months, Béla buys the boxcar that will carry the Eger fortune to Italy and then on to Haifa by ship. He buys the essential equipment for the macaroni factory. I see to the packing of the silver, the china with gold initials. I buy clothes for Marianne, enough for the next five years, and sew jewels into the pockets and hems.

We send the boxcar ahead and plan to follow, as soon as Bricha helps us find a way.

One late winter day when Béla is away on business, a certified letter comes for him from Prague, a letter I sign for, a letter I don't wait for him to read. Before the war, the letter says, Czechoslovakian citizens who had already immigrated to America were allowed to register any family members still in Europe, under a law that would allow people suffering persecution to apply for visas to come to America without being subject to the quota restrictions that limited the number of people who could find refuge in the United States. Béla's great-uncle Albert, who had been in Chicago since the early 1900s, had registered the Eger family. We are now one of two Czech families registered before the war invited to seek refuge in America. Béla must report right away to the American consulate in Prague for our documents.

Our boxcar is already en route to Israel. A new life is already on the horizon. We have already arranged everything. We have already chosen. But my heart races at this news, at this unexpected opportunity. We could go to America like Magda, but without the wait. Béla returns from his trip, and I beg him to go to Prague for the documents. "Just in case," I urge him. "Just as a precaution." Grudgingly, he goes. I put the papers in the top drawer of my dresser, with my underwear. Just in case.

CHAPTER 10

Flight

I come home from the park with Marianne on May 19, 1949, and Mariska is weeping.

"They arrested Mr. Eger!" she whimpers. "He's gone!"

For months we have recognized that our days of freedom were numbered. In addition to running Béla off the road the previous year, the Communists have by now seized Béla's business, confiscated our car, bugged our telephone. Our fortune safe in the boxcar on its way to Israel, we have stayed on, waiting for our travel arrangements from Bricha. We have stayed because we couldn't imagine leaving yet. And now I risk raising my daughter without her father. I will not accept it. I will not. First I must turn off the worry and fear that gather in me. I must shut off the possibility that Béla is being tortured or that he is already dead. I must become like my mother the morning we were evicted from our apartment and sent to the brick factory. I must become an agent of resourcefulness and hope. I must move like a person who has a plan.

I give Marianne a bath and eat lunch with her. I put her down for her nap. I am buying myself time to think and making sure she gets all the nourishment and creature comforts she can. Who knows if we will sleep tonight, or where? I am living minute by minute. I don't know what I will do next, only that I must find a way to get Béla out of jail and to keep our daughter safe. I gather everything that might come of use without arousing suspicion. While Marianne sleeps, I open my dresser drawer and take out the diamond ring Béla had made for me when we married. It's a beautiful ring—a perfect diamond, round, set in gold—but it has always made me feel self-conscious and so I never wear it. Today I put it on. I put the papers Béla retrieved from the American consulate in Prague inside my dress, flat against my back, held to my body by the belt on my dress. I can't look like a person who is on the run. I can't use our bugged phone to call anyone for help. But I can't bear to leave the house without contacting my sisters. I don't expect them to be able to help us, but I want them to know we are in distress, that I might not see them again. I call Klara. She picks up the phone and I improvise. I try not to cry, I try not to let my voice tremble or crack.

"I'm so happy that you're coming to visit," I say. There is no visit planned. I'm speaking in code. I hope she'll understand. "Marianne has been asking for her Auntie Klarie. Remind me, what time is your train?"

I hear her begin to correct or question me, then I hear the brief pause as she realizes that I'm trying to tell her something. Train, visit. What will she make of these scant clues? "We arrive this evening," she says. "I'll be at the station." Somehow, tonight, will she meet us on a train? Is this what we have just arranged? Or is our conversation too coded even for us to understand?

I tuck our passports into my purse and wait for Marianne to wake. She has been toilet-trained since she was nine months old, but when I dress her after her nap she allows me to put a diaper on her, and I fold my gold bracelet into it. I don't take anything else with me. I can't look like a person who is fleeing. Everything I say for the rest of the day, for as long as it takes to get us to safety, I will say in that language I find under duress, that way of being that is not authoritarian or domineering but also is not cowering or weak. To be passive is to let others decide for you. To be aggressive is to decide for others. To be assertive is to decide for yourself. And to trust that there is enough, that you are enough.

Oh, but I'm shaking. I leave the house with Marianne in my arms. If I act correctly, I won't be returning here to the Eger mansion, not today, maybe not ever. We will be on our way, tonight, to make our new home. I keep my voice low-key. I talk to Marianne nonstop. In the twenty months since Marianne's birth, besides nursing, this has been my success as a mother: I tell my daughter everything. I narrate what we are doing throughout the day. I name the streets and the trees. Words are treasures that I offer her again and again. She can speak in three languages: Hungarian, German, and Slovak. "*Kvetina*," she says, pointing at a flower, saying the word in Slovak. From her I relearn what it is to be safe *and* curious. And in return, this is what I can provide for her—I can't stave off danger, but I can help her know where she stands and what she's worth. I keep up the monologue so that there is no room for the voice of fear.

"Yes, a flower, and look at the oak, all leafed out, and there's the milk truck. We'll go see the man at the police station now, it's a big, big building, like our house, but with long hallways inside . . ." I talk as though this is an ordinary excursion, as though I can be to her the mother I need for myself.

The police station is intimidating. When the armed guards usher me into the building, I almost turn away and run. Men in uniforms. Men with guns. I can't tolerate this expression of authority. It spins me out, unplants me. I lose myself and my direction in the current of their threat. But every minute I wait heightens the danger for Béla. He has already shown that he is not a person who rolls over and complies. And the Communists have already shown that they are intolerant of dissent. To what lengths will they go to teach him a lesson, to extract from him some imagined piece of information, to bend him to their will?

And what about me? How will I be punished when I reveal my purpose here? I summon the confidence I found the day I bought penicillin from the black market dealer. Then, the biggest risk was that he would say no. I risked more if I *didn't* ask for what we needed to save Marianne's life. Today, asserting myself could lead to retaliation, imprisonment, torture. And yet, *not* to try, that is a risk too.

The warden sits on a stool behind a high counter. He is a large man. I am afraid Marianne will observe that he is fat, say it too loudly, and ruin our chances. I make eye contact. I smile. I will treat him not as he is, but as I trust he can be. I will talk to him as though I already have the thing that I want. "Thank you, sir," I say in Slovak, "thank you very much for giving my daughter back her father." His forehead creases in confusion. I hold his eyes. I take off my diamond ring. I hold it toward him. "A reunion between a father and a daughter is a beautiful thing," I continue, twisting the jewel back and forth so that it shines like a star in the dim light. He eyes the diamond and then stares up at me for an interminable moment. Will he call for his superior? Will he pull Marianne from my arms and arrest me too? Or will he seize something good for himself and help me? My chest tightens and my arms ache as he weighs his choices. Finally, he reaches for the ring and slips it into his pocket.

"Name?" he says.

"Eger."

"Come."

He takes me through a door and down some stairs. "We're going to get Daddy," I tell Marianne, as though we're meeting him at the train. It's a dismal, sad place. And the roles are topsy-turvy. How many of those locked up aren't criminals at all but the victims of misused power? I haven't been around prisoners since I was a prisoner myself. I feel ashamed, almost, to be on this side of the bars. And I am terrified that in a moment of arbitrary horror we might be made to switch places.

Béla is in a cell by himself. He's wearing his regular clothes—no uniform—and he jumps up from the cot when he sees us, reaching for Marianne's hands through the bars.

"Marchuka," he says. "Do you see my funny little bed?"

He thinks we are here for a visit. One of his eyes is black. There's blood on his lip. I see him wearing two faces—the innocent and happy one for Marianne, the quizzical one for me. Why have I brought a child into a prison? Why am I giving Marianne this image that she will always know by heart, even if she can't call it by its name? I try not to feel defensive. I try to make my eyes tell him he can trust me. And I try to shower him with love, the only thing bigger than fear. I have never loved him more than I do at this moment, when he knows instinctively how to make a game for Marianne, to reduce this bleak and terrifying place into something harmless.

The warden unlocks the cell. "Five minutes!" he yells loudly. He pats the pocket that holds the diamond ring. And then he retreats down the corridor, his back toward us.

I tug Béla through the cell door and I don't breathe until we are on the street again, Béla, Marianne, me. I help Béla wipe the blood off his lip with his dirty handkerchief. We begin walking toward the train station. We don't have to discuss it. It's as though we have planned it all, his arrest, our sudden escape. We are making everything up as we go along, but there's the giddy feeling of moving quickly through deep snow, stepping into leftover footprints, the surprise of finding that the tracks already laid out fit our feet and our speed. It's as though we have already taken this journey in another life and now we operate on memory. I am glad Béla can carry Marianne. My arms are almost numb.

The important thing is to get out of the country. To get away from the Communists. To get to the closest place where the Allies have a presence. At the train station I leave Béla and Marianne on a secluded bench and go alone to buy three tickets for Vienna and an armful of sandwiches. Who knows when we will eat again?

We still have forty-five minutes to wait for the next train. Forty-five more minutes for Béla's empty cell to be discovered. Of course they will send officers to the train station. The train station is where you go to track down a fugitive, which is what Béla is now. And I'm his accomplice. I count my breaths to keep from trembling. When I rejoin my family, Béla is telling Marianne a funny story about a pigeon that thinks he's a butterfly. I try not to look at the clock. I sit on the bench, Marianne is in Béla's lap, I lean against them, try to keep Béla's face obscured. The minutes tick slowly by. I unwrap a sandwich for Marianne. I try to eat a bite.

Then an announcement that makes my teeth chatter too violently to eat. "Béla Eger, please report to the information booth," the announcer drones. It cuts through the static of ticket transactions, of parents reprimanding their children, of separations and goodbyes.

"Don't look," I whisper. "Whatever you do, don't look up."

Béla tickles Marianne, trying to make her laugh. I'm worried they are making too much noise.

"Béla Eger, come immediately to information," the announcer calls. We can hear the urgency mounting.

At last the westbound train pulls into the station.

"Get on the train," I say. "Hide in the bathroom in case they search the train."

I try not to look around for the police officers as we hurry to board. Béla runs with Marianne on his shoulders. She shrieks delightedly. We have no luggage, which made sense on the streets, walking here, but now I'm worried that the absence of luggage will arouse suspicion. It will take nearly seven hours to reach Vienna. If we manage to get out of Prešov, there is still the threat that police might board at any stop to search the train. There was no time to procure fake identification. We are who we are.

We find an empty compartment, and I busy Marianne at the window, counting all the shoes on the platform. After springing Béla from jail, I can hardly tolerate the idea of his being out of my sight. I can't stand for the danger to continue, to mount. Béla kisses me, he kisses Marianne, and goes to hide in the bathroom. I wait for the train to start moving. If the train can just leave the station, we are an inch closer to freedom, a second closer to Béla's return.

The train won't move. *Mama, Mama,* I pray. *Help us, Mama. Help us, Papa.*

The compartment door folds open and a police officer gives us a quick glance before shutting the door. I hear his boots as they move down the aisle, I hear other doors opening and shutting, I hear him shouting Béla's name. I chatter at Marianne, I sing, I keep her looking out the window. And then I fear that we will see Béla in handcuffs, being pulled from the train. At last I see the conductor lift his stool from the platform and board the train. The car doors close. The train begins to move. Where is Béla? Is he still on the train? Has he managed to escape detection? Or is he on his way back to jail, to a certain beating—or worse? What if every turn of the wheels brings us farther apart, farther from a life we can make together?

By the time we reach Košice, Marianne is asleep in my arms. There is still no sign of Béla. I scan the platform for Klara. Is she here to meet us? Will Csicsi come? Has she understood the danger we're in? What preparations has she made in the hours since we spoke?

Just before the train pulls away from the Košice station, the compartment door opens, and Béla rushes in, giddy from adrenaline. "I have a surprise!" he calls before there is time to quiet him. Marianne opens her eyes, she is disoriented, she fusses.

I rock her, side to side, I reach for my husband. My husband who is safe.

"Don't you want to see my surprise?" He pulls the door open again. And there are my sister Klara, and Csicsi, and a suitcase, and her violin.

"Any seats free in here?" Csicsi asks.

"Little one!" Klara says, as she pulls me to her chest.

Béla wants to tell how he evaded the police search in Prešov, and Csicsi wants to recount how they discovered one another here in Košice, but I am superstitious. It seems like counting chickens before they've hatched. In myths, nothing good comes from gloating. You have to let the gods maintain the image of their singular power. I haven't even told Béla yet about the ring, about how I got him out of jail. He hasn't asked.

The train is moving again. Marianne falls back asleep with her head on Béla's lap. Csicsi and Klara whisper their plans: Vienna is the perfect place to await their visas for Australia, the time is right to leave Europe, to join Imre in Sydney. I can't let myself picture Vienna yet. I hold my breath at every station. Spišská Nová Ves. Poprad-Tatry. Liptovský Mikuláš. Žilina. Three more stops before Vienna. Trenčín yields no catastrophe. No crisis at Trnava. We're almost there. At Bratislava, the border crossing, the place of our honeymoon, the stop drags on. Marianne wakes up, feeling the stillness.

"Sleep, baby, sleep," Béla says.

"Hush," I say. "Hush."

On the platform, in the dark, we see a dozen Slovakian soldiers walking toward the train. They spread out, approaching the cars in pairs. Soon they will be knocking on our door. They will ask for our identification. If they don't recognize Béla's face, they will see his name on his passport. It is too late to hide.

"I'll be back," Csicsi says. He pushes out into the aisle, we hear his voice, the conductor's, we see him step down onto the platform just as the soldiers reach the door. I will never know what Csicsi says to them. I will never know if money or jewels change hands. All I know is that after a series of excruciating moments, the soldiers tip their hats at Csicsi, turn, and walk back to the station. How did I face a selection line, sometimes every day, sometimes more than that? At least in a selection line the verdict comes quickly.

Csicsi returns to the compartment. My heart has stopped its frenzied beating but I can't bring myself to ask him how he convinced the soldiers to turn away. Our safety feels too fragile to count on. If we speak our relief out loud we risk destroying it. We are silent as the train moves on to Vienna.

In Vienna we are little drops in the flow of 250,000 seeking refuge and passage to Palestine or North America since the end of the war. We take shelter at the Rothschild Hospital in the American-occupied part of the city. The hospital is being used as a center for refugees fleeing Eastern Europe, and the five of us are assigned to a room with three other families. Though it is already late at night, Béla leaves the room even before I have settled Marianne into a bed. He is intent on contacting Bandi and Marta, the friends from home with whom we have been planning to go to Israel, to tell them where we are. I rub Marianne's back while she sleeps, listening to Klara's whispered conversation with the other women who share our room. Here at the Rothschild

Hospital are thousands like us, all awaiting help from Bricha. When we sat at our table eating sauerkraut soup with Bandi and Marta on New Year's Eve, hatching the plan to start a new life in Israel, we were building something, not running away. But now, in a crowded room with other refugees, I realize the meaning of Bricha. Bricha is Hebrew for "flight." We are in flight.

Is our plan a sound one? The women in our room at Rothschild tell us about their friends who have already immigrated to Israel. It's not an easy place to be, they say. After a year, the Arab-Israeli War is finally winding down, but the country is still a war zone. People live in tents, do what they must in a time of deep political unrest and continuing hostilities between Arabs and Jews. That is not the life we prepared for when we packed our boxcar. What good will our silver and china be in a tent surrounded by violent conflict? And what of the jewels sewn into Marianne's clothes? They're worth only what others will pay for them. Who wants to eat on gold plates that bear our name? It's not the idea of hard work or poverty that creates a little drag of resistance in my stomach. It's the reality of more war. Why start again if it yields nothing more than the same suffering?

In the dark, waiting for Béla to return, I open the papers from the American consulate, the papers I was so adamant that Béla retrieve in Prague, that have crossed the border with us, strapped against my back. Two Czechoslovakian families qualified for immigration to America. Just two. The other family, Béla learned when he went to Prague, has already left Europe, they chose to immigrate to Israel instead of America. It is our turn, if we choose to go. I turn the papers around in my hand, look at the words, blurry in the dim light, wait for them to crumble in my hands, to rearrange. "America, Dicuka," I can hear my mother say. America is the hardest country to get into. The quotas are fierce. But if the letter is not a fraud, a hoax, we have a way in. Yet our fortune is in Israel. The letter must be a false invitation, I convince myself. No one wants you if you're penniless.

Béla comes in breathless, waking our roommates. He has managed to contact Bandi in the middle of the night. Tomorrow night our friends will travel to Vienna, we will meet them at the train station the following morning, and together we will travel to Italy where Bandi, with the help of Bricha, has secured our passage to Haifa by ship. We will go to Israel with Bandi and Marta as we have been planning since New Year's Eve. We will build our macaroni factory. We are lucky to be leaving Vienna almost as soon as we have arrived. We won't be waiting years, as Klara and Csicsi might have to in order to go to Australia.

But I don't feel joyful at the prospect of leaving Vienna in thirty-six hours, of having fled the postwar chaos of Prešov only to bring my daughter back to a volatile conflict zone. I sit on the edge of the bed, with the papers from the American consulate in my lap. I run my fingers over the ink. Béla watches me.

"It's a little late," he says. That is his only comment.

"You don't think we should discuss this?"

"What is there to discuss? Our fortune—our future—is in Israel."

He's right. Half right. Our fortune is in Israel, probably baking in a boxcar in the desert. Our future isn't. It doesn't exist yet. Our future is the sum of an equation that is part intention and part circumstance. And our intentions could shift. Or split.

When I finally lie down on the bed, Klara whispers to me across Marianne's sleeping body. "Little one," she says, "listen to me. You have to love what you are doing. Otherwise you shouldn't do it. It isn't worth it." What is she telling me to do? To argue with Béla over something we have already decided? To leave him? She is the one I expected—maybe counted on—to defend my choices to me, the ones I have already made. I know she doesn't want to go to Australia. But she will go to be with her husband. She of all people should understand why I am going to Israel even though I don't want to. But for the first time in our lives she is telling me not to do as she does, not to follow her lead.

In the morning, Béla leaves right away to procure the things we will need for our journey to Israel—suitcases, coats, clothes, other necessities provided for us refugees by the Jewish Joint Distribution Committee, the American charity that supports Rothschild. I go out in the city with Marianne, the documents from Prague tucked into my purse the way Magda used to hide away sweets—part temptation, part succor. What does it mean that we are the one Czech family allowed to immigrate? Who will go if we decline? No one? The Israel plan is a good one. It is the best we could do with what we had. But now there's an opportunity that didn't exist when we committed to the plan. Now we've been offered a new possibility, one that doesn't involve living in tents in a war zone.

I can't stop myself. Without Béla's permission, without his knowledge, I ask for directions to the U.S. consulate, I walk there with Marianne in my arms. I will at least satisfy the possibility that the papers are a mistake or a hoax.

"Congratulations," the officer says when I show him the documents, "you can go as soon as your visas are processed." He gives me the paperwork for our visa applications.

"How much will it cost?"

"Nothing, ma'am. You're refugees. You sail courtesy of your new country."

I feel dizzy. It's the good kind of dizzy, the way I felt the night before when the train left Bratislava with my family still intact. I take the applications back to our room at Rothschild, I show them to Klara and Csicsi, I study the questions, looking for the catch. It doesn't take long to find one: *Have you ever had tuberculosis (TB)?* Béla has. He hasn't had symptoms since 1945, but it doesn't matter how healthy he is now. You have to submit X-rays with the application. There are scars in his lungs. The damage is evident. And TB is never cured; like trauma, it could flare at any time.

Israel, then. Tomorrow.

Klara watches me put the applications under the mattress. "Remember when I was ten and I got accepted to Juilliard?" she says. "And Mama wouldn't let me go? Go to America, Dicu. Mama would want you to."

"But the TB," I say. I am trying to be loyal, not to the law but to Béla's wishes, to my husband's choice.

"When you can't go in through a door, go in through a window," Klara reminds me.

* * *

Night comes. Our second night, our last night in Vienna. I wait until Marianne is asleep, until Klara and Csicsi and the other families have gone to bed. I sit with Béla in two chairs by the door. Our knees touch. I try to memorize his face so that I can recite its contours to Marianne. His full forehead, the perfect arcs of his eyebrows, the kindness of his mouth.

"Precious Béla," I begin, "what I am about to say won't be easy to hear. There is no way around how hard it will be. And there is no way to talk me out of what I will say."

His beautiful forehead creases. "What's going on?"

"If you meet Bandi and Marta to go to Israel tomorrow, as we planned, I won't hold it against you. I won't try to talk you out of it. But I have made my choice. I will not go with you. I am taking Marchuka to America."

PART III

Freedom

CHAPTER 11

Immigration Day

Immigration day, October 28, 1949, was the most optimistic and promising day of my life. After living in the crowded room at the Rothschild Hospital for a month, and spending another five months in a tiny apartment in Vienna, waiting for our visas, we were on the threshold of our new home. A sunny blue sky lit the Atlantic as we stood on the deck of the USAT *General R. L. Howze*. Lady Liberty came into view, tiny in the distance like the little figurine in a music box. Then New York City became visible, a skyline emerging, intricate, where only horizon had been for weeks. I held Marianne up against the deck rail.

"We're in America," I told her. "The land of the free."

And I thought we finally were free. We had taken the risk. Now safety and opportunity were our rewards. It seemed a just and simple equation. Thousands of miles of ocean separated us from barbed wire, police searches, camps for the condemned, camps for the displaced. I did not yet know that nightmares know no geography, that guilt and anxiety wander borderless. For twenty minutes on the upper deck of a passenger ship, standing in the October sun, my daughter in my arms, New York in sight, I believed the past couldn't touch me here. Magda was already there. In July she had finally received her visa and sailed to New

York, where she now lived with Aunt Matilda and her husband in the Bronx. She worked in a toy factory, putting the heads on little giraffes. *It takes an Elefánt to make a giraffe*, she had joked in a letter. In another hour, maybe two, I would embrace my sister, my brave sister, her jokes at the ready to transcend pain. As Marianne and I counted the whitecaps between the ship and solid land, as I counted my blessings, Béla came up from the tiny cabin where he was packing the last of our things.

My heart swelled again with tenderness for my husband. In the weeks of travel, in the little cot in the room that rocked and bobbed across black water, through black air, I felt more passion for him than ever before in our three years together, more than on the train on our honeymoon when we conceived Marianne.

Back in May, in Vienna, he had been unable to decide, unable to choose, up until the last minute. He stood behind a pillar at the train station where he was to meet Bandi and Marta, suitcase in hand. He saw our friends arrive, saw them searching the platform for us. He continued to hide. He saw the train pull in, heard the announcement that passengers should board. He saw people getting onto the train. He saw Bandi and Marta at the door of a train car, waiting for him. Then he heard the clerk on the loudspeaker calling his name. He wanted to join our friends, he wanted to board the train and meet the ship and rescue the boxcar holding his fortune. But he was frozen there behind the pillar. The rest of the passengers filed on board, Bandi and Marta too. When the train doors closed, he finally forced himself into action. Against his better judgment, against all the bets he had made for what he hoped would be a safe and financially secure future, he took the biggest risk of his life. He walked away.

Now, minutes away from our new life in America, nothing seemed deeper or more profound than that we had made the same choice, to relinquish security in favor of opportunity for our daughter, to start over together from scratch. To have his commitment to our daughter, to this new venture, to me, touched me deeply.

And yet. (This "and yet" closing like a latch.) I had been ready to forsake our marriage in order to take Marianne to America. However painfully, I had been willing to sacrifice our family, our partnership—the very things Béla had been unable to accept losing. And so we began our new life on an unequal footing. I could feel that though his devotion to us could be measured in all that he had given up, he was still dizzy from what he had lost. And where I felt relief and joy, he felt hurt. Happy as I was to greet our new life, I could already feel that Béla's loss put a dangerous pressure on all the unknowns ahead.

So there was sacrifice at the heart of our choice. And there was also a lie: the report from the medical examiner, the X-rays we had pressed inside a folder with our visa applications. We couldn't allow the ghost of Béla's old illness, his TB, to deter our future, so Csicsi had posed as Béla and gone with me to the medical examiner. We now carried pictures of Csicsi's chest, clear as spring water. When the naturalization officers cleared Béla for immigration, it would be Csicsi's body and medical history they legitimized, another man's body they determined to be sound.

I wanted to breathe easily. To cherish our safety and good fortune as miracles, not guard them close and warily. I wanted to teach my daughter confidence in where she stood. There she was, hair whipping around her head, cheeks red from the wind.

"Liberty!" she called, pleased with her new word. On a whim I took the pacifier that hung on a ribbon around her neck and threw it into the sea.

If I had turned around, I might have seen Béla caution me. But I wasn't looking. "We're Americans now. American children don't use pacifiers," I said, heady and improvising, tossing my daughter's one token of security like it was parade confetti. I wanted Marianne to be what *I* wanted to be: someone who fits in, who isn't plagued by the idea of being different, of being flawed, of playing catch-up forever in a relentless race away from the claws of the past.

She didn't complain. She was excited by the novelty of our adventure, amused by my strange act, accepting of my logic. In America we'd do as the Americans do (as if I knew a single thing about what Americans do). I wanted to trust my choice, our new life, so I denied any trace of sadness, any trace of fear. When I walked down the wooden ramp to our new homeland, I was already wearing a mask.

I had escaped. But I wasn't yet free.

CHAPTER 12

Greener

November 1949. I board a city bus in Baltimore. Gray dawn. Wet streets. I am going to work, to the clothing factory, where I will spend all day cutting loose threads off the seams of little boys' boxer shorts, paid 7¢ per dozen. The factory reminds me of the thread factory in Germany where Magda and I worked after we were taken from Auschwitz—dry, dusty air, cold concrete, machines clattering so loudly that when the forewoman speaks she must shout. "Minimize bathroom breaks!" she yells. But I hear the forewoman of the past, the one who told us we would be worked until we were all used up, and then killed. I work without stopping. To maximize my productivity, to maximize my meager pay. But also because to work without a break is an old necessity, a habit impossible to overthrow. And if I can keep the noise and the urgency around me at all times, I will not have to be alone for even a moment with my own thoughts. I work so hard that my hands shake and shake in the dark when I get home.

Because Aunt Matilda and her husband didn't have the space or resources to take in my family—Magda was already an extra mouth to feed—we have begun our new life not in the Bronx, as I had imagined, but in Baltimore, where we live with Béla's brother George and his wife and two young daughters in a cramped walk-up apartment. George had been a well-known lawyer in Czechoslovakia, but in Chicago, where he first lived when he immigrated to America in the 1930s, he made a living as a Fuller Brush man, selling brushes and cleaning products door-to-door; now, in Baltimore, he sells insurance. Everything in George's life is bitter, fear based, discouraged. He follows me through the rooms of the apartment, watching my every move, barking at me to close the coffee can more tightly. He is angry about the past—about having been attacked in Bratislava, and mugged in Chicago in his early immigrant days. And he's angry about the present—he can't forgive us for having arrived penniless, for having turned our backs on the Eger fortune. I feel so self-conscious in his presence that I can't walk down the stairs without tripping.

One day as I board the bus to work, my head is so full of my own discomfort—girding up for the rattling pace of the factory, stewing over George's unpleasantness, obsessing over our relentless worries about money—that it takes me several moments to notice that the bus hasn't started to move, that we are still at the curb, that the other passengers are staring at me, scowling, shaking their heads. I begin to prickle with sweat. It is the feeling I had when I woke to hear armed *nyilas* banging on our door at dawn. The fear when the German soldier held a gun to my chest after I picked the carrots. The feeling that I have done wrong, that I will be punished, that the stakes are life and death. I am so consumed by the sensation of danger and threat that I can't put together what has happened—that I have boarded the bus the European way, taking my seat and waiting for the conductor to come and sell me a ticket. I have forgotten to put my token in the change box. Now the bus driver is yelling at me, "Pay or get off! Pay or get off!" Even if I could speak English, I would not be able to understand him. I am overcome by fear, by images of barbed wire and raised guns, by thick smoke rising from chimneys and obscuring my present reality, by the prison walls of the past closing in on me. It is the opposite of what happened to me when I danced for Josef Mengele my first night at Auschwitz. Then, I transported myself out of the barracks and onto the stage of the Budapest opera house. Then, my inner vision saved me. Now, my inner life makes me interpret a simple mistake, a misunderstanding, as catastrophe. Nothing in the present is really wrong, nothing that can't be easily fixed. A man is angry and frustrated because he has misunderstood me, because I can't understand him. There is shouting and conflict. But my life is not in danger. And yet, that is how I read the present situation. Danger, danger, death.

"Pay or get off! Pay or get off!" the driver shouts. He stands up from his seat. He is coming toward me. I fall to the ground, I cover my face. He is above me now, grabbing my arm, trying to yank me to my feet. I huddle on the floor of the bus, crying, shaking. A fellow passenger takes pity on me. She is an immigrant like me. She asks me first in Yiddish, then in German, if I have money, she counts the coins in my sweaty palm, she helps me back into my seat and sits with me until I'm breathing again. The bus pulls out onto the street.

"Stupid greener," someone says under her breath as she walks up the aisle to her seat.

When I tell Magda about the incident in a letter, I turn it into a joke—an episode of immigrant—"greener"—slapstick. But something changed in me that day. It will be more than twenty years before I will have the language and psychological training to understand that I was having a flashback, that the unnerving physical sensations—racing heart, sweaty palms, narrowing vision—I experienced that day (and that I will continue to experience many times in my life, even now, in my late eighties) are automatic responses to trauma. This is why I now object to pathologizing post-traumatic stress by calling it a disorder. It's not a disordered reaction to trauma—it's a common and natural one. But on that November morning in Baltimore I didn't know what was happening to me; I assumed that my collapse meant that I was deeply flawed. I wish I had known that I wasn't a damaged person, that I was suffering the fallout of an interrupted life.

At Auschwitz, at Mauthausen, on the Death March, I survived by drawing on my inner world. I found hope and faith in life within me, even when I was surrounded by starvation and torture and death. After my first flashback, I began to believe that my inner world was where the demons lived. That there was blight deep inside me. My inner world was no longer sustaining, it became the source of my pain: unstoppable memories, loss, fear. I could be standing in line at the fish counter, and when the clerk called my name I would see Mengele's face transposed over his. Walking into the factory some mornings I would see my mother beside me, as plain as day, I would see her turn her back and walk away. I tried to banish my memories of the past. I thought it was a matter of survival. Only after many years did I come to understand that running away doesn't heal pain. It makes the pain worse. In America I was farther geographically than I had ever been from my former prison. But here I became more psychologically imprisoned than I was before. In running from the past—from my fear—I didn't find freedom. I made a cell of my dread and sealed the lock with silence.

Marianne, however, was flourishing. I wanted her to feel normal, normal, normal. And she did. Despite my fear that she would discover that we were poor, that her mother was afraid all the time, that life in America wasn't what we had expected, she was a happy child. At her day care, which she was allowed to attend for free because the woman who ran it, Mrs. Bower, was sympathetic to immigrants, she learned English quickly. She became a little assistant to Mrs. Bower, tending to the other children when they cried or fussed. No one asked her to fill that role. She had an innate sensitivity to others' hurt, and an innate confidence in her own strength. Béla and I called her the little ambassador. Mrs. Bower would send her home with books—to help me learn English as much as to support Marianne. I try to read *Chicken Little*. I can't keep the characters straight. Who is Ducky Lucky? Who is Goosey Loosey? Marianne laughs at me. She teaches me again. She pretends exasperation. I pretend that I am only playing, that I am only pretending not to understand.

Even more than poverty, I feared my daughter's embarrassment. I feared that she would be ashamed of me. On the weekends, she came with me to the Laundromat and helped me operate the machines, she took me to the grocery store to find Jif Peanut Butter and a dozen other foods I'd never heard of, with names I couldn't spell or pronounce. In 1950, the year Marianne turned three, she insisted that we eat turkey for Thanksgiving, like her classmates. How can I tell her that we can't afford one? I stop at Schreiber's on the way home the day before Thanksgiving, and I'm in luck, they've put chicken on sale for 29¢ a pound. I choose the smallest one. "Look, sweetie!" I call when I get home. "We have a turkey. A baby turkey!" I want so badly for her—for all three of us—to fit in.

Alienation is my chronic condition, even among our Jewish immigrant friends. The winter Marianne is five, we are invited to a Hanukkah party, where all of the children take turns singing Hanukkah songs. The hostess invites Marianne to sing. I am so proud to see my intelligent and precocious daughter, who already speaks English as if it is her first language, happy and bright-eyed and eager, confidently accepting the invitation, taking her place in the center of the room. She is in kindergarten now and goes to an after-school program run by a Jewish man, who unbeknownst to me has become a Jew for Jesus. Marianne beams at the guests, then closes her eyes, begins to sing: "Jesus loves me, this I know, for the Bible tells me so . . ." The guests stare at her and at me. My daughter has learned the skill I most want her to have, the ability to be at home anywhere. And now it is exactly her lack of understanding of the codes that separate people that makes me want to slip under the floorboards and disappear. This embarrassment, this feeling of exile, even in my own community, didn't come from without. It came from within. It was the self-imprisoning part of me that believed I didn't deserve to have survived, that I would never be worthy enough to belong.

Marianne thrived in America, but Béla and I struggled. I still suffered with my own fear—the nightmarish memories, the panic that brewed just below the surface. And I feared Béla's resentment. He didn't struggle to learn English as I did. He had attended a boarding school in London for a time when he was a boy, and he spoke English as fluently as he spoke Czech, Slovak, Polish, German, and numerous other languages—but his stutter grew more pronounced in America, a signal to me that he was pained by the choice I had forced upon him. His first job was in a warehouse, where he lifted heavy boxes, an exertion we knew was dangerous for someone with TB. But George and his wife, Duci, who was a social worker and had helped us find our jobs, convinced us we were lucky to have work. The pay was terrible, the labor demanding and demeaning, but it was the immigrant reality. Immigrants weren't doctors or lawyers or mayors, no matter their training and expertise (except for my remarkable sister Klara, who secured a position as a violinist in the Sydney Symphony Orchestra soon after she and Csicsi immigrated). Immigrants drove taxis. Immigrants did piecework in factories. Immigrants stocked grocery store shelves. I internalized the feeling of unworthiness. Béla fought against it. He became short-tempered and volatile.

During our first winter in Baltimore, Duci comes home with a snowsuit she has bought for Marianne. It has a long zipper. Marianne wants to try it on right away. It takes ages to get the snug snowsuit on over the top of Marianne's clothes, but finally we are ready for the park. We trundle down the five flights of stairs to the street. When we reach the sidewalk, Marianne says she needs to pee.

"Why didn't you tell us before!" Béla explodes. He has never yelled at Marianne before.

"Let's get out of this house," I whisper that night.

"You got it, princess," he snarls. I don't recognize him. His anger frightens me.

No, the anger I am most afraid of is my own.

We manage to save enough money to move into a little maid's room at the back of a house in Park Heights, Baltimore's largest Jewish neighborhood. Our landlady was once an immigrant herself, from Poland, but she's been in America for decades already, since long before the war. She calls us greeners and laughs at our accents. She shows us the bathroom, expecting us to be amazed by indoor plumbing. I think of Mariska and the little bell in the Eger mansion that I used to ring when I wanted more bread. It is easier to feign astonishment, to fulfill our landlady's expectation of who we are, than to explain, even to myself, the gulf between then and now.

Béla and Marianne and I live together in the one room. We turn off the lights when Marianne goes to bed and we sit in the dark. The silence between us isn't the intimate kind, it's taut and burdened, a rope beginning to fray under the weight of its load.

We do our best to be a normal family. In 1950, we splurge and go to see a movie in the theater next door to the Laundromat on Park Heights Avenue. While our clothes spin in the machine, we take Marianne to see *The Red Shoes*, a movie written, we are proud to learn, by Emeric Pressburger, a Jewish Hungarian immigrant. I remember the film so well because it moved through me in two directions. Sitting in the dark, eating popcorn with my family, I felt a contentment that had grown elusive for me—a faith that all was well, that we could have a happy postwar life. But the film itself—the characters, the story—upended me with the force of recognition. Something broke through my careful mask, and I gazed into the full face of my hunger.

The movie is about a dancer, Vicky Page, who catches the attention of Boris Lermontov, the artistic director of a celebrated ballet company. She practices the high kick at the barre, she dances passionately in *Swan Lake*, she longs for Lermontov's attention and regard. I can't look away from the screen. I feel like I am watching my own life, the one I would have gone on to live if there hadn't been a Hitler, if there hadn't been a war. For a moment I think it is Eric in the seat next to mine, I forget I have a daughter. I am only twenty-three, but it feels as though the best parts of my life are over. At one point in the movie Lermontov asks Vicky, "Why do you want to dance?" She replies, "Why do you want to live?" Lermontov says, "I don't know exactly why, but I must." Vicky says, "That's my answer too." Before Auschwitz, even at Auschwitz, I would have said the same. There was a constant inner light, a part of me that always feasted and danced, that never relinquished the longing for life. Now my guiding purpose is simply to act in such a way that my daughter never knows my pain.

It's a sad movie. Vicky's dream doesn't turn out the way she thought it would. When she dances the lead role in Lermontov's new ballet, she is haunted by demons. This part of the movie is so terrifying I can barely watch. Vicky's red ballet shoes seem to take control of her, they dance her almost to death, she is dancing through her own nightmares—ghouls and barren landscapes, a dance partner made of disintegrating newspaper—but she can't stop dancing, she can't wake up. Vicky tries to give up dancing. She hides the red shoes in a drawer. She falls in love with a composer, she marries him. At the end of the film, she is invited to dance one more time in Lermontov's ballet. Her husband begs her not to go. Lermontov warns her, "Nobody can have two lives." She must choose. *What makes a person do one thing and not another?* I wonder. Vicky puts the red shoes on again. This time they dance her off the edge of a building to her death. The other dancers perform the ballet without her, a spotlight trained on the empty place on the stage where Vicky should be dancing.

It's not a film about trauma. In fact, I don't yet understand that I am living with trauma. But *The Red Shoes* gives me a vocabulary of images, it teaches me something about myself, the tension between my inner and outer experiences. And something about the way Vicky put on the red shoes for the last time and took flight—it didn't look like choice. It looked compulsive. Automatic. What was she so afraid of? What made her run? Was it something she couldn't live with, or something she couldn't live without?

"Would you have chosen dance over me?" Béla asks on the bus ride home. I wonder if he is thinking of the night in Vienna when I told him I was taking Marianne to America, with or without him. He already knows I am capable of choosing someone or something else.

I defuse his question with flirtation. "If you had seen me dance then, you wouldn't have asked me to choose," I say. "You've never seen a high kick like mine." I pretend, I pretend. Somewhere deep in my chest I suppress a scream. *I didn't get to choose!* the silence in me rages. *Hitler and Mengele chose for me. I didn't get to choose!*

Béla is the first to collapse under the pressure. It happens at work. He is lifting a box and he falls to the ground. He can't breathe. At the hospital, an X-ray reveals that his TB has returned. He looks more unraveled and pale than he did the day I got him out of jail, the day we fled to Vienna. The doctors transfer him to a TB hospital, and when I take Marianne to visit him every day after work, I am rigid with the fear that she will see him coughing up blood, that she will feel the possibility of death despite our efforts to hide from her how sick he is. She is four years old, she can already read, she brings picture books from Mrs. Bower's to entertain her father, she tells the nurses when he has finished his food, when he needs more water. "You know what would cheer Daddy up?" she says to me. "A baby sister!" We haven't allowed ourselves to try for another child, we are too poor, and now I am relieved that we don't have the pressure of another person's hunger weighing on Béla's recovery, on my pitiful paychecks. But it breaks my heart to see my daughter yearning for a companion. To see her loneliness. It makes me long for my own sisters. Magda has a better job now, in New York, using the tailoring skills she learned from our father to make coats at London Fog. She doesn't want to start over again in a new city, but I beg her to come to Baltimore. In Vienna, in 1949, that is how I briefly imagined my life might turn out—bringing Marianne up with my sister instead of my husband. Then, it was a choice, a sacrifice, to spare my daughter life in a war zone. Now, if Béla dies, or if he becomes an invalid, it will be a necessity. We live in a slightly bigger apartment now, and even with two of us working we struggle to eat. I can't imagine how I will afford to pay for it alone. Magda agrees to think about coming.

"Don't worry," Béla says, coughing into a handkerchief. "I won't let our girl grow up without a father. I will not." He coughs and stutters so badly he can barely get out the words.

Béla does recover, but he is still weak. He won't be able to resume his job at the warehouse—but he will live. The medical staff at the TB hospital, taken by Béla's charm and humor, promise that before he is discharged they will help him figure out a career path that can lift us out of poverty and give him plenty of healthy years. They administer an aptitude test that Béla thinks is silly until the results come back. He is best suited to a career as an orchestra conductor or an accountant, the test reveals.

"We could make a new life in the ballet," he jokes. "You could dance, I'd conduct the orchestra."

"Do you ever wish you'd studied music when you were young?" It's a dangerous game to play what-if with the past.

"I did study music when I was young."

How have I forgotten this? He studied violin, like my sister. He wrote about it in those letters when he courted me. Hearing him talk about it now is like being told he used to go by a different name.

"I was pretty good. My teachers told me I could have gone to conservatory, and I might have, if there wasn't the family business to run."

My face gets hot. I am suddenly angry. I don't know why. I want to say something that will sting, but I don't know if it is myself I want to punish, or him. "Just think," I say, "if you'd kept it up, you might have met Klara first instead of me."

Béla tries to read my face. I can see him trying to decide whether to tease me or reassure me. "Do you really want to try to convince me that I'm not happy beyond happy to be married to you? It was a violin. It doesn't matter now."

Then I understand what it is that has upset me. It is the seeming effortlessness with which my husband has put to rest an old dream. If he ever suffered anguish over giving up music, he kept it hidden from me. What was wrong with me that I was still so hungry for what *wasn't*?

* * *

Béla shows his old boss at the warehouse the results of the aptitude test, and the boss introduces Béla to his accountant, a generous man who agrees to employ Béla as his assistant while Béla takes CPA classes and works toward his license.

I am restless. I have been so consumed with money worries and Béla's illness, so wrapped up in the cramped routine of hours at the factory and counting coins to buy groceries, that the good news unmoors me. The release of worry leaves me with a gaping cavity that I don't know how to fill. Béla has new prospects, a new path, but I don't. I change jobs several times in an effort to earn more, to feel better about myself. The extra money helps and the advancements do lift me for a while. But the feeling never lasts. At an insurance company, I am promoted from my station at the ditto machine to bookkeeper. My supervisor has noticed how hard I work, she will train me. I feel happy in the company of the other secretaries, happy to be one of them, until my new friend advises me, "Don't ever sit next to the Jews at lunch. They smell." I don't belong after all. I must hide who I am. At the luggage company where I work next, I have a Jewish boss, and I think I will finally fit in. I feel confident, accepted. Although I am a clerk, not a receptionist, one day the phone is ringing and ringing, and seeing how taxed the secretaries are, I jump in to answer the phone. My boss storms out of his office. "Who gave you permission?" he yells. "Are you trying to ruin my reputation? No greener will represent this company. Am I making myself clear?" The problem isn't that he chews me out. The problem is that I believe his assessment of my worthlessness.

In the summer of 1952, shortly after Béla's recovery and a few months before Marianne turns five, Magda does move to Baltimore. She stays with us for a few months until she can find a job. We set up a bed for her in the dining area, near the front door. Our apartment is always stuffy in the summer, even at night, and Magda cracks the door a little before she goes to bed. "Careful," Béla warns. "I don't know what kind of palace you were living in in the Bronx, but this isn't a safe neighborhood. If you leave that door open, someone might walk right in."

"Don't I wish," Magda purrs, batting her eyelashes. My sister. Her pain visible only in the humor she uses to transcend it.

We host a small party to welcome her—George and Duci come (George shakes his head at the small expense), and some of our neighbors in the apartment building, including our landlords, who bring their friend Nat Shillman, a retired Navy engineer. Magda tells a funny story about her first week in America, when Aunt Matilda bought her a hot dog on the street. "In Europe, when you buy a hot dog from a vendor like that, you always get two hot dogs, and they're covered in kraut and onions. Matilda goes to pay for my hot dog, and she comes back and there's just one puny hot dog on a flimsy little bun. I thought she was too cheap to pay full price for two, or that she was making a point about my weight. I held a grudge for months, till the day I bought my own hot dog and learned that's how it is here."

All eyes are on Magda, on her expressive face, waiting for the next funny thing she'll say. And she has more; she always does. Nat is clearly fascinated by her. When the guests leave and Marianne is asleep, I sit with Magda on her bed, gossiping the way we did when we were girls. She asks what I know of Nat Shillman. "I know, I know, he's Daddy's age," she says, "but I have a good feeling about him."

We talk until I am half asleep on her bed. I don't want to stop. There is something I need to ask Magda, something that has to do with the cavity in me, but if I ask her about the fear, the emptiness, then I must acknowledge it, and I am so used to pretending it isn't there. "Are you happy?" I finally work up the courage to ask her. I want her to say that she is, so that I can be too. I want her to say that she'll never be happy, not really, so that I'll know the hole isn't only in me.

"Dicuka, here's some advice from your big sister. Either you're sensitive, or you're not. When you're sensitive, you hurt more."

"Are we going to be okay?" I ask. "Someday?"

"Yes," she says. "No. I don't know. One thing's true: *Hitler fucked us up for sure.*"

Béla and I are now bringing in $60 a week, enough to try for a second child. I get pregnant. My daughter is born February

10, 1954. When I awaken from the anesthesia that American doctors routinely administered to all women in labor at that time, she is in the nursery. But I demand to hold my baby, I demand to nurse her. When the nurse brings her to me, I see that she is perfect and sleepy, not as big as her sister was when she was born, her nose so tiny, her cheeks so smooth.

Béla brings Marianne, now six years old, to see the baby. "I got my sister! I got my sister!" Marianne celebrates, as though I have put away money in an envelope and ordered her a sister from a catalog, as though I have the capacity to always grant her wishes. She will soon also have a cousin, because Magda, who married Nat Shillman in 1953, is pregnant and will give birth to a daughter in October. She names her Ilona, after our mother.

We name our own new daughter Audrey, after Audrey Hepburn. I am still dazed from the drugs the doctors used to sedate me. Even the intensity of labor, of meeting and nursing my baby for the first time, have taken on the numb quality of my life in hiding.

It is a reflex to expect the bad with the good. The first months of Audrey's life, Béla studies for his CPA test as though preparing for the ultimate test, the one crucial trial that will determine forever whether or not he will find his place, his peace with himself and our choices.

He doesn't pass the test. Moreover, he is told that with his stutter, his accent, he will never get a job, no matter if he is able the earn his license.

"There's always going to be a block in the road," he says, "no matter what I do."

I object. I reassure him. I say we'll find a way, but I can't stop my sister Klara's voice from creeping into my head. *Two cripples. How is that going to work out?* I cry in the bathroom. I do it silently, come out cheerful. I don't know that fears kept hidden only grow more fierce. I don't know that my habits of providing and placating—of pretending—are only making us worse.

CHAPTER 13

You Were There?

In the summer of 1955, when Marianne was seven and Audrey was one, we loaded up our old gray Ford and left Baltimore for El Paso, Texas. Demoralized by the lack of job prospects, tired of his brother's judgment and resentments, worried about his own health, Béla had contacted his cousin, Bob Eger, hoping for advice. Bob was the adopted son of Béla's great-uncle Albert, who had immigrated to Chicago with two of his brothers in the early 1900s, leaving the fourth brother—Béla's grandfather—in Prešov to run the wholesaling business that Béla had inherited after the war. It was the Chicago Egers who had supported George's immigration to America in the 1930s, and it was also they who had secured our opportunity for visas by registering the Eger family before the war. I was grateful for the generosity and foresight of the Chicago Egers, without whom we never could have made a home in America.

But when Bob, who now lived with his wife and two children in El Paso, told Béla, "Come west!" I was worried that we might be walking into another dead end disguised as opportunity. Bob reassured us. He said the economy was booming in El Paso, that in a border town immigrants were less segregated and marginalized, that the frontier was a perfect place to start from scratch, to reinvent one's life. He even helped Béla find a job as a CPA's assistant at twice his Baltimore salary. "The desert air will be good for my lungs," Béla said. "We'll be able to afford to rent a house, not another tiny apartment." And so I agreed.

We tried to make the upheaval into a fun adventure, a vacation. We drove scenic highways, we stopped at motels with swimming pools, and got off the road early enough in the day to have a refreshing swim before dinner. Despite my anxieties over the move, the cost of gas and motels and restaurant meals, the miles stretching once again between Magda and me, I found myself smiling more often. Not the mask of a smile worn to reassure my family. The real kind, deep in my cheeks and my eyes. I felt a new camaraderie with Béla, who taught Marianne corny jokes and bounced Audrey in the water when we swam.

In El Paso, the first thing I noticed was the sky. Open, uncluttered, vast. The mountains that girded the city to the north drew my gaze too. I was always looking up. At certain times of day, the angle of the sun would flatten the range into a faint cardboard cutout, a movie set, the peaks a uniform dull brown. And then the light would shift, the mountains rainbow into pink, orange, purple, red, gold, deep blue, the range popping into relief like an accordion stretched to expose all its folds.

The culture, too, had dimension. I had expected the dusty, out-of-touch frontier village of a Western movie, a place with stoic, lonely men and lonelier women. But El Paso felt more European, more cosmopolitan, than Baltimore. It was bilingual. Multicultural without the stark segregation. And there was the border itself, the union of worlds. El Paso, Texas, and Juárez, Chihuahua, weren't separate cities so much as two halves of the same whole. The Rio Grande cut through the middle, dividing the city between two countries, but the border was as arbitrary as it was distinct. I thought of my hometown: from Košice, to Kassa, to Košice again, the border changing everything, the border changing nothing. My English was still basic and I didn't speak Spanish at all, but I felt less marginalized and ostracized here than I had in Baltimore, where we lived in a Jewish immigrant neighborhood, where we had expected to find shelter but instead felt exposed. In El Paso we were just part of the mix.

One afternoon soon after our move, I am at the neighborhood park with Audrey when I hear a mother call to her kids in Hungarian. I watch her, this other Hungarian mother, for a few minutes, expecting to recognize her, but then I chide myself. What a naïve assumption, that just because her voice is familiar, a mirror of my own, we might have anything in common. Yet I can't stop tracking her as she and her children play, can't let go of the feeling that I know her.

Suddenly, I remember something I haven't thought of since the night of Klara's wedding: the postcard tucked into Magda's mirror in Košice. The cursive script across the picture of the bridge: *El Paso*. How had I forgotten that ten years ago, Laci Gladstein moved here, to this city? Laci, the young man who was liberated with us at Gunskirchen, who was on the top of the train with Magda and me from Vienna to Prague, who held our hands in comfort, who I thought might marry Magda one day, who had come to El Paso to work in his aunt and uncle's furniture store to save for medical school. *El Paso*, the place I thought looked in the postcard like the end of the world, the place where I now live.

Audrey pulls me out of my reverie, demanding to get on the swings. As I lift her up, the Hungarian woman approaches the swing set with her son. I speak quickly to her, in Hungarian, before I can stop myself.

"You're Hungarian," I say. "Maybe you know an old friend of mine who came to El Paso after the war."

She looks at me in that amused way that adults look at children, as though I am delightfully, impossibly naïve. "Who is your friend?" she asks. She is playing along.

"Laci Gladstein."

Tears spring into her eyes. "I'm his sister!" she cries. She has read my code. *Old friend. After the war.* "He's a doctor," she says. "He goes by Larry Gladstone now."

How can I explain the way I felt in this moment? Ten years had passed since I rode with Laci on top of a train with other displaced survivors. In that decade, he had fulfilled his dream of becoming a doctor. Hearing this made no hope or ambition seem out of reach. He had reinvented himself in America. So could I.

But that is only half the story. Standing in a park in the hot desert sun, I was indeed at the end of the world, farther in time and space than I'd ever been from the girl left for dead in a pile of bodies in a muggy forest in Austria. And yet I had never, since the war, been closer to her, either, because here I was almost acknowledging her to a stranger, here I was meeting a ghost from the past in broad daylight, while my daughter demanded to go higher and higher in the swing. Maybe moving forward also meant circling back.

* * *

I find Larry Gladstone in the phone book and wait a week or more before I make the call. His wife, an American, answers the phone. She takes a message, she asks several times how to spell my name. I tell myself he won't remember me. That evening, Bob and his family come over to our house for dinner. Marianne has asked me to make hamburgers, and I make them the way my mother would have, the ground beef mixed with egg and garlic and breadcrumbs, rolled up like meatballs, served with Brussels sprouts and potatoes cooked with caraway seeds. When I bring the meal to the table, Marianne rolls her eyes. "Mom," she says, "I meant *American* hamburgers." She wants flattened patties served between tasteless white buns, with greasy french fries and a puddle of bland ketchup. She is embarrassed in front of Dickie and Barbara, her American cousins. Her disapproval stings. I have done what I have promised myself never to do. I have made her feel ashamed. The phone rings and I escape the table to answer it.

"Edith," the man says. "Mrs. Eger. This is Dr. Larry Gladstone."

He speaks in English, but his voice is the same. It brings the past into my kitchen, the sting of the wind from the top of the train. I am dizzy. I am hungry, as I was then, half starved. My broken back aches. "Laci," I say, my own voice far away, as though it is coming through a radio in another room. Our shared past is pervasive yet unmentionable.

"We meet again," he says. We switch to Hungarian. He tells me about his wife and her philanthropic work, their three daughters, I tell him about my children and Béla's aspirations to become a CPA. He invites me to visit his office, he welcomes my family to join his family for dinner. So begins—again—a friendship that will last the rest of our lives. When I hang up the phone, the sky is turning rose and gold. I can hear my family's voices in the dining room. Bob's son Dickie is asking his mother about me, am I really an American, why is my English so bad? My body tenses, the way it does when the past is too near. It's like a hand thrown out in front of my children when the car brakes too fast. A reflex to protect. Since my pregnancy with Marianne, when I defied the doctor's warning, when I chose that my life would always stand for more life, I resolved not to let the death camps cast a shadow over my children. That conviction has hardened into a single purpose: *My children can't ever know.* They will never picture me skeletal with hunger, dreaming of my mother's strudel under a smoke-thickened sky. It will never be an image they have to hold in their minds. I will protect them. I will spare them. But Dickie's questions remind me that while I can choose my own silence, and I can choose the kinship or camouflage of others' silence, I can't choose what other people say or do when I'm not there. What might my daughters overhear? What might others tell them despite my efforts to keep the truth locked away?

To my relief, Dickie's mother moves the conversation in a new direction. She prompts Dickie and his older sister Barbara to tell Marianne about the best teachers at the school she will start in the fall. Has Béla instructed her to maintain the conspiracy of silence? Or is it something she has intuited? Is it something she does for my sake, my children's sake, her own? Later, as their family gathers at the door to leave, I hear Dickie's mother whisper to him in English, "Don't *ever* ask Auntie Dicu about the past. It's not something we talk about." My life is a family taboo. My secret is safe.

There are always two worlds. The one that I choose and the one I deny, which inserts itself without my permission.

In 1956, Béla passes the CPA test, earns his license, and a few months before our third child—Johnny, a son—is born, we buy a modest three-bedroom rambler on Fiesta Drive. There is nothing but desert behind the house—pink and purple ceniza blooms, red yucca flowers, the throb of rattlesnakes. Inside, we choose light-colored furnishings for the living room and the den. Over fresh papaya that Béla crosses the border to buy in the Juárez produce markets on Sunday mornings, we read the headlines. In Hungary, an uprising, Soviet tanks rolling in to quash the anti-Communist rebellion. Béla is terse with the girls, his stutter edging back. It is hot, I am very pregnant. We turn on the swamp cooler and gather around the TV in the den to watch the summer Olympics broadcast from Melbourne.

We tune in just as Ágnes Keleti, a Jew from Budapest on the women's gymnastics team, warms up for her floor routine. She is thirty-five, six years older than I am. If she had grown up in Kassa, or I in Budapest, we would have trained together. "Pay attention!" Béla tells the girls. "She's Hungarian, like us." To watch Ágnes Keleti take the floor is to watch my other half, my other self. The one who wasn't sent to Auschwitz. (Keleti, I later find out, bought identification papers from a Christian girl in Budapest and fled to a remote village where she waited out the war, working as a maid.) The one whose mother lived. The one who picked up the seam of her old life after the war, who hasn't let her hardships or her age destroy her dream. She lifts her arms, extends her body long, she is poised to begin. Béla cheers wildly. Audrey imitates him. Marianne studies me, how I lean, lean toward the TV. She doesn't know I was a competitive gymnast once, much less that the same war that interrupted Ágnes Keleti's life also interrupted—still intrudes on—mine. But I sense my daughter's awareness of my held breath, of the way I follow Keleti's body with my body, not just with my eyes. Béla and Marianne and Audrey applaud each flip. I am breathless when Keleti is slow and controlled, when she leans all the way down over her legs to touch the floor, and then revolves from a seated forward bend to a backward arch, and up into a handstand, all grace and fluid motion. Her routine is over.

Her Soviet competitor takes the floor. Because of the uprising in Hungary, the tensions between Hungarian and Soviet athletes are especially fraught. Béla boos loudly. Little Audrey, two years old, does the same. I tell them both to hush. I watch Larisa Latynina the way the judges do, the way Keleti must be watching her. I see that her high kick is maybe a little higher than Keleti's, I see the buoyancy of her flips, the way she lands in a full split. Marianne sighs with appreciation. Béla boos again. "She's really good, Daddy," Marianne says. "She's from a country of oppressors and bullies," Béla says. "She didn't choose where she was born," I say. Béla shrugs. "Try twirling like that when *your* country's under siege," he says. "In this house we cheer for Hungarians." In the end, Keleti and Latynina share the gold. Latynina's shoulder brushes Keleti's as they stand side by side at the awards ceremony. Keleti grimaces from the pedestal. "Mom, why are you crying?" Marianne asks me. "I'm not," I say.

Deny. Deny. Deny. Who am I protecting? My daughter? Or myself?

Marianne grows ever more curious, and is a voracious reader. When she has read every book in the children's section of the El Paso Public Library, she begins scrambling around the bookcases in our house, reading my philosophy and literature, Béla's history. In 1957, when she is ten, she sits Béla and me down on the beige couch in the den. She stands before us like a little teacher. She opens a book that she tells us she found hidden behind the other books on one of our shelves. She points to a picture of naked, skeletal corpses piled up in a heap. "What is this?" she asks. I am sweating, the room spins. I could have predicted this moment would come, but it is as surprising to me, as arresting and terrifying, as if I had walked into the house to discover that the live alligator pit from San Jacinto Plaza had been installed in our living room. To face the truth, to face my daughter facing the truth, is to face a beast. I run from the room. I vomit in the bathroom sink. I hear Béla telling our daughter about Hitler, about Auschwitz. I hear him say the dreaded words: *Your mother was there.* I could crack the mirror. *No! No! No!* I want to scream. *I wasn't there!* What I mean is, *This isn't yours to carry!* "Your mother is very strong," I hear Béla tell Marianne. "But you must understand that you are a survivor's daughter, you must always, always protect her." This could have been an opportunity. To soothe Marianne. To unburden her from the need to worry about or pity me. To tell her how much her grandparents would have loved her. To tell her, *It's all okay, we are safe now.* But I can't leave the bathroom. I don't trust myself. If I say a word about the past, I will stoke the rage and the loss, I will fall into the dark, I will take her there with me.

I focus on the children, on the things I can do to make all of us feel secure and accepted and happy in our new home.

There are the daily rituals, the hallmarks of the week and seasons, the things we do for joy, the things we count on: Béla's unusual practice of shaving his bald head in the morning while he drives Audrey to school. Béla on a shopping run to the Safeway that was built in the vast desert behind our house. Inevitably, I've forgotten to add something to the list, and I call him at the store. The grocery clerks know my voice. "Mr. Eger, your wife's on the phone," they call over the PA. I tend our garden, I mow the lawn, I work part time in Béla's office. He becomes the loved and trusted accountant for all the successful immigrants in El Paso—Syrians, Mexicans, Italians, European Jews. On Saturdays he brings the kids along to meet with clients, and if I didn't already know how much Béla was adored, I would see their love for him in the affection they shower on our children. Sundays, Béla drives to Juárez to buy fresh fruit from Chuy the grocer, and then we have a big family brunch at our house, we listen to Broadway musicals albums, we sing along to the show tunes (Béla can sing without stuttering), and then we go to the YMCA for a family swim. We go to San Jacinto Plaza in downtown El Paso on Christmas Day. We don't celebrate Christmas with gifts, but the kids still write letters to Santa. We exchange practical gifts—socks and clothes—for Hanukkah, and we bring in the New Year with lots of food and the Sun Carnival parade—the Sun Queen, the high school bands, the Rotary Club men riding by on motorcycles. In spring, there are picnic outings to White Sands and Santa Fe. In the fall, back-to-school clothes shopping at Amen Wardy. Running my hands over the racks, I can feel the best fabrics by touch, I have a knack for finding the finest garments for the lowest price. (Béla and I both have these tactile rituals—for him, choosing produce; for me, choosing clothes.) We go to farms in Mexico for fall harvest, we fill ourselves with homemade tamales. Food is love. When our kids bring home good report cards, we take them for a banana split at the soda fountain behind our house.

When Audrey is nine, she tries out for a year-round swimming team and becomes a competitive swimmer. By the time she is in high school, she will be training six hours a day, as I used to do in gymnastics and ballet. When Marianne is thirteen, we build an addition to our house, adding a master suite so that Marianne and Audrey and Johnny have their own rooms. We buy a piano. Marianne and Audrey both take lessons, we host chamber music concerts like my parents did when I was a girl, we have bridge parties. Béla and I join a book club hosted by Molly Shapiro, well known in El Paso for her salons, where she brings artists and intellectuals together. I take an ESL class at the University of Texas. My English finally improves enough that in 1959 I feel I can enroll as an undergraduate student. It's long been my dream to continue my education—another dream deferred, but this one now seems possible. I take my first psychology class, sit in a row of basketball players, take notes in Hungarian, ask for Béla's help writing every paper. I am thirty-two years old. We are happy on the outside, on the inside often too.

*   *   *

But there is the way Béla looks at our son. He wanted a son, but he didn't expect this son. Johnny had athetoid cerebral palsy, probably caused by encephalitis before birth, and this affected his motor control. He struggled to do things Marianne and Audrey had learned to do with little fuss—dress himself, talk, use a fork or a spoon to feed himself. He looked different from them too. His eyes drooped. He drooled. Béla was critical of Johnny, impatient with his struggles. I remembered the ridicule I had faced for being cross-eyed, and I ached for my son. Béla would yell in frustration over Johnny's challenges. (He yelled in Czech, so the children, who had picked up a little Hungarian in our home, despite my wish for them to speak only flawless American English, wouldn't understand the words—though of course they understood his tone.) I would retreat into our bedroom. I was a master hider. In 1960, when Johnny was four, I took him to see Dr. Clark, a specialist at Johns Hopkins, who told me, "Your son will be whatever you make of him. John's going to do everything everyone else does, but it's going to take him longer to get there. You can push him too hard, and that will backfire, but it will also be a mistake not to push him hard enough. You need to push him to the level of his potential." I dropped out of school so that I could get Johnny to his speech therapy appointments, his occupational therapy appointments, to every kind of clinic I could think of, to every kind of specialist who might help. (Audrey says now that her most vivid childhood memories aren't in the swimming pool—they're in waiting rooms.) I chose not to accept that our son was forever compromised. I felt sure that he could thrive if we believed he could. But when he was young, eating with his hands, chewing with his mouth open because that was the best he could manage, Béla gazed at him with such disappointment, such sadness, I felt I had to protect my son from his father.

Fear pulled a current through our comfortable lives. Once, when Audrey was ten, she had a friend over, and I walked past the open door of her room just as an ambulance raced past our house, siren wailing. I covered my head, a stubborn habit from the war, something I still do. Before I had consciously registered the siren or my reaction to it, I heard Audrey yelling to her friend, "Quick, get under the bed!" She threw herself on the floor and rolled under the bed skirt. Her friend laughed, followed her down, probably thinking it was a peculiar game. But I could tell that Audrey wasn't joking. She really thought sirens signaled danger. That you have to take cover. Without meaning to, without any conscious awareness, I had taught her that.

What else were we unconsciously teaching our children, about safety, values, love?

The night of Marianne's high school prom, she stands on our front porch in her silk dress, a beautiful orchid corsage on her wrist. As she steps off the porch with her date, Béla calls, "Have a great time, honey. You know, your mother was in Auschwitz when she was your age and her parents were dead."

I scream at Béla when Marianne has left. I call him bitter and cold, I tell him he had no right to ruin her joy on her special night, to ruin the vicarious pleasure I took in her joy. If he can't censor himself, I won't either. If he can't bless our daughter with happy thoughts, I tell him, then he might as well be dead. "The fact that you were at Auschwitz and she's not *is* a happy thought," Béla defends. "I want Marianne to feel glad for the life she has." "Then don't poison it!" I yell. Worse than Béla's comment is the fact that I never talk to Marianne about it afterward. I pretend not to notice that she is also living two lives—the one she lives for herself and the one she lives for me because I wasn't allowed to live it.

In the fall of 1966, when Audrey is twelve, Marianne a sophomore at Whittier College, and Johnny, ten, fulfilling Dr. Clark's prediction that with the right support, he could be physically and academically stable, I have time again to devote to my own progress. I return to school. My English is now good enough to write my papers without Béla's help (when he helped me, the best grade I got was a C, but now I earn As). I feel that I am finally getting ahead, finally transcending the limitations of my past. But once again the two worlds I've done my best to keep separate collide. I'm sitting in a lecture hall, waiting for my introductory political science class to begin, when a sandy-haired man sits down behind me.

"You were there, weren't you?" he says.

"There?" I feel the panic start to rise.

"Auschwitz. You're a survivor, aren't you?"

I am so rattled by his question that I don't think to ask him one in return. What makes him think I'm a survivor? How does he know? How did he guess? I have never said a single word about my experience to anyone in my present life, not even my kids. I don't have a number tattooed on my arm.

"Aren't you a Holocaust survivor?" he asks again.

He is young, maybe twenty—roughly half my age. Something in his youth, in his earnest nature, in the kind intensity of his voice, reminds me of Eric, how we sat in a movie theater together after curfew, how he took a picture of me on the shore doing the splits, how he kissed my lips for the first time, his hands resting on the thin belt at my waist. Twenty-one years after liberation, I feel pounded by loss. The loss of Eric. The loss of our young love. The loss of the future—the vision we shared of marriage and family and activism. For the entire year of my imprisonment, for the year I somehow escaped a death that seemed mandatory and inevitable, I held to Eric's remembered verse: *I'll never forget your eyes, I'll never forget your hands.* Memory was my lifeline. And now? I have shut out the past. To remember is to concede to the horror again and again. But in the past, too, is Eric's voice. In the past is the love that I felt and sang in my mind all those months that I starved.

"I am a survivor," I say, shaking.

"Have you read this?" He shows me a small paperback: *Man's Search for Meaning* by Viktor Frankl. It sounds like a philosophy text. The author's name doesn't ring a bell. I shake my head. "Frankl was at Auschwitz," the student explains. "He wrote this book about it, just after the war. I think you would find it of interest," he says, offering it to me.

I take the book in my hand. It is slim. It fills me with dread. Why would I willingly return to hell, even through the filter of someone else's experience? But I don't have the heart to reject this young man's gesture. I whisper a thank you and tuck the little book into my bag, where it sits all evening like a ticking bomb.

I start to make dinner, I feel distracted and out of my body. I send Béla to Safeway for more garlic, and then again for more peppers. I barely taste my meal. After dinner, I quiz Johnny on his spelling words. I do the dishes. I kiss my children good night. Béla goes to the den to listen to Rachmaninoff and read *The*

Nation. My bag sits in the hall by the front door, the book still inside. Even its presence in my house is causing me discomfort. I won't read it. I don't have to. I was there. I will spare myself the pain.

Sometime after midnight, my curiosity wins out over my fear. I creep into the living room, where I sit for a long time in a pool of lamplight holding the book. I begin to read. *This book does not claim to be an account of facts and events but of personal experiences, experiences which millions of prisoners have suffered time and again. It is the inside story of a concentration camp, told by one of its survivors.* The back of my neck prickles. He is speaking to me. He is speaking for me. *How was everyday life in a concentration camp reflected in the mind of the average prisoner?* He writes about the three phases of a prisoner's life—beginning with what it is like to arrive at a death camp and feel the "delusion of reprieve." Yes, I remember so well how my father heard the music playing on the train platform and said this couldn't be a bad place, remember the way Mengele wagged his finger between life and death, and said, as casually as you please, "You'll see your mother very soon." Then there is the second phase—learning to adapt to the impossible and inconceivable. To endure the kapos' beatings, to get up no matter how cold or hungry or tired or ill, to eat the soup and save the bread, to watch our own flesh disappearing, to hear everywhere that the only escape is death. Even the third phase, release and liberation, wasn't an end to the imprisonment, Frankl writes. It can continue in bitterness, disillusionment, a struggle for meaning and happiness.

I am staring directly at the thing I have sought to hide. And as I read, I find I don't feel shut down or trapped, locked back in that place. To my surprise, I don't feel afraid. For every page I read, I want to write ten. What if telling my story could lighten its grip instead of tightening it? What if speaking about the past could heal it instead of calcify it? What if silence and denial aren't the only choices to make in the wake of catastrophic loss?

I read how Frankl marches to his work site in the icy dark. The cold is harsh, the guards are brutal, the prisoners stumble. In the midst of physical pain and dehumanizing injustice, Frankl flashes on his wife's face. He sees her eyes, and his heart blooms with love in the depth of winter. He understands *how a man who has nothing left in this world may still know bliss, be it only for a brief moment, in the contemplation of his beloved.* My heart opens. I weep. It is my mother speaking to me from the page, from the oppressive dark of the train: *Just remember, no one can take away from you what you've put in your mind.* We can't choose to vanish the dark, but we can choose to kindle the light.

In those predawn hours in the autumn of 1966, I read this, which is at the very heart of Frankl's teaching: *Everything can be taken from a man but one thing: the last of the human freedoms—to choose one's attitude in any given set of circumstances, to choose one's own way.* Each moment is a choice. No matter how frustrating or boring or constraining or painful or oppressive our experience, we can always choose how we respond. And I finally begin to understand that I, too, have a choice. This realization will change my life.

CHAPTER 14

From One Survivor to Another

No one heals in a straight line.

One January evening in 1969, when Audrey comes home from a babysitting job, Béla and I ask her and John to sit on the brown Danish couch in the living room. I can't look at Béla, I can't look at my children, I stare at the clean modern lines of the couch, its thin little legs. Béla starts to cry.

"Did someone die?" Audrey asks. "Just tell us."

Johnny kicks his feet nervously against the couch.

"Everything's fine," Béla says. "We love you both very much. Your mother and I have decided that we need to live in separate houses for a while." He stutters as he speaks, the sentences last a year.

"What are you saying?" Audrey asks. "What's going on?"

"We need to explore how to have more peace in our family," I say. "This isn't your fault."

"You don't love each other anymore?"

"We do," Béla says. "*I* do." This is his jab, the one knife he points at me.

"You're not happy all of a sudden? I thought you were happy. Or have you just been lying to us our whole lives?" Audrey has been clutching her babysitting money in her hand—when she turned twelve, Béla opened a checking account for her and said he would double any dollar that she made—but now she throws her money on the couch, as though we have contaminated every good or valuable thing.

* * *

It was an accrual of experiences, not a sudden recognition, that led me to divorce Béla. My choice had something to do with my mother—what she had chosen and what she hadn't been allowed to choose. Before she married my father, she was working for a consulate in Budapest, she was earning her own money, she was part of a cosmopolitan social and professional circle. She was quite liberated for her time. But then her younger sister got married, and the pressure was on her to do what her society and family expected of her, to marry before she became an embarrassment. There was a man she loved, someone she met through her work at the consulate, the man who had given her the inscribed copy of *Gone with the Wind*. But her father forbade her to marry him because he wasn't Jewish. My father, the celebrated tailor, fit her for a dress one day, he admired her figure, and she opted to leave the life she had chosen for herself in favor of the life she was expected to live. In marrying Béla, I feared I had done the same thing—forgone taking responsibility for my own dreams in exchange for the safety Béla provided me. Now the qualities that had drawn me to him, his ability to provide and caretake, felt suffocating, our marriage felt like an abdication of myself.

I didn't want the kind of marriage my parents had—lonely, lacking in intimacy—and I didn't want their broken dreams (my father's, to be a doctor; my mother's, to be a career woman, to marry for love). But what did I want for myself? I didn't know. And so I erected Béla as a force to push against. In place of discovering my own genuine purpose and direction, I found meaning in fighting against him, against the ways I imagined that he limited me. Really, Béla was supportive of my schooling, he paid for my tuition, he loved talking with me about the philosophy and literature I was reading, he found my reading lists and analyses interesting complements to his favorite subject: history. Maybe because Béla occasionally expressed some resentment for the time I gave to school, or because in the interest of my own health he sometimes cautioned me to slow down, the notion took root and grew in me that if I wanted to progress in my life, it would have to be on my own. I was so hungry, so tired of discounting myself.

I remember traveling with Audrey to a swim meet in San Angelo in 1967, when she was thirteen. The other parent chaperones got together in the hotel in the evening and drank and caroused. If Béla had been there, I realized, we would have been at the center of the activity, not because either of us liked to be around heavy drinking, but because Béla was a natural charmer—he saw a room of people and he couldn't stay away. Any room that he occupied became a social sphere, people drawn into convivial relationship because of the atmosphere he created. I admired this about him, and I resented it, too, resented the ways I became silent so that his voice could ring. Just like in my family growing up, there was room for one star. At our weekly prime rib and dancing dates with friends in El Paso, I got to share the light when everyone made room for Béla and me on the dance floor. Together, we were sensational, our friends said, it was hard to look away. We were admired as a couple—but there wasn't space for just me. That night in San Angelo, I found the noise and drunkenness of the other parents unpleasant, and I was about to retreat to my room. I was lonely, feeling a little sorry for myself. Then I flashed on Frankl's book. On my freedom to choose my own response to any situation.

I did something I had never done before. I knocked on the door of Audrey's hotel room. She was surprised to see me, but she invited me in. She and her friends were playing cards, watching TV. "When I was your age," I said, "I was an athlete too." Audrey's eyes opened wide. "You girls are so lucky and beautiful. You know what it is to have a strong body. To work hard. To be a team." I told them what my ballet teacher had told me a lifetime ago: "All your ecstasy in life is going to come from the inside." I said good night and started to walk out the door, but before I left the room, I did a high kick. Audrey's eyes glittered with pride. Her friends clapped and cheered. I wasn't the quiet mom with the strange accent. I was the performer, the athlete, the mom whose daughter admired her. Inside, I equated that feeling of self-worth and elation with Béla's absence. If I wanted to feel that glow more often, perhaps I needed to be with him less often.

That hunger for self fueled me in my undergraduate studies too. I was voracious, always in search of more knowledge, and also the respect and approval that might signal to me that I was of value. I stayed up all night working on papers that were already good, for fear that they wouldn't—or would only—be good enough. When a psychology professor announced to our class at the beginning of the semester that he only gave C's, I marched to his office, told him I only earned As, and asked what I could do to continue my exceptional academic performance. He invited me to work with him as an assistant, augmenting my classroom learning with field experience usually granted only to graduate students.

One afternoon, some of my classmates invited me to join them for a beer after class. I sat with them in the darkened bar near campus, my chilled glass on the table, enthralled by their youthful energy, their political passion. I admired them, social justice advocates, pacifists. I was happy to be included. And sad too. This stage of my life had been cut short. Individuation and independence from my family. Dating and romance. Participation in social movements that were bringing about real change. I had lost my childhood to the war, my adolescence to the death camps, and my young adulthood to the compulsion to never look back. I had become a mother before I had grieved my own mother's death. I had tried too fast and too soon to be whole. It wasn't Béla's fault that I had chosen denial, that I often kept myself, my memories, my true opinions and experiences hidden, even from him. But now I held him responsible for prolonging my stuckness.

That day over beers, one of my fellow students asked me how Béla and I had met. "I love a good love story," she said. "Was it love at first sight?" I don't remember how I answered her, but I do know that the question made me think, again, about the kind of love I wished I'd had. With Eric there had been sparks, a flush all over my body when he was near. Even Auschwitz didn't kill the romantic girl in me, the girl who told herself each day that she might meet him again. But after the war, that dream died. When I met Béla, I wasn't in love; I was hungry. And he brought me Swiss cheese. He brought me salami. I could remember feeling happy in those early years with Béla—when I was pregnant with Marianne, walking to the market every morning to buy flowers, talking to her in my womb, telling her how she was going to blossom like a flower. And she had, all of my children had. And now I was forty years old, the age my mother had been when she died, and I still hadn't blossomed, still hadn't had the love I thought I was due. I felt cheated, denied of an essential human rite, trapped in a marriage that had become a meal consumed with no expectation of nourishment, with no hope of erasing hunger.

My sustenance came from an unexpected source. One day in 1968, I came home to find a letter in the mailbox addressed to me in a European-looking hand, sent from Southern Methodist University, in Dallas. There was no name above the return address, only initials: *V. F.* When I opened the letter, I almost fell over. *From one survivor to another*, the salutation read. The letter was from Viktor Frankl.

Following my predawn immersion in *Man's Search for Meaning* two years earlier, I had written an essay called "Viktor Frankl and Me." I had written it for myself, it was a personal exercise, not an academic one, my first attempt to speak about my past. Timidly, cautiously hopeful for the possibility of personal growth, I had shared it with some professors and some friends, and eventually it had found its way into a campus publication. Someone had anonymously mailed a copy of my article to Frankl in Dallas, where, unbeknownst to me, he had been a visiting professor since 1966. Frankl was twenty-three years my senior—he had been thirty-nine years old, already a successful physician and psychiatrist, when he was interned at Auschwitz. Now he was the celebrated founder of Logotherapy. He had practiced, lectured, and taught all over the world. And he had been moved enough by my little essay to contact me, to relate to me as a fellow survivor, as a peer. I had written about imagining myself onstage at the Budapest opera house the night I was forced to dance for Mengele. Frankl wrote that he had done something similar at Auschwitz—in his worst moments, he had imagined himself a free man, giving lectures in Vienna on the psychology of imprisonment. He had also found a sanctuary in an inner world that both shielded him from his present fear and pain, and inspired his hope and sense of purpose—that gave him the means and a reason to survive. Frankl's book and his letter helped me find words for our shared experience.

So began a correspondence and a friendship that would last for many years, in which we would try together to answer the questions that ran through our lives: *Why did I survive? What is the purpose in my life? What meaning can I make from my suffering? How can I help myself and others to endure the hardest parts of life and to experience more passion and joy?* After exchanging letters for several years, we met for the first time at a lecture he gave in San Diego in the 1970s. He invited me backstage to meet his wife and even asked me to critique his talk—a hugely important moment, to be treated by my mentor as a peer. Even his first letter nourished in me the seed of a calling: the search to make meaning in my life by helping others to make meaning; to heal so that I could heal others; to heal others so that I could heal myself. It also reinforced my understanding, however misapplied when I divorced Béla, that I had the power and opportunity—as well as the responsibility—to choose my own meaning, my own life.

* * *

I had taken my first conscious step toward finding my own way in the late 1950s, when I noticed Johnny's developmental challenges and needed help in meeting them. A friend recommended a Jungian analyst who had studied in Switzerland. I knew next to nothing about clinical psychology in general or Jungian analysis in particular, but after looking into the subject a bit, several Jungian ideas appealed to me. I liked the emphasis on myths and archetypes, which reminded me of the literature I had loved as a girl. And I was intrigued by the notion of bringing the conscious and unconscious parts of one's psyche together into a balanced whole. I remembered the images of dissonance between Vicky Page's inner and outer experience in *The Red Shoes*, and of course I was suffering in the grip of my own inner conflicts. I wasn't consciously entering therapy to heal that tension in myself—I really just wanted to know what to do for my son and how to heal the rift between Béla and me over what to do. But I also felt drawn to Carl Jung's vision of therapeutic analysis: *It is a matter of saying yea to oneself, of taking oneself as the most serious of tasks, of being conscious of everything one does, and keeping it constantly before one's eyes in all its dubious aspects—truly a task that taxes us to the utmost.* "Saying yea" to myself. I wanted to do that. I wanted to blossom and improve.

My therapist gave me dream homework, and I studiously recorded my dreams. Almost always, I was flying. I could choose how high or low to the ground to fly, how fast or how slow. I could choose which landscapes to fly over—European cathedrals, forested mountains, ocean beaches. I looked forward to sleep so that I could have these dreams in which I was joyful and strong, flying free, in control. I found in those dreams my power to transcend the limiting assumptions that others often imposed on my son. And I found my desire to transcend what I perceived to be the limitations imposed on me. I didn't yet know that the limitations that needed transcending weren't without— they were within. So when, years later, under the influence of Viktor Frankl, I began to question what I wanted out of life, it was easy for me to think that saying no to Béla would be one way of saying yes to myself.

In the months after the divorce, I felt better. For several years I had been suffering from migraines (my mother had also struggled with debilitating headaches; I assumed they were hereditary), but right after Béla and I separated, the migraines disappeared, departing like a season. I thought it was because now I was living free from Béla's weather—his yelling and cynicism, his irritation and disappointment. My headaches disappeared and so did my need to hide, to retreat. I invited fellow students and our professors to my house, I hosted raucous parties, I felt at the center of a community, open to the world.

I was living the way I wanted to live, I thought. But soon a fog set in. My surroundings looked gray-washed. I had to remind myself to eat.

One Saturday morning in May 1969, I sit at home alone in the den. It's my graduation day. I am forty-two years old. I am graduating with a BS in psychology from the University of Texas–El Paso, I am graduating with honors. Yet I can't make myself walk in the ceremony. I am too ashamed. "I should have done this years ago," I tell myself. What I really mean—the subtext of so many of my choices and beliefs—is, "I don't deserve to have survived." I am so obsessed with proving my worth, with earning my place in the world, that I don't need Hitler anymore. I have become my own jailor, telling myself, "No matter what you do, you will never be good enough."

What I miss the most about Béla is the way he dances. Especially the Viennese waltz. As cynical and angry as he can be, he also lets joy in, he lets his body wear it, express it. He can surrender to the tempo and still lead, hold steady. I dream of him some nights. Of his childhood, the stories he told me in letters when he courted me. I see his father collapse into an avalanche, his breath lost in all that white. I see his mother panic in a Budapest market and confess her identity to the SS. I think of the sad tension in Béla's family stemming from his mother's role in their deaths. I think of Béla's stutter, the way his early trauma marked him. One summer day Béla comes to pick up John. He's driving a new car. In America, we have always owned frugal cars—dumpy cars, our children say. Today he's driving an Oldsmobile with leather seats. He bought it used, he says, defensive, proud. But my look of disbelief isn't about the car. It's about the elegant woman sitting in the passenger seat. He's found someone else.

I am grateful for the necessity of working to support myself and my children. Work is an escape. And it gives me a clear purpose. I become a seventh- and eighth-grade social studies teacher in the El Paso barrio. I receive job offers from more coveted schools in the wealthy parts of town, but I want to work with students who are bilingual, who are facing the kinds of obstacles Béla and I did when we came to America: poverty, prejudice. I want to connect my students to their choices, to show them that the more choices they have, the less they'll feel like victims. The most difficult part of my job is countering the negative voices in my students' lives—sometimes even their own parents' voices—that say they will never make it as students, that education for them isn't a viable course. *You're so puny, you're so ugly, you'll never find a husband.* I tell them about my crossed eyes, about my sisters' silly chant, how the problem wasn't that they sang these songs to me—the problem was that I believed them. But I don't let my students know how deeply I identify with them, how hate obliterated my childhood, how I know the darkness that eats you when you've been taught to believe that you don't matter. I remember the voice that rose up through the Tatra Mountains, *If you're going to live, you have to stand for something.* My students give me something to stand for. But I am still numb and anxious, isolated, so brittle and sad.

The flashbacks persist, they happen sometimes when I'm driving. I see a policeman in uniform at the side of the road and my vision tunnels, I feel like I will faint. I don't have a name for these experiences, I don't yet understand that they are a physiological manifestation of the grief that I haven't dealt with yet. A clue my body sends as a reminder of the feelings that I have blocked from conscious life. A storm that assaults me when I deny myself permission to feel.

What are my disowned feelings? They are like strangers living in my house, invisible except for the food they steal, the furniture they leave out of place, the mud they trail down the hall. Divorce doesn't liberate me from their uneasy presence. Divorce empties the room of other distractions, of the habitual targets of my blame and resentment, and forces me to sit alone with my feelings.

Sometimes I call Magda. She and Nat have divorced too, and she is remarried to Ted Gilbert, a man closer to her age, a kind listener and stepfather. She and Nat have maintained a close friendship. He comes to her house for dinner two or three times a week. "Be careful what you do when you're restless," my sister cautions. "You can start to think the wrong things. Unimportant things. He's too this, he's too that, I've suffered enough. You end up missing the same things that drove you crazy."

It's like she has read my mind, the little edge of doubt, the concession that maybe divorce isn't fixing what I thought was broken.

One night a woman calls my house. She is looking for Béla. Do I know where he might be? It's his girlfriend, I realize. She's calling my house as though I keep tabs on my ex-husband, as though I owe her information, as though I am his secretary. "Don't ever call me again!" I shout. After I hang up, I am agitated, I can't sleep. I try to have a flying dream, a lucid dream, but I can't take flight, I keep falling, waking. It is a terrible night. And a useful one. Audrey's sleeping over at a friend's house, Johnny is already in bed. There is nowhere to go to escape from my discomfort; I just have to feel it. I cry, I feel sorry for myself, I am furious. I feel every wave of jealousy, of bitterness, of loneliness, of indignation, of self-pity, and on and on. And in the morning, although I haven't slept, I feel better. Calmer. Nothing has changed. I still feel abandoned, however illogically, by the husband *I* chose to leave. But my storminess and agitation have run their course.

They aren't permanent features. They move, they change. I feel more at peace.

I will have many more nights and days like this one. Times when I am alone, when I begin to practice the work of not pushing my feelings away, no matter how painful. That is the gift of my divorce: the recognition that I have to face up to what's inside me. If I am really going to improve my life, it isn't Béla or our relationship that has to change. It's me.

I see the need for change, but I don't know what kind of change will help me feel freer and more joyful. I try a new therapist, for fresh perspective on my marriage, but her approach isn't useful—she wags her finger at me, telling me that forcing Béla to do the grocery shopping was emasculating, that I should never have mowed the lawn and taken his male responsibilities from him. She picks at the things that were working in my marriage and recasts them as problems and faults. I try a new job, this time at a high school, where I teach introductory psychology and serve as a school counselor. But the sense of purpose I felt at the beginning of my profession begins to be eroded by the bureaucracy of schools, the huge class sizes and case loads, the inability to work effectively with individual students. There's more I have to offer—I know this, although I don't yet know what it is I am meant to do.

This theme prevails: that my deepest and most important work, professionally and personally, is still to come, and still blurry, undefined. My friends Lili and Arpad are the first people to name for me what this work will entail, though I am not yet ready to acknowledge it, much less take it on. One weekend they invite me to visit them in Mexico. For years, Béla and I have vacationed with them together; this time, I go alone. The Sunday I am to return home, we linger over breakfast—coffee, fruit, the eggs I've cooked with Hungarian peppers and onions.

"We're worried about you," Lili says, her voice easy, gentle.

I know she and Arpad were surprised by the divorce, I know they think I made a mistake. It's hard not to read her concern as judgment. I tell them about Béla's girlfriend, she's a writer or a musician, I can never remember which, she isn't a person to me, she is an idea: Béla has moved on and left me behind. My friends listen, they are sympathetic. Then they share a glance, and Arpad clears his throat.

"Edie," he says, "forgive me if I'm getting too personal, and you can tell me to mind my own business. But I wonder, have you ever considered that it might be beneficial for you to work through your past?"

Work through it? I lived it, what other work is there to do? I want to say. *I've broken the conspiracy of silence. And talking hasn't made the fear or flashbacks go away.* In fact, talking seems to have made my symptoms worse. I haven't broken my silence with my children or friends in a formal way, but I no longer live in fear that they will ask me about the past. And I have tried to embrace opportunities to share my story. Recently, when a friend from my undergraduate days who went on to pursue a master's in history asked to interview me for a paper she was writing about the Holocaust, I accepted. I thought it might be a relief to tell my whole story. But when I left her house, I was shaking. I came home and vomited, just as I had a decade before when Marianne showed us the book with pictures of concentration camp inmates. "The past is past," I tell Lili and Arpad now. I'm not ready to heed or even understand Arpad's advice to "work through" the past. But, like Viktor Frankl's letter, it plants a seed within me, something that will sprout and take root with time.

One Saturday I am sitting at the table in the kitchen, grading my students' psychology exams, when Béla calls. It's his day with Audrey and John. My mind leaps to fear.

"What's wrong?" I say.

"Nothing's wrong. They're watching TV." He goes quiet, he waits for his voice to catch up. "Come to dinner," he finally says.

"With *you*?"

"With me."

"I'm busy," I say. I am. I have a date with a sociology professor. I have already called Marianne, asking for advice. What should I wear? What should I say? What should I do if he invites me to go home with him? *Do not* sleep with him, she has warned me. Especially not on a first date.

"Edith Eva Eger," my ex-husband pleads, "please, please let the kids spend the night with friends and agree to come to dinner with me."

"Whatever it is, we can discuss it on the phone, or when you drop the kids off."

"No," he says. "No. This is not a conversation for the phone or the front door."

I assume it has to do with the children, and I agree to meet him at our favorite prime rib restaurant, our old date spot.

"I'm picking you up," he says.

He arrives exactly on time, dressed for a date in a dark suit and silk tie. He leans in to kiss my cheek and I don't want to move away, I want to stay near his cologne, his cleanly shaved chin.

In the restaurant, at our old table, he takes my hands. "Is it possible," he asks, "that we have more to build together?"

His question sends my mind spinning, as though we are already on the dance floor. Try again? Reunite? "What about *her*?" I ask.

"She's a lovely person. She's fun. She's a very good companion."

"So?"

"Let me finish." Tears begin to well in his eyes and fall down his face. "She's not the mother of my children. She didn't spring me out of jail in Prešov. She's never heard of the Tatra Mountains. She can't pronounce chicken paprikash, much less make it for dinner. Edie, she isn't the woman I love. She isn't you."

The compliments feel good, the embrace of our shared past, but what strikes me most deeply is Béla's readiness for risk. This has always been true of him, as far as I can tell. He chose to fight Nazis in the forest. He risked death by disease and bullets to stop what was unconscionable. I was conscripted into risk. Béla chose risk knowingly, and he chooses it again at this table, allowing himself to be vulnerable to the possibility of my rejecting him. I have become so used to measuring all the ways he falls short that I have stopped counting who he is, what he offers. *I have to leave this marriage or I'm going to die,* I had thought. And perhaps the months and years I've spent apart from him have helped me come of age, have helped me discover that there is no we until there is an I. Now that I have faced myself a little more fully, I can see that the emptiness I felt in our marriage wasn't a sign of something wrong in our relationship, it was the void I carry with me, even now, the void that no man or achievement will ever fill. Nothing will ever make up for the loss of my parents and childhood. And no one else is responsible for my freedom. I am.

In 1971, two years after our divorce, when I am forty-four years old, Béla kneels and presents me with an engagement ring. We have a Jewish ceremony instead of the city hall union we decided on more than twenty years before. Our friends Gloria and John Lavis are our witnesses. "This is your *real* wedding," the rabbi says. He means because it is a Jewish wedding this time, but I think he also means that this time we are really choosing each other, we aren't in flight, we aren't running away. We buy a new house in Coronado Heights, decorate it in bright colors, red, orange, put in solar panels and a swimming pool. For our honeymoon we travel to Switzerland, to the Alps, and stay at a hotel with hot springs. The air is cold. The water is warm. I sit in Béla's lap. Jagged mountains stretch out against the sky, colors shifting over them as over water. Our love feels as stable as the mountain range, as enveloping and fluid as a sea, adapting, shifting to fill the shape we give it. It isn't that the substance of our marriage has changed. We have.

CHAPTER 15

What Life Expected

*I*t did not really matter what we expected from life, but rather what life *expected from us*, Viktor Frankl writes in *Man's Search for Meaning*. In 1972, a year after Béla and I remarried, I was named Teacher of the Year in El Paso, and while I was honored by the award and felt privileged to serve my students, I couldn't let go of the conviction that I still hadn't discovered what life expected from me. "You've won top recognition at the beginning of your career, not the end," the principal of my school said. "We'll expect to see great things from you. What's next?"

It was the same question I was still asking myself. I had begun working with my Jungian therapist again, and despite his admonition that degrees don't replace inner work, inner growth, I had been toying with the idea of graduate school. I wanted to understand why people choose to do one thing and not another, how we meet everyday challenges and survive devastating experiences, how we live with our past and our mistakes, how people heal. What if my mother had had someone to talk to? Could she have had a happier marriage with my father, or chosen a different life? And what about my students—or my own son— the ones who said *can't* instead of *can*. How could I help people to transcend self-limiting beliefs, to become who they were meant to be in the world? I told my principal I was considering getting my doctorate in psychology. But I couldn't speak my dream without a caveat. "I don't know," I said, "by the time I finish school I'll be fifty." He smiled at me. "You're going to be fifty anyhow," he said.

In the next six years, I discovered that my principal and my Jungian therapist were both right. There was no reason to limit myself, to let my age restrict my choices. I listened to what my life was asking of me, and in 1974 I earned an MA in educational psychology from the University of Texas–El Paso, and in 1978 a PhD in clinical psychology from Saybrook University.

My academic journey introduced me to the work of Martin Seligman and Albert Ellis, and brought me inspiring teachers and mentors in Carl Rogers and Richard Farson, all of whom helped me to understand parts of myself and my own experience. Martin Seligman, who later founded a new branch of our field called Positive Psychology, did some research in the late 1960s that answered a question that had nagged at me since liberation day at Gunskirchen in May 1945: Why did so many inmates wander out of the gates of the camp only to return to the muddy, festering barracks? Frankl had noted the same phenomenon at Auschwitz. Psychologically, what was at work to make a liberated prisoner reject freedom?

Seligman's experiments—which were done with dogs and unfortunately preceded current protections against cruelty to animals—taught him about the concept he called "learned helplessness." When dogs who were given painful shocks were able to stop the shocks by pressing a lever, they learned quickly to stop the pain. And they were able, in subsequent experiments, to figure out how to escape painful shocks administered in a kennel cage by leaping over a small barrier. Dogs who hadn't been given a means to stop the pain, however, had learned the lesson that they were helpless against it. When they were put in a kennel cage and administered shocks, they ignored the route to escape and just lay down in the kennel and whimpered. From this Seligman concluded that when we feel we have no control over our circumstances, when we believe that nothing we do can alleviate our suffering or improve our lives, we stop taking action on our own behalf because we believe there is no point. This is what happened at the camps, when former inmates left through the gates only to return to prison, to sit vacantly, unsure what to do with their freedom now that it had finally come.

Suffering is inevitable and universal. But how we respond to suffering differs. In my studies, I gravitated toward psychologists whose work revealed our power to effect change in ourselves. Albert Ellis, who founded Rational Emotive Behavior Therapy, a precursor to cognitive behavior therapy, taught me the extent to which we teach ourselves negative feelings about ourselves—and the negative and self-defeating behaviors that follow from these feelings. He showed that underlying our least effective and most harmful behaviors is a philosophical or ideological core that is irrational but is so central to our views of our self and the world that often we aren't aware that it is only a belief, nor are we aware of how persistently we repeat this belief to ourselves in our daily lives. The belief determines our feelings (sadness, anger, anxiety, etc.), and our feelings in turn influence our behavior (acting out, shutting down, self-medicating to ease the discomfort). To change our behavior, Ellis taught, we must change our feelings, and to change our feelings, we change our thoughts.

I watched Ellis conduct a therapy session onstage one day, working with a confident and articulate young woman who was frustrated by her dating experiences. She felt she wasn't able to attract the kind of men she wanted to have a long-term relationship with, and she was seeking advice on how to meet and connect with eligible men. She said that she tended to feel shy and tense when she met a man she thought might be a good fit, and that she behaved in a guarded and defensive manner that masked her true self and her true interest in getting to know him. In just a few minutes, Dr. Ellis guided her to the core belief underlying her dating encounters—the irrational belief that, without realizing it, she kept repeating to herself, over and over, until she became convinced of its truth: *I'm never going to be happy.* After a lousy date she wasn't only telling herself, *Oops, I did it again, I was stiff and uninviting,* she was also reverting to her core belief that she could never achieve happiness so there was no point trying. It was the fear produced by this core belief that made her so reluctant to risk showing her genuine self, which in turn made it more likely that her self-defeating belief might come true.

It was profound to see her self-image shift visibly right there on the stage. She seemed to slip out of the negative belief like she was shrugging off an old bathrobe. Suddenly her eyes were brighter, she sat taller, her chest and shoulders were more open and expansive, as if she were creating a greater surface area for happiness to land. Dr. Ellis cautioned her that she was unlikely to have an amazing date right out of the gate. He also said that accepting the discomfort of disappointing dates was part of the work of ridding herself of the negative belief.

The truth is, we will have unpleasant experiences in our lives, we will make mistakes, we won't always get what we want. This is part of being human. The problem—and the foundation of our persistent suffering—is the belief that discomfort, mistakes, disappointment signal something about our worth. The belief that the unpleasant things in our lives are all we deserve. Although my way of building rapport is different from Dr. Ellis's, his skill at guiding patients to reframe and reform their damaging thoughts has influenced my practice profoundly.

Carl Rogers, one of my most influential mentors, was a master of helping patients to fully accept themselves. Rogers theorized that when our need to self-actualize comes into conflict with our need for positive regard, or vice versa, we might choose to repress or hide or neglect our genuine personalities and desires. When we come to believe that there is no way to be loved *and* to be genuine, we are at risk of denying our true nature.

Self-acceptance was the hardest part of healing for me, something I still struggle with. Perfectionism emerged in my childhood as a behavior to satisfy my need for approval, and it became an even more embedded coping mechanism for dealing with my survivor's guilt. Perfectionism is the belief that something is broken—you. So you dress up your brokenness with degrees, achievements, accolades, pieces of paper, none of which can fix what you think you are fixing. In trying to combat my low self-esteem, I was actually reinforcing my sense of unworthiness. In learning to offer my patients total love and acceptance, I fortunately learned the importance of offering the same to myself.

Rogers was brilliant at being able to validate patients' feelings, to help them reframe their self-concept without denying their truth. He offered unconditional positive regard, and in the safety of that total acceptance, his patients were able to shed their masks and inhibitions and inhabit their own lives more authentically. From Dr. Rogers I learned two of my most important phrases in any therapeutic encounter: *I hear you say . . .* and *Tell me more.* I also learned how to read my patients' body language and how to use my own body to communicate my unconditional love and acceptance. I don't cross my arms or my legs—I open myself. I make eye contact, I lean forward, I create a bridge between myself and my patients, so that they know I am with them 100 percent. I mirror my patients' states (if they want to sit quietly, I sit quietly too; if they wait to rage and scream, I scream with them; I adapt my language to my patients' language) as a sign of total acceptance. And I model a way of being (breathing, opening, moving, listening) that can promote growth and healing.

Studying Seligman and Ellis, and working with Rogers, among others, helped me to become a good listener and synthesizer, and helped me to derive my eclectic and intuitive insight- and cognitive-oriented therapeutic approach. If I had to name my therapy I'd probably call it Choice Therapy, as freedom is about CHOICE—about choosing compassion, humor, optimism, intuition, curiosity, and self-expression. And to be free is to live in the present. If we are stuck in the past, saying, "If only I had gone there instead of here . . ." or "If *only* I had married someone else . . . ," we are living in a prison of our own making. Likewise if we spend our time in the future, saying, "I won't be happy until I graduate . . ." or "I won't be happy *until*

I find the right person." The *only* place where we can exercise our freedom of choice is in the present.

These are the tools my patients use to liberate themselves from role expectations, to be kind and loving parents to themselves, to stop passing on imprisoning beliefs and behaviors, to discover that love comes out as the answer in the end. I guide patients to understand both what *causes* and what *maintains* their self-defeating behaviors. The self-defeating behaviors first emerged as useful behaviors, things they did to satisfy a need, usually a need for one of the As: approval, affection, attention. Once patients can see why they developed a certain behavior (belittling others, attaching oneself to angry people, eating too little, eating too much, etc.), they can take responsibility for whether or not they maintain the behavior. They can choose what to give up (the need for approval, the need to go shopping, the need to be perfect, etc.)—because even freedom doesn't come for free! And they can learn to take better care of themselves and to discover self-acceptance: *Only I can do what I can do the way I can do it.*

For me, learning that *only I can do what I can do the way I can do it* meant overthrowing the compulsive achiever in me, who was always chasing more and more pieces of paper in the hopes of affirming my worth. And it meant learning to reframe my trauma, to see in my painful past evidence of my strength and gifts and opportunities for growth, rather than confirmation of my weakness or damage.

In 1975, I traveled to Israel to conduct interviews with Holocaust survivors for my dissertation. (Béla accompanied me; I thought that his facility with languages, including Yiddish, which he had picked up from his El Paso clients, would make him an invaluable translator.) I wanted to explore my professor Richard Farson's calamity theory of growth, which says: *Very often it is the crisis situation . . . that actually improves us as human beings. Paradoxically, while these incidents can sometimes ruin people, they are usually growth experiences. As a result of such calamities the person often makes a major reassessment of his life situation and changes it in ways that reflect a deeper understanding of his own capabilities, values, and goals.* I planned to interview my fellow concentration camp survivors to discover how a person survives and even thrives in the wake of trauma. How do people create lives of joy, purpose, and passion, no matter what wounds they have suffered, no matter what sorrows they have experienced? And in what ways does the trauma itself give people an opportunity for positive growth and change? I wasn't yet doing what my friend Arpad had advised me to do—grapple deeply with my own past—but I was getting one step closer in interviewing people with whom I shared a traumatic past, laying a foundation for my own healing to come.

How did the experience of calamitous events contribute to my subjects' everyday functioning? I met survivors who had gone back to school, who had opened businesses (as Béla and I had planned to do), who had built tremendous close friendships, who faced daily life with a sense of discovery. Israel wasn't an easy place for survivors; it's not easy to live amid prejudice and not become an aggressor yourself. I met people who faced the political and cultural conflicts with courage and peacefulness, who took turns standing guard at a school all night so bombs wouldn't greet their children in the morning. I admired them for whatever it was that allowed them not to give up or give in, I admired their strength for living through another war and for not allowing horrific experiences in the past to destroy what came after. Having endured imprisonment, dehumanization, torture, starvation, and devastating loss did not dictate the kind of life that was possible for them.

Of course, not everyone I interviewed was thriving. I saw a lot of silent parents, a lot of children who didn't know how to feel about their parents' silence and numbness, who blamed themselves. And I met a lot of survivors who remained in the past. "Never, ever will I forgive," many told me. To them forgiveness meant forgetting or condoning. Many of the people I interviewed harbored revenge fantasies. I had never fantasized about revenge, but especially during those first challenging years in Baltimore, I had fantasized about confronting my oppressors—I wanted to find Mengele in Paraguay, where he had fled to escape prosecution under the Nuremberg Trials. I imagined posing as an American journalist to gain entry to his house. Then I would reveal my identity. "I'm the girl who danced for you," I would say. "You murdered my parents. You murdered so many children's parents. How could you be so cruel? You were a medical doctor. You took the Hippocratic Oath to do no harm. You're a cold-blooded killer. Do you have no conscience?" I would rage and rage at his withered, retreating body, I would make him face his shame. It's important to assign blame to the perpetrators. Nothing is gained if we close our eyes to wrong, if we give someone a pass, if we dismiss accountability. But as my fellow survivors taught me, you can live to avenge the past, or you can live to enrich the present. You can live in the prison of the past, or you can let the past be the springboard that helps you reach the life you want now.

All of the survivors I met had one thing in common with me and with one another: We had no control over the most consuming facts of our lives, but we had the power to determine how we experienced life after trauma. Survivors could continue to be victims long after the oppression had ended, or they could learn to thrive. In my dissertation research, I discovered and articulated my personal conviction and my clinical touchstone: We can choose to be our own jailors, or we can choose to be free.

Before we leave Israel, Béla and I visit Bandi and Marta Vadasz, the friends Béla had left waiting at the train station in Vienna. They live in Ramat Gan, near Tel Aviv. It is a poignant encounter, a meeting with our unlived life, the life we almost had. Bandi is still very political, still a Zionist, eager to discuss the anticipated peaceful agreement between Israel and Egypt over Israel's occupation of the Sinai Peninsula. He can recite with precision details of Arab bombings in Jerusalem and Tel Aviv. He and Béla keep us at the table long after we've finished eating, enthusiastically debating Israel's military strategy. The men talk about war. Marta turns to me, she takes my hand. Her face is plumper than it was in her youth, her red hair duller now, going gray.

"Editke, the years have been kinder to you," she says with a sigh.

"It's my mother's good genes," I say. And then the selection line flashes through my mind, the smoothness of my mother's face. This moment is a ghost that trails me through the years.

Marta must notice that my mind has traveled someplace else, that a darkness holds me. "I'm sorry," she says. "I didn't mean to say you've had it easy."

"You gave me a compliment," I reassure her. "You're how I have always remembered you. So kind." When her baby was born dead, she didn't let my healthy baby sour our friendship, she was never jealous or bitter. I took Marianne with me every afternoon to visit her, every afternoon of her year of mourning.

She seems to read my mind. "You know," she says, "nothing in my life was harder than losing my baby after the war. That grief was so terrible." She pauses. We sit together in silence, in our shared and separate pain. "I don't think I ever thanked you," she finally says. "When we buried my child, you told me two things that I've never forgotten. You said, 'Life will be good again.' And you said, 'If you can survive this, you can survive anything.' I've said those phrases to myself over and over." She reaches into her purse for photographs of her children, two daughters born in Israel in the early 1950s. "I was too afraid to try again right away. But life has a way of working out, I guess. I grieved and grieved. And then I took all the love I had for my baby, and I decided I wasn't going to plant that love in my loss. I was going to plant it in my marriage, and then in the children who lived."

I hold her fingers in my hand. I hold the beautiful image of the seed. The seed of my life and love has been forced into difficult soil, but it has taken root and grown. I look at Béla across the table, I think of our children, of the news Marianne has recently told me, that she and her husband, Rob, are going to try to start a family. The next generation. This is where my love for my parents will live.

"Next year in El Paso," we promise as we part.

At home, I wrote my dissertation and completed my final clinical internship at the William Beaumont Army Medical Center at Fort Bliss, Texas. I had been fortunate to secure both master's- and doctoral-level internships at William Beaumont. It was a competitive and desirable placement, a prestigious post, where the best of the best speakers and teachers cycled through. I didn't realize that the true benefit of the position would be that it would require me to look more deeply within.

One day I arrive at work and slip on my white coat and my name tag, DR. EGER, DEPARTMENT OF PSYCHIATRY. During my time at William Beaumont, I have developed a reputation as a person willing to go above and beyond the technical requirements of my position—to stay up all night on suicide watch, to take the most discouraging cases, the ones that others have given up on.

Today I have been assigned two new patients, both Vietnam veterans, both paraplegics. They have the same diagnosis (lower T-injury of the spinal cord), the same prognosis (compromised fertility and sexual function, unlikely to walk again, good control of hands and trunk). On my way to see them, I am unaware that one of them will have a life-changing effect on me. I meet Tom first. He is lying on his bed, curled up in a fetal position, cursing God and country. He seems imprisoned—by his injured body, by his misery, by his rage.

When I go to the other vet's room, I find Chuck out of bed and sitting in his wheelchair. "It's interesting," he says. "I've been given a second chance in life. Isn't it amazing?" He is brimming over with a sense of discovery and possibility. "I sit in this wheelchair, and I go out on the lawn, out on the grounds, and the flowers are much closer. I can see my children's eyes."

The way I tell this story now, when I'm talking to my current patients, or addressing an audience from the stage, is that every person is part Tom and part Chuck. We are overwhelmed by loss and think we will never recover a sense of self and purpose, that we will never mend. But despite—and, really, because of—the struggles and the tragedies in our lives, each of us has the capacity to gain the perspective that transforms us from victim to thriver. We can choose to take responsibility for our hardships and our healing. We can choose to be free. What I still have trouble admitting, however, is that when I first met Tom, his rage thrilled me.

"Fuck America!" Tom screams as I enter his room that day. "Fuck God!" I think to myself: He is letting all that anger out. And witnessing his fury calls out the huge rage in me, the need to express it, release it. *Fuck Hitler! Fuck Mengele!* It would be such a relief. But I am the doctor here. I have to assume a role, present myself as in control and having solutions, even though inside I want to punch a wall, kick down a door, scream and cry and fall apart on the floor. I look at my badge, *Dr. Eger, Department of Psychiatry*, and for a moment it seems to read, *Dr. Eger, Impostor.* Who is the real me? Do I know who I am? I'm so scared of the feeling, of the mask falling apart, of seeing how broken I am, of all the rage that pushes at me: *Why me? How could this happen?* My life has been changed irrevocably, and I'm furious.

It was thrilling to watch Tom because he was so overt about expressing what I'd been hiding. I'd been too afraid of others' disapproval or anger, afraid of anger itself as a destructive force. I hadn't let myself feel the feelings, afraid that if I started to let them out, I might never stop, I'd become a monster. In a way, Tom was freer than I was, because he was giving himself permission to feel the rage, to say the words, the ones that I could barely allow myself to think, much less speak. I wanted to get down on the floor and rage with him.

In therapy I timidly say I want to try it, I want to express that rage, but with a professional there to help pull me out if I get stuck in it. I get on the floor. I try to yell, but I can't, I'm too scared, I curl into a smaller and smaller ball. I need to feel a limit around me, a boundary, I need to feel something to push against. I tell my therapist to sit on me. He is heavy, his weight almost suffocates me. I think I'm going to pass out. I am about to tap the floor, to beg him to let me up, to give up this silly experiment. But then a scream comes out of me, so long and full and anguished that it frightens me, what awful wounded thing would make a noise like that? But I can't stop making the sound. It feels good. More than thirty years of silenced ghosts come roaring out of me now, the full-throated outpouring of my sorrow. It feels good. I scream, I scream, I push against the weight bearing down on me. My therapist doesn't make it easy, and the effort makes me cry and sweat.

What happens? What happens when the long-denied part of me is let out?

Nothing happens.

I feel the force of the rage, and it doesn't kill me after all.

I'm okay. I'm okay. I'm alive.

It still isn't easy for me to talk about the past. It is deeply painful to confront the fear and the loss all over again each time I remember or recount it. But from this moment on, I understood that feelings, no matter how powerful, aren't fatal. And they are temporary. Suppressing the feelings only makes it harder to let them go. Expression is the opposite of depression.

In 1978, my son, John, graduated from the University of Texas, one of the top ten students, and I earned my PhD in clinical psychology. It was a triumphant year for our family. I decided to pursue my licensure in California because it was the toughest state (there I was, putting on the red shoes again!), and beyond the ego needs of proving my worth (as though a piece of paper could accomplish that), California licensure had the practical advantage of allowing me to practice anywhere in the country. I remembered Béla's struggle to earn his CPA license, and I girded myself for a difficult journey.

I needed three thousand clinical hours to sit for the exam, but I doubled the requirement. I didn't even sign up to take the exam until I had six thousand hours—almost all at William Beaumont, where I had developed such a good reputation that I was asked to conduct sessions behind one-way glass, so that my fellow clinicians could observe my way of building rapport, establishing trust, and guiding patients toward new choices. Then it was time to face the written test. I was terrible at multiple-choice tests—I had to study for months even to pass the driving test. Somehow, through gritty persistence or sheer luck, I passed the written exam. But not on my first try.

Finally, I sat for the oral exam, which I thought would be the easiest part of the process. Two men conducted the interview, one who wore blue jeans and had long hair pulled back in a ponytail, and another who wore a suit and had a crew cut. They grilled me for hours. The man with long hair spoke sharply, tersely, asking me all the questions about statistics, ethics, and legal matters. The man with the crew cut asked all the philosophical questions, the ones that got my mind working more creatively, my heart more engaged. Overall, though, it was an unpleasant experience. I felt stiff and numb and vulnerable. The examiners didn't make it easy—their expressionless faces, cold voices, and emotional distance were alienating. It was hard to put my energy into the next question when each previous one left me churning with self-criticism, with the desire to go back and revise what I had said, to say something, anything, that would elicit a nod of recognition or encouragement. When the exam finally ended, I felt dazed, my hands shook, I was both starving and nauseated, my head hurt. I was sure I had blown it.

Just as I reached the front door, I heard footsteps behind me, someone running to catch up. Had I left my purse behind in my disorientation? Were they telling me already that I had failed? "Dr. Eger," the man with the crew cut called. I braced myself, as though awaiting a punishment. He reached me, paused to catch his breath. My jaw and shoulders clenched. At last the man extended his hand. "Dr. Eger, it was an honor. You have a wealth of knowledge. Your future patients are very lucky indeed."

When I got back to my hotel, I jumped on the bed like a little girl.

CHAPTER 16

The Choice

My joyous optimism, my sense of professional accomplishment, my feeling that I was reaching a full embodiment and expression of myself all withered when I established my private practice and met my first patient. I visited him in the hospital where he had been living for a month, awaiting diagnosis and undergoing treatment for what turned out to be stomach cancer. He was terrified. He felt betrayed by his body, threatened by his mortality, overwhelmed by the uncertainty and loneliness of illness. And I couldn't reach him where he was. All of my skill in establishing a climate of warmth and trust, in building a bridge between me and my patient, had disappeared. I felt like a child dressed up in a doctor's white coat. A fake. My expectations of myself were so high, my fear of failure so toppling, that I couldn't see past my own self-absorption to reach the man who was asking for my help and my love. "Will I ever be healthy again?" he asked, and my mind flipped like a Rolodex, spinning through theories and techniques, my eyes pointed at the wall, trying to mask how nervous and scared I was. I was of no help to him. He didn't invite me back. I realized, as I had when I met Tom, the paraplegic veteran, that my professional success had to come from a deeper place within me—not from the little girl trying to please others and win approval but from my whole and authentic self, the one who was vulnerable and curious, who was accepting of herself and ready to grow.

In other words, I began to formulate a new relationship with my own trauma. It wasn't something to silence, suppress, avoid, negate. It was a well I could draw on, a deep source of understanding and intuition about my patients, their pain, and the path to healing. My first years of private practice helped me to reframe my wound as something necessary and useful, and to shape and develop my most enduring therapeutic principles. Often the patients I worked with mirrored my own discoveries about the journey to freedom. Equally often they taught me that my search for freedom wasn't complete—and they pointed me in the direction of further healing.

Although Emma was the identified patient, I met her parents first. They had never spoken to anyone, least of all a stranger, about the secret in their family: Emma, their oldest child, was starving herself to death. They were private, reserved people, a conservative German American family, their faces creased with worry, eyes filled with fear.

"We're looking for practical solutions," Emma's father told me that first visit. "We have to get her to start eating again."

"We heard that you're a survivor," Emma's mother added. "We thought Emma could learn something from you, that you might inspire her."

It was heartbreaking to see their panic for Emma's life, to see their shock. Nothing in life had prepared them for a child with an eating disorder; they had never considered that something like this could happen to their daughter and their family, and none of their existing parenting tools was having a positive effect on Emma's health. I wanted to reassure them. I wanted to ease their distress. But I also wanted them to begin to see a truth that might be even more painful for them to acknowledge than Emma's illness—that they had a part in it. When a child is grappling with anorexia, the identified patient is the child, but the real patient is the family.

They wanted to tell me every detail of Emma's behaviors that concerned them: the food she refused to eat, the food she pretended to eat, the food they would find tucked inside napkins after family meals, the food they discovered stuffed into her dresser drawers, the ways she pulled away from them and retreated behind closed doors, the terrifying changes in her body. But I asked them instead to talk about themselves, which they did with obvious discomfort.

Emma's father was short and compact—he was a soccer player, I learned. He looked a little like Hitler, I realized with unease—he had a thin mustache and dark, pressed hair, and a way of barking when he talked, as though behind every communication was the insistence on not being ignored. Later I would have individual sessions with each of Emma's parents, and I would ask her father how he had decided on his career as a police officer. He told me that as a boy he had walked with a limp, and his father had called him Shrimpy-Limpy. He chose to be a police officer because it required risk taking and physical strength; he wanted to prove to his father that he wasn't a shrimp or a cripple. When you have something to prove, you aren't free. Even though I didn't yet know anything about his childhood during our first visit, I could tell that Emma's father was living in a prison of his own making—he was living within a limited image of who he should be. He behaved more like a drill sergeant than a supportive husband or concerned father. He didn't ask questions; he ran an interrogation. He didn't acknowledge his fears or vulnerabilities; he asserted his ego.

His wife, who wore a tailored cotton dress with buttons down the front and a thin belt, a look that was both timeless and no-nonsense, seemed hyperattuned to his tone and speech. He talked for a few minutes about his frustrations at work when he was skipped over for a promotion, and I could see her searching for a careful balance point between affirming his indignation and stoking his anger. She had clearly learned that her husband needed to be right, that he couldn't handle being confronted or contradicted. In our private session, I would be impressed by her resourcefulness—she mowed the lawn and did many of their home repairs, she made her own clothes—and the seeming contradiction between her skills and the power she gave over to her husband, the price she paid to keep the peace. Her habit of avoiding conflict with her husband at all costs was as damaging to her daughter's health and their family dynamic as were his domineering behaviors. They were partners in making control—not empathic connection, not unconditional love—the language of the family.

"This is a waste of time," Emma's father finally said during our first visit, after answering my questions about his job, their family routines, how they celebrated holidays. "Just tell us what to do."

"Yes, just tell us how we can get Emma to come to the table at mealtime," her mother begged. "Tell us how we can make her eat."

"I can see how worried you are about Emma. I can see how desperate you are for answers and fixes. And I can tell you that if you want Emma to get well, your first job is to understand that with anorexia, the issue isn't only what Emma eats; it's also about what's eating her." I couldn't just fix her and send her back, her healthy self, I told them. I invited them to help me, to be my cotherapists, to observe their daughter, but not with the agenda of making her do or be anything different, just paying attention to her emotional states and behaviors. Together we could build a clearer picture of her emotional landscape and get more familiar with the psychological aspects of the disease. By enlisting their help and cooperation, I hoped to lead them toward an understanding of their part in her illness. I was nudging them toward taking responsibility for the way they contributed to what was eating Emma.

The following week, I met Emma for the first time. She was fourteen years old. It was like meeting my own ghost. She looked like I had at Auschwitz—skeletal, pale. She was wasting away. Her long, stringy blond hair made her face look even thinner. She stood in the doorway of my office, her too-long sleeves pulled all the way down over her hands. She looked like a person with a secret.

With any new patient, it's important to be sensitive to his or her psychological boundaries from the very first moments of our initial encounter. I must intuit immediately if this is a person who wants me to take her hand or keep my physical distance, if this is a person who needs me to give him an order or a gentle suggestion. For a patient with anorexia—a disease that is all about control, about relentless rules for what and when you eat or don't eat, for what you reveal or conceal—these first moments are critical. For one thing, anorexia has an inescapable physiological dimension. Because of the lack of nutrients entering the body, and because the bulk of the few calories consumed go to autonomic functions (breathing, elimination), the brain is deprived of blood flow, and this leads to distorted thinking and, in severe cases, paranoia. As a psychologist beginning a therapeutic relationship with a person with anorexia, I have to remember that I'm communicating with a person who likely has distorted cognitive functioning. It's easy for a habitual gesture—putting a hand on someone's shoulder as I guide her to a comfortable chair, for example—to be misinterpreted as threatening or invasive. As I greeted Emma for the first time, I tried to simultaneously warm and neutralize my body language. Because someone with anorexia is an expert at control, it's important to disarm her need for control by offering freedom. At the same time, it's vital to create a structured environment where there is safety in clear rules and rituals.

Having met her parents, I knew that the home language was full of criticisms and blame, so I began our session with a compliment. "Thank you for coming," I said. "I'm so happy to finally meet you. And thank you for being right on time."

When she had chosen a seat on the couch, I told her that anything she told me was confidential—unless her life was in danger. And then I made a soft, open-ended invitation. "You know, your parents are so worried about you. I'm interested to know the real story. Is there anything you'd like to tell me?"

Emma didn't respond. She stared at the carpet, tugging her sleeves even farther over her hands.

"It's okay to be silent," I said.

More silence stretched between us. I waited. I waited some more. "You know," I said after a while, "it's fine for you to take as long as you need. I have a little paperwork I need to do. I'm going to go work in the other room. When you're ready, let me know."

She eyed me suspiciously. In a home with punitive discipline, children grow accustomed to hearing threats, and these threats can escalate quickly or, at the other extreme, prove empty. Although I was speaking kindly, she was looking to see if my words and tone were going to escalate into an angry criticism or admonition, or if I wasn't really going to leave the room, if I was just a pushover.

I think she was surprised when I simply stood up, crossed the room, and opened the door. Only then, my hand on the doorknob, did she speak.

"I'm ready," she said.

"Thank you," I said, returning to my chair. "I'm happy to hear that. We have forty minutes left. Let's use them well. Is it okay if I ask you a couple questions?"

She shrugged.

"Tell me about a typical day. What time do you wake up?"

She rolled her eyes, but she answered my question. I continued in this vein. Did she have a clock radio, or an alarm clock, or did her mother or father come to wake her up? Did she like to lie in bed for a while under the covers, or did she jump right out of bed? I asked her mundane questions, getting a sense of her daily life—but none of my questions had anything to do with food. It is so hard for someone with anorexia to see anything in life outside of food. I already knew from her parents that her focus on food was controlling her family, that all of their attention was consumed by her illness. I had a feeling she expected me, too, to be interested only in her illness. With my questions I was trying to shift her attention to other parts of her life, and to dismantle or at least soften her defensive structures.

When I had worked through a day in her life, I asked her a question that she didn't know how to answer. "What do you like to do?" I asked.

"I don't know," she said.

"What are your hobbies? What do you like to do in your free time?"

"I don't know."

I walked over to the whiteboard that I keep in my office. I wrote, *I don't know.* As I asked her more questions about her interests, her passions, her desires, I put a check mark for every time she said, "I don't know."

"What are your dreams for your life?"

"I don't know."

"If you don't know, then guess."

"I don't know. I'll think about it."

"A lot of girls your age write poems. Do you write poems?"

Emma shrugged. "Sometimes."

"Where would you like to be in five years? What kind of a life and career appeal to you?"

"I don't know."

"I'm noticing that you say these words a lot: *I don't know.* But when the only thing you can think is *I don't know*, that saddens me. It means you're not aware of your options. And without options or choices, you aren't really living. Can you do something for me? Can you take this pen and draw me a picture?"

"I guess." She walked to the board and pushed her thin hand out from her sleeve to take the pen.

"Draw me a picture of yourself, right now. How do you see yourself?"

She uncapped the pen and drew quickly, her lips pursed. She turned so I could see her drawing: a short, fat girl with a void, blank face. It was a devastating contrast—skeletal Emma beside a blank, fat cartoon.

"Can you remember a time when you felt different? When you felt happy and pretty and fun loving?"

She thought and thought. But she didn't say, "I don't know." Finally she nodded her head. "When I was five."

"Could you draw me a picture of that happy girl?"

When she stepped away from the board, I saw a picture of a dancing, twirling girl in a tutu. I felt my throat catch, a spasm of recognition.

"Did you take ballet?"

"Yes."

"I'd love to hear more about that. How did you feel when you were dancing?"

She closed her eyes. I saw her heels pull together in first position. It was an unconscious motion, her body remembering.

"What are you feeling right now as you remember? Can you give that feeling a word?"

She nodded, her eyes still closed. "Free."

"Would you like to feel that way again? Free? Full of life?"

She nodded. She put the pen on the tray and tugged her sleeves down over her hands again.

"And how does starving yourself get you closer to this goal of freedom?" I said it as warmly, as kindly as I could. It wasn't a recrimination. It was an effort to bring her into an unflinching awareness of her self-sabotage and of how far she had taken it. And it was an effort to help her answer the most important questions at the outset of any journey toward freedom: *What am I doing now? Is it working? Is it bringing me closer to my goals, or farther away?* Emma didn't answer my question in words. But in her teary silence I could sense her recognizing that she needed and wanted to change.

When I met with Emma and her parents all together for the first time, I greeted them with enthusiasm. "I have very good news!" I said. I shared with them my hope, my confidence in their ability to work as a team. And I made my own participation in the teamwork conditional upon their agreeing that Emma would also be in the care of the medical staff at an eating disorder clinic, because anorexia is a serious, potentially fatal condition. If Emma ever got below a certain weight, which would be determined in consultation with the staff at the clinic, she would have to be hospitalized. "I can't risk you losing your life over something that can be prevented," I told Emma.

A month or two after I started working with Emma, her parents invited me to their home for a family meal. I met all of Emma's siblings. I noticed that Emma's mother introduced each of her children with qualifiers: this is Gretchen, the shy one, and Peter, the funny one, and Derek, the responsible one. (Emma had already been introduced to me: the sick one.) You give children a name, and they play the game. This is why I find it useful to ask my patients, "What was your ticket of admission in your family?" (In my childhood, Klara was the prodigy, Magda was the rebel, and I was the confidante. I was most valuable to my parents when I was a listener, a container for their feelings, when I was invisible.) Sure enough, at the table Gretchen was shy, Peter was funny, Derek was responsible.

I wanted to see what would happen if I broke the code, if I invited one of the children into a different role. "You know," I said to Gretchen, "you have such a beautiful profile."

Their mother kicked me under the table. "Don't say that," she admonished me under her breath. "She'll end up conceited."

After dinner, while Emma's mother cleaned up in the kitchen, Peter, who was still a toddler, was pulling on her skirt, asking for her attention. She kept putting him off, and his attempts to get her to stop what she was doing and pick him up became more and more frantic. Finally he toddled out of the kitchen and went straight for the coffee table, where there were some porcelain knickknacks. His mom ran after him, swooped him up, spanked him, and said, "Didn't I tell you not to touch those?"

The spare-the-rod-spoil-the-child approach to discipline had created a climate in which the children seemed to get only negative attention (bad attention, after all, is better than no attention). The strict environment, the black-and-white nature of the rules and roles imposed on the children, the palpable tension between the parents—all made for an emotional famine in the home.

I also witnessed the highly inappropriate attention that Emma's father paid her. "Hey there, Hottie," he said to her when she joined us in the living room after dinner. I saw her shrink into the couch, trying to cover herself. Control, punitive discipline, emotional incest—no wonder Emma was dying in the midst of plenty.

Like all families, Emma and her family needed rules, but very different ones from those they were operating under. So I helped Emma and her parents to make a family constitution that they would help one another to enforce, a list of family rules that would improve the climate in their home. First, they talked about the behaviors that weren't working. Emma told her parents how much hearing them yell and blame frightened her, and how resentful she felt when they changed the rules or expectations at the last minute—what time she had to be home, what chores she had to finish before she could watch TV. Her father talked about how isolated he felt in the family—he felt like the only one disciplining the kids. Interestingly, Emma's mother said something similar, that she felt like she was parenting all alone. From the list of hurtful habits and behaviors—the things they wanted to stop doing—we built a short list of things they agreed to start doing:

1. Instead of blaming others, take responsibility for your own actions and speech. Before you say or do something, ask, *Is it kind? Is it important? Does it help?*
2. Use teamwork to reach common goals. If the house needs cleaning, each member of the family has an age-appropriate job. If the family is going out to a movie, choose together which movie to see, or take turns getting to choose. Think of the family as a car where all the wheels are integrated and work together to move

where it needs to go—no one wheel takes control, no
one wheel bears all the weight.

3. Be consistent. If curfew has already been established,
the rule can't change at the last minute.

In general, Emma's family's constitution was about giving up
the need to control someone else.

I treated Emma for two years. In that time she completed
the outpatient program at the eating disorder clinic. She stopped
playing soccer—something her father had forced her into when
she started middle school—and went back to ballet class (and
then on to more dance classes: belly dancing, salsa). The creative
expression, the pleasure she took in moving to the music and
rhythm, led to an enjoyment of her body, which gave her a
healthier self-image. Near the end of our time together, when
she was sixteen, she met a boy in school and fell in love, and
this relationship gave her another motivation to live and to be
healthy. By the time she stopped working with me, her body had
filled out and her hair was thick and shining. She had become the
present-day version of her picture of the twirling, dancing girl.

The summer after Emma's junior year of high school, her
family invited me to a barbeque at their house. They put out a
wonderful spread—ribs, beans, German potato salad, homemade
rolls. Emma stood with her boyfriend, filling a plate with food,
laughing, flirting. Her parents, siblings, and friends sprawled on
the lawn and in folding chairs, feasting. Food was no longer the
negative language of the family. Emma's parents, though they
hadn't completely transformed the tone of their parenting or
their marriage, had learned to give Emma what she had learned

to give herself—the space and trust to find her way toward the good in life. And without having to live consumed by their fear of what might happen to Emma, they had grown free to live their own lives. They had a weekly bridge night with a group of friends and had let go of much of the worry and anger and need to control that had poisoned their family life for so long.

I was relieved and moved to see Emma restored to Emma. And her journey also prompted me to reflect on me. Edie. Was I at one with my own inner dancing girl? Was I living with her curiosity and ecstasy? Around the same time that Emma left my practice, my first grandchild, Marianne's daughter, Lindsey, began a toddler ballet class. Marianne sent me a picture of Lindsey in a little pink tutu, her sweet chubby feet tucked into a pair of tiny pink slippers. I wept when I saw the picture. Joyful tears, yes. But there was also an ache in my chest that had more to do with loss. I could picture Lindsey's life spreading out from this moment—her performances and recitals (sure enough, she would continue to study ballet and perform in *The Nutcracker* every winter of her childhood and adolescence)—and the happiness I felt for her in anticipation of all she had to look forward to could not be uncoupled from the sorrow I felt at my own interrupted life. When we grieve, it's not just over what happened—we grieve for what didn't happen. I housed a year of horror within me. And I housed a vacant, empty place, the vast dark of the life that would never be. I held the trauma and the absence, I couldn't let go of either piece of my truth, nor could I hold either easily.

I found another mirror and teacher in Agnes, a woman I met at a spa in Utah where I was speaking to breast cancer survivors about the importance of self-care to promote healing. She was young, in her early forties, her black hair pulled back in a low bun. She had on a neutral-colored smock dress buttoned up to her neck. If she hadn't been the first in line for a private appointment in my hotel room after my talk, I might not have noticed her at all. She kept herself in the background. Even when she stood in front of me, her body was barely visible beneath her clothes.

"I'm sorry," she said, when I opened my door to invite her in. "I'm sure there are other people who deserve more of your time."

I showed her to the chair by the window and poured her a glass of water. She seemed embarrassed by my small caretaking gestures. She sat on the very edge of her chair and held the water glass stiffly in front of her, as though to take a sip would be an imposition on my hospitality. "I don't really need a whole hour. I just have a quick question."

"Yes, honey. Tell me how I can be useful."

She said she had been interested in something I'd said in my talk. I'd shared an old Hungarian saying I learned as a girl: *Don't inhale your anger to your chest.* I had given an example of the self-imprisoning beliefs and feelings I had held on to in my life: my anger and my belief that I had to earn others' approval, that nothing I did would be good enough to make me worthy of love. I'd invited the women in the audience to ask themselves, *What feeling or belief am I holding on to? Am I willing to let it go?* Agnes asked me now, "How do you know if there's something you're holding on to?"

"It's a beautiful question. When we're talking about freedom, there's no one-size-fits-all. Do you have a guess? Does your gut tell you that there's something inside that's trying to get your attention?"

"It's a dream." She said that ever since her cancer diagnosis a few years ago, and even now that her disease was in remission, she'd been having a recurring dream. In it she is preparing to perform surgery. She puts on blue scrubs and a face mask. She tucks her long hair inside a disposable cap. She stands at a sink, scrubbing and scrubbing her hands.

"Who's the patient?"

"I'm not sure. It's different people. Sometimes it's my son. Sometimes it's my husband or my daughter, or someone from the past."

"Why are you performing the surgery? What's the patient's diagnosis?"

"I don't know. I think it changes."

"How do you feel when you're performing the operation?"

"Like my hands are on fire."

"And how do you feel when you wake up? Do you feel energized, or tired?"

"It depends. Sometimes I want to go back to sleep so I can keep working, the surgery isn't finished yet. Sometimes I feel sad and tired, like it's a futile procedure."

"What do you think this dream is about?"

"I used to want to go to medical school. I thought about applying after college. But we had to pay for my husband's business degree, and then we had kids, and then the cancer. It was never the right time. That's why I wanted to talk to you. Do you think I'm having this dream because I should pursue medical school now, this late in my life? Or do you think I'm having this dream because it's time to finally put the fantasy of becoming a doctor to rest?"

"What appeals to you about medicine?"

She thought before she answered. "Helping people. But also finding out what's really going on. Finding out the truth. Finding what's under the surface and fixing the problem."

"There aren't absolutes in life—or in medicine. As you know, diseases can be difficult to treat. Pain, surgery, treatments, physical changes, mood swings. And there's no guarantee of recovery. What has helped you live with cancer? What truths or beliefs are you using to guide you through your illness?"

"Not to be a burden. I don't want my pain to hurt anyone else."

"How would you like to be remembered?"

Tears sprang into her light gray eyes. "As a good person."

"What does 'good' mean to you?"

"Giving. Generous. Kind. Selfless. Doing what's right."

"Does a 'good' person ever get to complain? Or be angry?"

"Those aren't my values."

She reminded me of myself, before the paraplegic veteran had brought me to an encounter with my own rage. "Anger isn't a value," I told Agnes. "It's a feeling. It doesn't mean you're bad. It just means you're alive."

She looked skeptical.

"I'd like you to try something. An exercise. You're going to turn yourself inside out. Whatever you usually hold in, you're going to get out, and whatever you usually get rid of, you're going to put back in." I took the pad of hotel stationery off the desk and handed it to her with a pen. "Each person in your immediate family gets one sentence. I want you to write down something you haven't told that person. It might be a desire or a secret or a regret—it might be something small, like, 'I wish you'd put your dirty socks in the laundry.' The only rule is it has to be something you've never said out loud."

She smiled faintly, nervously. "Are you going to make me actually say these?"

"What you do with them is entirely up to you. You can tear them up like confetti and flush them down the toilet, or set them on fire. I just want you to get them out of your body by writing them down."

She sat in silence for a few minutes and then began to write. Several times she crossed something out. Finally she looked up.

"How do you feel?"

"A little dizzy."

"Topsy-turvy?"

"Yes."

"Then it's time to fill yourself back up again. But with the things you usually give to other people. You're going to put all that love and protection and nurturing back inside." I asked her to picture herself getting very small, so tiny that she could climb inside her own ear. I told her to crawl down the canal, and down her throat and esophagus, all the way to her stomach. As she journeyed within, I asked her to put her tiny loving hands on each part of her body that she passed. On her lungs, her heart. On her spine, along the inside of each leg and arm. I coached her to lay her compassionate hands on each organ, muscle, bone, vein. "Bring love everywhere. Be your own unique, one-of-a-kind nurturer," I said.

It took awhile for her to settle in, to let her attention move away from the surface experience. She kept shifting in her chair, brushing a stray hair away from her forehead, clearing her throat. But then her breathing deepened and slowed, her body became still. She grew deeply relaxed as she ventured within, her face looked untroubled. Before I guided her back out through her ear canal, I asked if there was anything she wanted to tell me about what she had felt or discovered inside.

"I thought it would be so dark in here," she said. "But there's so much light."

A few months later she called with devastating news: Her breast cancer was no longer in remission. It had returned and was spreading rapidly. She said, "I don't know how long I have." She told me she planned to do the inside-out exercise every day so that she could empty herself of the inevitable anger and fear she felt, and fill herself back up with love and light. She said that, paradoxically, the more honest she was with her family about her more negative feelings, the more grateful she became. She told her husband how resentful she had been that his career had taken priority. Telling him openly made it easy to see that holding on to the resentment served nobody, and she found she could see more vividly all the ways he had supported her throughout their marriage. She found she could forgive him. With her teenage son, she didn't mask her fears about death, she didn't give him the reassurances that left no room for doubt. She talked openly about her uncertainties. She told him that sometimes we just don't know. To her daughter, who was younger, in middle school, she expressed how angry she was about the moments she would miss—hearing about her first dates, seeing her open her college acceptance letters, helping her put on her wedding dress. She didn't repress her rage as an unacceptable emotion. She found her way to what was beneath it—the depth and urgency of her love.

When her husband called to tell me Agnes had died, he said he would never get over the grief, but that her passing was peaceful. The quality of love in their family relationships had deepened in her last months of life. She had taught them a truer way of relating to one another. After I hung up the phone, I wept. Through no one's fault, a beautiful person was gone too soon. It was unfair. It was cruel. And it made me wonder about my own mortality. If I died tomorrow, would I die at peace? Had I really learned for myself what Agnes had discovered? Within my own darkness, had I found the light?

Emma helped me question how I was relating to my past. Agnes helped me confront how I was relating to my present. And Jason Fuller, the catatonic army captain who came to my office for the first time one hot afternoon in 1980, who sat silent and frozen for long minutes on the white couch, who obeyed the order I finally gave him to come to the park with me to take my dog for a walk, taught me how to face a decision that would determine my future. What I learned from him that day would affect the quality of my life in all of my remaining years, and the quality of the legacy I have chosen to pass on to my children, grandchildren, and great-grandchildren.

As we walked around the park, Jason's gait loosened. So did his face, every step bringing more color and softness. He looked younger all of a sudden, less hollowed out. Still, he didn't talk. I didn't plan ahead for what would happen when we returned to my office. I just kept us moving, breathing, every minute that Jason stayed with me an indication that if he felt safe enough, he might be reached.

After one slow loop around the park, I led us back to my office. I poured us some water. Whatever lay ahead, I knew it couldn't be rushed. I had to provide a place of absolute trust, where Jason could tell me anything, any feeling, where he knew he was safe, where he knew he wouldn't be judged. He sat on the couch again, facing me, and I leaned forward. How could I keep him here with me? Not just physically in my office. But ready for openness, for discovery? Together, we had to find a way to move toward insight and healing, a way for Jason to flow with whatever emotions and situations were overwhelming him into catatonia. And if I was to guide him toward wellness, I couldn't force him to talk. I had to flow with his current state of mind, his current choices and conditions, and stay open to opportunities for revelation and change.

"I wonder if you can help me," I finally said. This is an approach I sometimes take with a reluctant patient, a tough customer. I take the attention away from the patient's problem. I become the one with the problem. I appeal to the patient's sympathy. I wanted Jason to feel like he was the one with strength and solutions, and I was just a person, curious and somewhat desperate, asking to be helped. "I really want to know how you want to spend your time here with me. You're a young man, a soldier. I'm just a grandmother. Could you help me out?"

He started to speak, but then his throat clotted up with emotion and he shook his head. How could I help him to stay with whatever external or internal turmoil existed without running away or shutting down?

"I wonder if you could help me understand a little better how I could be useful to you. I'd like to be your sounding board. Would you please help me a little?"

His eyes cinched up as though he was reacting to a bright light. Or clenching back tears. "My wife," he finally said, his throat closing down again around the words.

I didn't ask in what way his wife was troubling him. I didn't ask for the facts. I went straight for the feeling under his words. I wanted him to take me directly, deeply, to the truth in his heart. I wanted him to be the person I trusted he was capable of being—a person who could unfreeze and feel. You can't heal what you can't feel. I had learned this the hard way, after decades of choosing to be frozen and numb. Like Jason, I had bottled my feelings, I had put on a mask.

What was under Jason's mask, his frozenness? Loss? Fear?

"It looks like you're sad about something," I said. I was guessing, suggesting. Either I was right, or he would correct me.

"I'm not sad," he muttered. "I'm mad. I'm mad as hell. I could *kill* her!"

"Your wife."

"That bitch is cheating on me!" There. The truth was out. It was a beginning.

"Tell me more," I said.

His wife was having an affair, he told me. His best friend had tipped him off. He couldn't believe he had missed the signs.

"Oh God," he said. "Oh God, oh God."

He stood. He paced. He kicked at the couch. He had broken through his rigidity and was now becoming manic, aggressive. He pounded the wall until he winced in pain. It was as though a switch had been hit, the full strength of his emotion surging on like floodlights. He was no longer sealed off and contained. He was explosive. Volcanic. And now that he was thrashing around unprotected in all that hurt, my role had changed. I had guided him back into his feelings. Now I had to help him experience them without drowning in them, without totally losing himself in the intensity. Before I could say a word, he stiffened in the middle of the room and yelled, "I can't take it! I'm going to kill her. I'll kill both of them."

"You're so mad you could kill her."

"Yes! I'm going to kill that bitch. I'm going to do it right now. Look what I've got." He wasn't speaking hyperbolically. He meant it quite literally. From under his belt he pulled a handgun. "I'm going to kill her right now."

I should have called the police. The warning sirens I had felt in my gut when Jason first walked through the door had not rung false. And now it might be too late. I didn't know if Jason and his wife had children, but what I pictured as Jason brandished the gun was the children crying at their mother's funeral, Jason behind bars, the children losing both of their parents in the heat of one moment's impulse for revenge.

But I didn't call the police. I didn't even call my assistant to let her know I might need help. There wasn't time.

I wouldn't shut him down. I would ride the wave of his intention to its consequence. "What if you kill her right now?" I said.

"I'm going to do it!"

"What will happen?"

"She deserves it. She's got it coming. She's going to regret every lie she ever told me."

"What will happen to you if you kill your wife?"

"I don't care!" He was pointing the gun at me, right at my chest, gripping it with both hands, his finger frozen near the trigger.

Was I a target? Could he take his rage out on me? Pull the trigger by mistake, send a bullet flying? There wasn't time to be afraid.

"Do your children care?" I was acting on instinct.

"Don't mention my children," Jason hissed. He lowered the gun a fraction. If he pulled the trigger now he would shoot my arm, my chair, not my heart.

"Do you love your children?" I asked. Anger, however consuming, is never the most important emotion. It is only the very outer edge, the thinly exposed top layer of a much deeper feeling. And the real feeling that's disguised by the mask of anger is usually fear. And you can't feel love and fear at the same time. If I could appeal to Jason's heart, if I could get him to feel love for even a second, it might be long enough to interrupt the signal of fear that was about to become violence. Already his fury was on pause. "Do you love your children?" I asked again.

Jason wouldn't answer. It was as though he was stuck in the crosshairs of his own competing feelings.

"I have three kids," I said. "Two daughters, one son. What about you?"

"Both," he said.

"A daughter and a son?"

He nodded.

"Tell me about your son," I said.

Something broke loose in Jason. A new feeling. I saw it pass over his face.

"He looks like me," Jason said.

"Like father, like son."

His eyes were no longer focused on me or the gun, his vision was someplace else. I couldn't tell what the new feeling was yet, but I could sense that something had shifted. I followed the thread.

"Do you want your son to be like you?" I asked.

"No!" he said. "God, no."

"Why not?"

He shook his head. He wasn't willing to go where I was leading him.

"What *do* you want?" I said it quietly. It was a question that can be terrifying to answer, a question that can change your life.

"I can't take this! I don't want to feel like this!"

"You want to be free from pain."

"I want that bitch to pay! I'm not going to let her make a fool of me." He raised the gun.

"You'll get your life back in control."

"Damn right I will."

"Damn right I will."

I was sweating now. It was up to me to help him drop the gun. There was no script to follow. "She did you wrong."

"Not anymore! It ends now."

"You'll protect yourself."

"That's right."

"You'll show your son how to handle things. How to be a man."

"I'll show him how to not let other people hurt him!"

"By killing his mom."

Jason froze.

"If you kill his mother, won't you be hurting your son?"

Jason stared at the gun in his hand. In visits to come, he would tell me what filled his mind at this moment. He would tell me about his father, a violent man who beat into Jason, sometimes with his words, sometimes with his fists, that *this* is what a man does: A man is invulnerable; a man doesn't cry; a man is in control; a man calls the shots. He would tell me that he had always intended to be a better father than his father had been. But he didn't know how. He didn't know how to teach and guide his children without intimidation. When I asked him to consider how his choice to seek revenge would affect his son, he was suddenly compelled to search for a possibility that, up until then, he hadn't been able to summon. A way to live that didn't perpetuate violence and insecurity, that would bring him—and his son—not to the imprisoning seduction of revenge but to the wide open sky of his promise and potential.

If I understand anything about that afternoon, about the whole of my life, it's that sometimes the worst moments in our lives, the moments that set us spinning with ugly desires, that threaten to unglue us with the sheer impossibility of the pain we must endure, are in fact the moments that bring us to understand our worth. It's as if we become aware of ourselves as a bridge between all that's been and all that will be. We become aware of all we've received and what we can choose—or choose not—

to perpetuate. It's like vertigo, thrilling and terrifying, the past and the future surrounding us like a vast but traversable canyon. Small as we are in the big scheme of universe and time, each of us is a little mechanism that keeps the whole wheel spinning. And what will we power with the wheel of our own life? Will we keep pushing the same piston of loss or regret? Will we reengage and re-enact all the hurts from the past? Will we abandon the people we love as a consequence of our own abandonment? Will we make our children pick up the tab for our losses? Or will we take the best of what we know and let a new crop flourish from the field of our life?

Craving revenge, holding a gun, picturing himself in his son's face, Jason was suddenly able to see the choices available to him. He could choose to kill or choose to love. To vanquish or to forgive. To face a grief, or to pass the pain on, again and again. He dropped the gun. He was crying now, huge, rippling sobs, waves of sorrow crashing over his body. He couldn't stand with the immensity of the feeling. He fell to the ground, to his knees, he bent his head. I could almost see the different feelings breaking over him in waves, the hurt and shame and broken pride and ruined trust and loneliness, the image of the man he couldn't be and would never be. He couldn't be a man who had never lost. He would always be a man whose father beat and humiliated him when he was young, whose wife cheated on him. Just as I will always be a woman whose mother and father were gassed and burned and turned to smoke. Jason and I would always be what every person is, someone who will bear suffering. We can't erase the pain. But we are free to accept who we are and what has been done to us, and move on. Jason knelt, crying. I joined him on the floor. The people we loved and relied on had disappeared or let us down. He needed to be held. I held him. I pulled him to my chest and he sank into my lap and I held him and we cried until our tears had soaked my silk blouse through.

Before Jason left my office, I demanded that he give me the gun. (I would hang on to the gun for years, so long that I forgot it was still in my closet. When I was packing my office in preparation for my move to San Diego, I would discover the gun, still loaded, in the drawer of a filing cabinet, a reminder of the volatility and pain we often choose to hide away, the potential for damage that persists until we consciously face and dismantle it.) "Are you safe to leave now?" I asked him. "Are you safe to go home?"

"I'm not sure."

"It's going to be uncomfortable for you without a gun. Do you have somewhere else to go if the rage comes back? If you feel like you have to hurt or kill someone?"

He said he could go to his friend's house, the one who had told him about the affair and advised him to see me.

"We need to practice what you will say to your wife." We made a script. He wrote it down. He would tell her, "I feel so sad and upset. I hope we can find a time to talk about it tonight." He wasn't allowed to say more until they were alone together, and only then if he could communicate with words instead of violence. He was to call me immediately if he felt incapable of going home. If the homicidal feelings came back, he was to find a safe place to sit down or take a walk. "Close the door. Or go outside. Be by yourself. Breathe and breathe and breathe. The feelings will pass. Promise me you will call me if you start to feel out of control. Get yourself out of the situation, make yourself safe, and call me."

He started to cry again. "No one ever cared about me like you do."

"We're going to be a good team together," I told him. "I know you're not going to let me down."

Jason came back to my office two days later, and so began a therapeutic relationship that would last for five years. But before I knew how his story would turn out, I had a turning point of my own to confront.

Once Jason left and I had stowed the gun and sat down in my chair, breathing deeply, slowly, regaining my calm, I sorted through the mail my assistant had given me just before Jason's unexpected arrival. And there I found another letter that changed the course of my life. It was from U.S. Army chaplain David Woehr, a former colleague at William Beaumont, who was then heading the Religious Resource Center in Munich, where he was responsible for administering clinical training to all of the U.S. Army chaplains and chaplains' assistants currently serving in Europe. The letter was an invitation to address six hundred chaplains at a workshop Dave would be leading in a month. In any other circumstance, I would have accepted, would have been honored and humbled to be of use. Because of my clinical experience at William Beaumont, and my success in treating active-duty personnel and combat veterans, I had been asked a number of times to speak to larger military audiences and had always felt that it was not just an honor but also my moral obligation—as a former prisoner of war, as a person liberated by U.S. soldiers—to do so. But Dave's workshop was scheduled to meet in Germany. And not just anywhere in Germany. In Berchtesgaden. Hitler's former retreat in the mountains of Bavaria.

CHAPTER 17

Then Hitler Won

It isn't the cold air coming through the cooling vent in my office that makes me shiver. Soon I will be fifty-three years old. I am no longer the young orphaned mother fleeing war-torn Europe. I am no longer the immigrant hiding from her past. I am Dr. Edith Eva Eger now. I have survived. I have worked to heal. I use what I have learned from my traumatic past to help others heal. I am often called in by social service organizations and medical and military groups to treat patients with PTSD. I have come a great distance since escaping to America. But I haven't been back to Germany since the war.

That evening, to distract myself from my worry over how Jason is handling the confrontation with his wife, to ease my own swirling indecision, I call Marianne in San Diego and ask her what she thinks I should do about Berchtesgaden. She is a mother now, and a psychologist. We often consult each other about our most challenging patients. Just as for Jason in the long moments when he held the gun, the decision before me now has a lot to do with my children—with the kind of wound they will carry with them after I'm gone: a healed one or an open one.

"I don't know, Mom," Marianne says. "I want to tell you to go. You survived, and now you get to go back and tell your story. That's such a triumph. But . . . do you remember that Danish family, the friends of my host family back in college? They returned to Auschwitz thinking it would bring them peace. But it just stirred up all the trauma. It was very stressful. They both suffered heart attacks when they got home. They died, Mom."

Berchtesgaden isn't Auschwitz, I remind her. I'd be more in the geography of Hitler's past than my own. Yet even my daily routines in El Paso can trigger flashbacks. I hear sirens and I go cold, I see barbed wire around a construction site and I am no longer in the present, I am watching the blue bodies hanging from the fence, I am stuck in the fear, I am struggling for my life. If mundane triggers can bring my trauma back, what would it be like to be surrounded by people speaking German, to wonder if I am walking among former Hitler Youth, to be in the very rooms where Hitler and his advisers once lived?

"If you think there's something to be gained, then go. I support you," Marianne says. "But it's got to be for you. You don't have to prove anything to anyone else. You're not required to go."

When she says it, the relief is immediate. "Thank you, Marchuka," I say. I am safe now, I am happy. I have done my work. I have grown. Now I can let go. I can be finished. I can say that I am honored by the invitation, but it is too painful for me to accept. Dave will understand.

But when I tell Béla that I have decided to decline the invitation, he grabs my shoulder. "If you don't go to Germany," he says, "then Hitler won the war."

It's not what I want to hear. I feel like I've been sucker-punched. But I have to concede that he's right about one thing: It's easier to hold someone or something else responsible for your pain than to take responsibility for ending your own victimhood. Our marriage has taught me that—all the times when my anger or frustration at Béla has taken my attention away from my own work and growth, the times when blaming him for my unhappiness was easier than taking responsibility for myself.

Most of us want a dictator—albeit a benevolent one—so we can pass the buck, so we can say, "You made me do that. It's not my fault." But we can't spend our lives hanging out under someone else's umbrella and then complain that we're getting wet. A good definition of being a victim is when you keep the focus outside yourself, when you look outside yourself for someone to blame for your present circumstances, or to determine your purpose, fate, or worth.

And that is why Béla tells me that if I don't go to Berchtesgaden, then Hitler has won. He means that I am sitting on a seesaw with my past. As long as I can put Hitler, or Mengele, or the gaping mouth of my loss on the opposite seat, then I am somehow justified, I always have an excuse. *That's* why I'm anxious. *That's* why I'm sad. *That's* why I can't risk going to Germany. It's not that I'm wrong to feel anxious and sad and afraid. It's not that there isn't real trauma at the core of my life. And it's not that Hitler and Mengele and every other perpetrator of violence or cruelty shouldn't be held accountable for the harm they cause. But if I stay on the seesaw, I am holding the past responsible for what I choose to do now.

Long ago, Mengele's finger did point me to my fate. He chose for my mother to die, he chose for Magda and me to live. At every selection line, the stakes were life and death, the choice was never mine to make. But even then, in my prison, in hell, I could choose how I responded, I could choose my actions and speech, I could choose what I held in my mind. I could choose whether to walk into the electrified barbed wire, to refuse to leave my bed, or I could choose to struggle and live, to think of Eric's voice and my mother's strudel, to think of Magda beside me, to recognize all I had to live for, even amid the horror and the loss. It has been thirty-five years since I left hell. The panic attacks come at any time of day or night, they can subsume me as easily in my own living room as in Hitler's old bunker, because my panic isn't the result of purely external triggers. It is an expression of the memories and fears that live inside. If I keep myself in exile from a particular part of the globe, I am really saying that I want to exile the part of myself that is afraid. Maybe there is something I can learn by getting closer to that part.

And what of my legacy? Only hours ago, Jason faced a turning point in his life—the moment when he held a gun in his hand but didn't pull the trigger, when he considered the legacy he wanted to pass on to his children, when he chose something other than violence. What legacy do I want to pass on? What will I leave in the world when I am gone? I have already chosen to relinquish secrets and denial and shame. But have I really made peace with the past? Is there more to resolve so that I don't perpetuate more pain?

I think of my mother's mother, who died suddenly in her sleep. Of my mother, whose grief over the trauma of that sudden childhood loss marked her with hunger and fear from a very early age, and who passed on to her own children a vague inchoate sense of loss. And what will I pass on, besides her smooth skin, her thick hair, her deep eyes, besides the pain and grief and rage at having lost her too young? And what if I have to return to the site of my trauma to stop the cycle, to create a different kind of legacy?

I accept the invitation to Berchtesgaden.

CHAPTER 18

Goebbels's Bed

Over the phone, Rev. Dr. David Woehr briefed me for my visit. I would address six hundred Army chaplains gathered for a clinical pastoral retreat at an Armed Forces Recreation Center in the General Walker Hotel, high in the mountains of Bavaria, which had served as a guesthouse and meeting place for Hitler's SS officers. Béla and I would be provided accommodations at the nearby Hotel zum Türken, which had once been reserved for Hitler's cabinet and diplomatic visitors. This was where British prime minister Neville Chamberlain stayed in 1938 when he met with Hitler and returned home with the triumphant and tragically misguided news that he had secured "peace for our time," and where Adolf Eichmann himself had likely briefed Hitler on the Final Solution. The Berghof, or the Eagle's Nest, Hitler's former residence, was a short walk away.

My audience would be made up of healing arts professionals. Army chaplains serve as behavioral health providers in addition to spiritual counselors, and for the first time, Dave told me, chaplains were required to receive a year of clinical pastoral education to complement their seminary studies. The chaplains needed training in psychology as well as in religious doctrine, and Dave was leading weeklong retreats on clinical psychology to the chaplains stationed in Europe. I would give the keynote address.

Dave told me more about the chaplains and the soldiers they served. These weren't the soldiers of my youth, or the soldiers I was accustomed to treating at William Beaumont; these were peacetime soldiers, soldiers of the cold war, of war behind the scenes. They weren't living through daily violence, but nevertheless were on high alert, keeping the peace but at the ready for war. Most cold war soldiers were stationed at the sites of prepositioned missiles. These missiles were mounted on mobile launchers, already hidden at strategic sites. It was a matter of routine for these military personnel to live with the perpetual threat of war, the middle-of-the-night sirens that could signal another alert drill or an actual attack. (Like the showers at Auschwitz. Water or gas? We never knew.) The chaplains I was to address had the responsibility of supporting the spiritual and psychological needs of soldiers doing their best to deter an all-out war, doing their best to be prepared for whatever happened.

"What do they need to hear?" I asked. "What would it be helpful for me to talk about?"

"Hope," Dave said. "Forgiveness. If chaplains can't talk about this stuff, if we don't understand it, we can't do our job."

"Why me?"

"It's one thing to hear about hope and forgiveness from the pulpit, or from a religious scholar," Dave explained. "But you're one of the few people who can talk about holding on to hope even when you'd been stripped of everything, when you were starving and left for dead. I don't know anyone else with that kind of credibility."

A month later, when Béla and I are on a train from Berlin to Berchtesgaden, I feel like the least credible person, the last person on Earth qualified to talk about hope and forgiveness. When I close my eyes, I hear the sound of my nightmares, the constant turning of wheel against track. I see my parents, my father who refuses to shave, my mother's inward gaze. Béla holds my hand. He touches a finger to the gold bracelet he gave me when Marianne was born, that I tucked into Marianne's diaper when we fled Prešov, the bracelet I wear every day. It's a token of triumph. We made it. We survived. We stand for life. But not even Béla's comfort, nor the kiss of the smooth metal on my skin, can mitigate the dread collecting in my gut.

We share the train compartment with a German couple about our age. They are pleasant, they offer us some of the pastries they've brought, the woman compliments me on my outfit. What would they say if they knew that when I was seventeen I sat on the top of a German train under a hail of bombs, a human shield in a thin striped dress, forced to protect Nazi ammunition with my life? And where were they when I shivered on the top of the train? Where were they during the war? Were they the children who spat at Magda and me when we marched through German towns? Were they Hitler Youth? Do they think about the past now, or are they in denial, as I was for so many years?

The dread in me turns to something else, a fiery and jagged feeling, fury. I remember Magda's rage: *After the war, I'm going to kill a German mother.* She couldn't erase our loss, but she could flip it on its head, she could retaliate. At times I shared her desire for confrontation, but not her desire for revenge. My devastation manifested as a suicidal urge, not a homicidal one. But now anger collects in me, a gale-force fury, it gathers strength and speed. I am sitting inches away from people who might be my former oppressors. I am afraid of what I might do.

"Béla," I whisper, "I think I've come far enough. I want to go home."

"You've been afraid before," he says. "Welcome it, welcome it." Béla is reminding me of what I believe too: This is the work of healing. You deny what hurts, what you fear. You avoid it at all costs. Then you find a way to welcome and embrace what you're most afraid of. And then you can finally let it go.

We arrive in Berchtesgaden and take a shuttle van to the Hotel zum Türken, which is now a museum as well as a hotel. I try to ignore the ominous history of this place and lift my face to the physical grandeur, to the mountain peaks rising around us. The rocky, snowy range reminds me of the Tatra Mountains where Béla and I first met when he reluctantly chaperoned me to the TB hospital.

Inside the hotel, Béla and I have a good laugh when the concierge addresses us as Dr. and Mrs. Eger.

"It's Dr. and *Mr.* Eger," Béla says.

The hotel is like a time machine, an anachronism. The rooms are still appointed as they were in the 1930s and 1940s, with thick Persian rugs and no telephones. Béla and I are assigned to the room that Joseph Goebbels, Hitler's minister of propaganda, slept in, with the same bed, the same mirror and dresser and nightstand that once were his. I stand in the doorway of the room, I feel my inner peace shatter. What does it mean that I am standing here now? Béla runs his hand over the dresser top, the bedspread, he goes to the window. Is history grabbing his skull the way it is mine? I grab for the bedpost to keep from falling to my knees. Béla turns back to me. He winks, he bursts into song.

It's . . . springtime for Hitler, and Germany! he sings. It's from Mel Brooks's *The Producers. Deutschland is happy and gay!*

He does a tap-dance routine in front of the window, he holds a pretend cane in his hands. We saw *The Producers* together when it opened in 1968, the year before our divorce. I sat in a movie theater with a hundred laughing people, Béla laughing loudest of all. I couldn't even crack a smile. Intellectually, I understood the purpose of the satire. I knew that laughter can lift, that it can carry us over and through difficult times. I knew that laughter can heal. But to hear this song now, in this place, it is too much. I am furious at Béla, less for his absence of tact, more for his ability to move so quickly and successfully out of anguish. I have to get away.

I head out alone for a walk. Just outside the hotel lobby is a path that leads to the Berghof, the Eagle's Nest, Hitler's old residence. I will not choose that path. I will not give Hitler the satisfaction of acknowledging his home, his existence. I am not stranded in the past. I follow a different trail instead, to a different peak, toward the open sky.

And then I stop myself. Here I am, forever giving a dead person the power to cut off my own discovery. Isn't this why I have come to Germany? To get closer to the discomfort? To see what the past still has to teach me?

I slide along the gravel path toward the unassuming remains of Hitler's once grand estate, perched at the edge of a cliff. Now all that exists of the house is an old retaining wall covered in moss, pieces of rubble and pipes poking out of the ground. I look out over the valley as Hitler must have done. Hitler's house is gone—American GIs burned it to the ground in the last days of the war, but not before raiding Hitler's stores of wine and cognac. They sat on the terrace and raised their glasses, behind them his house obscured by smoke and flames. The house is gone, but what of Hitler? Can I still feel his presence here? I test my gut for nausea, my spine for chills. I listen for his voice. I listen for the echoing register of his hate, for the relentless call of evil. But it's quiet here today. I gaze up the mountain, I see wildflowers fed by the first cold trickles of melting snow from the surrounding peaks. I am walking on the same steps that Hitler once took, but he isn't here now, *I* am. It *is* springtime, though not for Hitler. For me. The thick crust of silent snow has melted; dead quiet winter has yielded to the burst of new leaves and the jolting rush of fast water. Within the layers of the terrible sorrow I carry in me always, another feeling shoots through. It is the first melting trickle of long-frozen snow. Pulsing down the mountainside, the water speaks, the chambers of my heart speak. *I am alive*, the bubbling stream says. *I made it.* A song of triumph is filling me, pushing its way out of my heart, out through my mouth to the sky up above and the valley below.

"I release you!" I shout to that old sorrow. "I release you!"

"Tempora mutantur, et nos mutamur in illis," I say to the chaplains when I give my keynote address the next morning. "It's a Latin phrase I learned as a girl. Times are changing and we are changing with them. We are always in the process of becoming." I ask them to travel back with me forty years, to the

same mountain village where we sit right now, maybe to this very room, when fifteen highly educated people contemplated how many of their fellow humans they could incinerate in an oven at one time. "In human history, there is war," I say. "There is cruelty, there is violence, there is hate. But never in the history of humankind has there ever been a more scientific and systematic annihilation of people. I survived Hitler's horrific death camps. Last night I slept in Joseph Goebbels's bed. People ask me, how did you learn to overcome the past? Overcome? Overcome? I haven't overcome anything. Every beating, bombing, and selection line, every death, every column of smoke pushing skyward, every moment of terror when I thought it was the end—these live on in me, in my memories and my nightmares. The past isn't gone. It isn't transcended or excised. It lives on in me. But so does the perspective it has afforded me: that I lived to see liberation because I kept hope alive in my heart. That I lived to see freedom because I learned to forgive."

Forgiveness isn't easy, I tell them. It is easier to hold grudges, to seek revenge. I tell of my fellow survivors, the courageous men and women I met in Israel, who looked pained when I mentioned forgiveness, who insisted that to forgive is to condone or to forget. Why forgive? Doesn't that let Hitler off the hook for what he did?

I tell of my dear friend Laci Gladstein—Larry Gladstone— and the single time in the decades since the war when he spoke to me explicitly about the past. It was during my divorce, when he knew money was a struggle for me. He called to say that he knew of a lawyer representing survivors in reparations cases, he encouraged me to step forward as a survivor, to claim my due. That was the right choice for many, but not for me. It felt like blood money. As if one could put a price on my parents' heads. A way to stay chained to those who had tried to destroy us.

It is too easy to make a prison out of our pain, out of the past. At best, revenge is useless. It can't alter what was done to us, it can't erase the wrongs we've suffered, it can't bring back the dead. At worst, revenge perpetuates the cycle of hate. It keeps the hate circling on and on. When we seek revenge, even non-violent revenge, we are revolving, not evolving.

I even thought when I arrived yesterday that my presence here is a healthy kind of revenge, a comeuppance, a settling of the scores. And then I stood overlooking the cliff at the Berghof, and it came to me that revenge doesn't make you free. So I stood on the site of Hitler's former home and forgave him. This had nothing to do with Hitler. It was something I did for me. I was letting go, releasing the part of myself that had spent most of my life exerting the mental and spiritual energy to keep Hitler in chains. As long as I was holding on to that rage, I was in chains with him, locked in the damaging past, locked in my grief. To forgive is to grieve—for what happened, for what didn't happen—and to give up the need for a different past. To accept life as it was and as it is. I do not of course mean that it was acceptable for Hitler to murder six million people. Just that it happened, and I do not want that fact to destroy the life that I clung to and fought for against all odds.

The chaplains rise to their feet. They shower me in warm applause. I stand in the light on the stage, thinking that I will never feel so elated, so free. I don't know that forgiving Hitler isn't the hardest thing I'll ever do. The hardest person to forgive is someone I've still to confront: myself.

Our last night in Berchtesgaden, I can't sleep. I lie awake in Goebbels's bed. A crack of light breaks in from under the door and I can see the pattern of vines on the old wallpaper, the way they intertwine, the way they rise. *Tempora mutantur, et nos mutamur in illis.* If I am changing, what am I in the process of becoming?

I rest in the wakeful uncertainty. I try to open myself, to let my intuition speak. For some reason I think of a story I heard of a very talented Jewish boy, an artist. He was told to go to Vienna to art school, but he didn't have any money for the journey. He walked from Czechoslovakia to Vienna, only to be denied a seat at the exams because he was Jewish. He begged. He had come so far, he had walked the whole way, could he at least take the test, could he be allowed that much? They let him sit for the exam, and he passed. He was so talented that he was offered a spot at the school despite his ancestry. Sitting beside him at the exam was a boy named Adolf Hitler, who was not accepted at the school. But the Jewish boy was. And all his life, this man, who had left Europe and lived in Los Angeles, had felt guilty, because if Hitler hadn't suffered this loss, if he hadn't lost to a Jew, he might not have felt the need to scapegoat Jews. The Holocaust might not have happened. Like children who have been abused, or whose parents divorce, we find a way to blame ourselves.

The self-blame hurts others, too, not just ourselves. I remember a former patient, a man and his family I treated briefly a year or so ago. They sat before me like abandoned pieces from different puzzles: the intimidating colonel in his decorated uniform; the silent blonde wife, her collarbones jutting out from her white blouse; their teenage daughter, her dyed black hair ratted and sprayed into a wild nest, her eyes ringed in black eyeliner; a quiet son, eight years old, studying a comic book in his lap.

The colonel pointed at his daughter. "Look at her. She's promiscuous. She's a drug addict. She won't respect our rules. She mouths off to her mother. She doesn't come home when she's told. It's becoming impossible to live with her."

"We've heard your version," I said. "Let's hear from Leah."

As if taunting him by reading from a script that would confirm every one of her father's claims, Leah launched into a story about her weekend. She'd had sex with her boyfriend at a party, where there'd been underage drinking and where she'd also dropped acid. She'd stayed out all night. She seemed to take pleasure in listing the details.

Her mother blinked and picked at her manicured nails. Her father's face flushed red. He rose from his seat next to hers. He towered over her, shaking his fist. "You see what I have to put up with?" he roared. His daughter saw his anger, but I saw a man on his way to a heart attack.

"You see what *I* have to put up with?" Leah said, rolling her eyes. "He doesn't even try to understand me. He never listens to me. He just tells me what to do."

Her brother stared harder at his comic book, as if force of will could take him out of the war zone his family life had become and put him in the fantasy world of his book, where the lines between good and evil were clearly drawn, where the good guys would win, eventually. He had said the least of anyone in the family, and yet I had a hunch that he was the one with the most important things to say.

I told the parents I would spend the next part of the session with them, without their children in the room, and I took Leah and her brother into my adjoining office, where I gave them drawing paper and markers. I gave them an assignment, something I thought might help them let off steam after the tense minutes with their parents. I asked them each to draw a portrait of their family but without using people.

I returned to the parents. The colonel was yelling at his wife. She appeared to be wasting away, disappearing, and I was concerned she might be in the early stages of an eating disorder. If I asked her a question directly, she deferred to her husband. Each family member was in his or her own stockade. I could see the evidence of their inner pain in the ways they accused one another and hid themselves. But in trying to get them closer to the sources of their pain, I only seemed to be inviting them to open fire or recede even further.

"We've talked about what you see going on with your children," I said, interrupting the colonel. "What about what's going on with you?"

Leah's mother blinked at me. Her father gave me a cold stare.

"What do you wish to achieve, as parents?"

"To teach them how to be strong in the world," the colonel said.

"And how are you doing with that?"

"My daughter's a slut and my son's a sissy. How do you think?"

"I can see that your daughter's behaviors are scaring you. What about your son? How is he disappointing you?"

"He's weak. He's always backing down."

"Can you give me an example?"

"When we play basketball together, he's a sore loser. He doesn't even try to win. He just walks away."

"He's a boy. He's much smaller than you. What happens if you let him win?"

"What would that teach him? That the world bends over for you if you're soft?"

"There are ways to teach kids to go farther, to stretch their capacities, with a gentle push, not a kick in the ass," I said.

The colonel grunted.

"How do you want your children to see you?"

"Like I'm in charge."

"A hero? A leader?"

He nodded.

"How do you think your children actually see you?"

"They think I'm a goddamn pussy."

Later in the session I brought the family back together, and I asked the kids to share their family portraits. Leah had drawn only one object: an enormous bomb detonating in the middle of the page. Her brother had drawn a ferocious lion and three cowering mice.

The colonel's face turned red again. His wife looked down at her lap. He stammered and stared at the ceiling.

"Tell me what's going on for you right now."

"I fucked up this family, didn't I?"

I half expected that I would never see the colonel or his family again. But he called the following week to schedule a private session. I asked him to tell me more about how he felt when his children had showed us their pictures.

"If my kids are afraid of me, how are they supposed to handle themselves in the world?"

"What leads you to believe they can't protect themselves?"

"Leah can't say no to boys or drugs. Robbie can't say no to bullies."

"What about you? Can you protect yourself?"

He puffed out his chest so his medals glinted in the sunlight. "You're looking at the proof."

"I don't mean on the battlefield. I mean in your home."

"I don't think you understand the pressure I'm under."

"What would it take for you to feel safe?"

"Safety isn't the issue. If I'm not in control, people die."

"Is that what safety would feel like to you? Freedom from the fear that people are going to get hurt on your watch?"

"It's not just a fear."

"Take me where you are. What are you thinking of?"

"I don't think you want to hear this."

"You don't have to worry about me."

"You won't understand."

"You're right, no one can ever understand someone else completely. But I can tell you that I was once a prisoner of war. Whatever it is you want to tell me, I've probably heard—and seen—worse."

"In the military, it's kill or be killed. So when I got the order, I didn't question it."

"Where are you when you get this order?"

"Vietnam."

"Are you inside? Outside?"

"In my office at the air base."

I watched his body language as he took me into the past. I watched his energy, his level of agitation, so that I could be attuned to any distress that signaled we were going too far too fast. He had closed his eyes. He seemed to be sinking into a trance.

"Are you sitting or standing?"

"I'm sitting when I get the call. But I stand up right away."

"Who's calling you?"

"My commanding officer."

"What does he say?"

"That he's putting my men on a rescue mission in the bush."

"Why do you stand up when you hear the order?"

"I feel hot. My chest is tight."

"What are you thinking?"

"That it isn't safe. That we're going to be attacked. That we need more air support if we're heading to that part of the bush. And they're not giving it to us."

"Are you mad about that?"

His eyes snapped open. "Of course I'm mad. They send us in there, they feed us a bunch of bullshit about America being the strongest army in the world, that the gooks don't stand a chance."

"The war wasn't what you expected."

"They lied to us."

"You feel betrayed."

"Hell yes, I feel betrayed."

"What happened the day you got the order to send your troops on the rescue mission?"

"It was night."

"What happened that night?"

"I'll tell you what happened. It was an ambush."

"Your men got hurt?"

"Do I have to spell it out? They died. They all died that night. And I'm the one who sent them in there. They trusted me, and I sent them in there to die."

"War means people die."

"You know what I think? Dying is easy. I have to live every day thinking about all those parents burying their sons."

"You were following an order."

"But I knew it was the wrong decision. I knew those boys needed more air support. And I didn't have the balls to demand it."

"What did you give up to become a colonel?"

"What do you mean?"

"You made a choice to become a soldier and a military leader. What did you have to give up to get here?"

"I had to be away from my family a lot."

"What else?"

"When you have six thousand men relying on you for their lives, you don't have the luxury of being afraid."

"You've had to give up your feelings. To give up letting others see them."

He nodded.

"You said before that dying is easy. Do you ever wish you were dead?"

"All the fucking time."

"What's stopping you?"

"My kids." His face contorted in anguish. "But they think I'm a monster. They'd be better off without me."

"Do you want to know how I see it? I think your children would be very much better off with you. With *you*, the man I am coming to know and admire. The man who can risk talking about his fear. The man who has the guts to forgive and accept himself."

He was silent. Perhaps this was the first moment he had encountered the possibility of freeing himself from the guilt he felt over the past.

"I can't help you go back in time to save your troops. I can't guarantee your children's safety. But I can help you protect one person: yourself."

He stared at me.

"But to save yourself, you are going to have to give up the image of who you think you're supposed to be."

"I hope this works," he said.

Shortly after, the colonel was reassigned and his family left El Paso. I don't know what happened to them. I hope something good, as I cared for them deeply. But why am I thinking of them now? What does their story have to do with me? Something about the colonel's guilt, about his prison of self-blame, is calling for my attention. Is my memory pointing to work I have already done, or work that I have yet to do? I have come so far since the end of my literal imprisonment, since the American GI rescued me in 1945. I have taken off my mask. I have learned to feel and express, to stop bottling my fears and my grief. I have worked to express and release my rage. And I have traveled back here, to my oppressor's old home. I have even forgiven Hitler, released him to the universe, if only for today. But there's a knot, a darkness, that extends from my gut to my heart, there's a tightness in my spine—it's an unrelenting sense of guilt. I was victimized, I wasn't the victimizer. Whom is it that I think I have wronged?

Another patient flashes into my mind. She was seventy-one years old and a chronic source of concern to her family. She exhibited all the symptoms of clinical depression. She slept too much and ate too much and isolated herself from her children and grandchildren. And when she did interact with her family, she was so full of anger that her grandchildren were afraid of her. Her son approached me after my lecture in their city to ask if I could spare an hour to meet with his mother. I wasn't sure in what way I could be useful to her in a single, short visit until the man revealed that, like me, his mother had lost her own mother when she was only sixteen. I felt a surge of compassion for his mother, this stranger. It struck me that she was the person I could easily have become, that I almost became—so steeped in loss that I hid from the people who loved me the most.

The woman, Margaret, came to see me in my hotel room that afternoon. She was meticulously dressed, but there was a hostility that bristled out of her like quills. She unleashed a litany of complaints about her health, her family members, her housekeeper, her postman, her neighbors, the headmistress of the girls' school up the street. She seemed to find injustice and inconvenience everywhere in her life. The hour was wasting away, and she was so caught up in the small disasters that we hadn't touched on what I knew to be her larger grief.

"Where is your mother buried?" I asked suddenly.

Margaret pulled away as though I was a dragon breathing on her face with flame. "In the cemetery," she finally said, recomposed.

"Where is the cemetery? Nearby?"

"In this very town," she said.

"Your mother needs you right now."

I didn't give her a chance to object. We hailed a taxi. We sat and watched the wet, busy streets through the windows. She kept up a running criticism of other drivers, the speed of the traffic signals, the quality of the shops and businesses we passed, even the color of someone's umbrella. We drove through the iron gates of the cemetery. The trees were mature and towering. A narrow cobblestone road led from the gate into the field of the dead. Rain fell.

"There," Margaret said at last, pointing up the muddy hill to a crowd of headstones. "Now tell me what in God's name we're doing here."

"Do you know," I said, "mothers can't rest in peace unless they know the people they have left behind are fully embracing life?" Take off your shoes, I told her. Take off your stockings. Stand barefoot on your mother's grave. Make direct contact so she can finally rest in peace.

Margaret got out of the taxi. She stood on the rain-slick grass. I gave her privacy. I looked back only once, when I saw Margaret crouched on the ground, holding her mother's headstone in her hands. I don't know what she said to her mother, if she said anything at all. I only know she stood barefoot on her mother's grave, that she connected her bare skin to this site of loss and grief. That when she got back in the taxi she was barefoot still. She cried a little, then fell silent.

Later I would receive a beautiful letter from Margaret's son. *I don't know what you said to my mother*, he would write, *but she's a different person, she is more peaceful, more joyful.*

It was a whim, a lucky experiment. My goal was to help her reframe her experience—to reframe her problem as an opportunity, to put her in the position of helping her mother—and in helping her mother to be free, to help herself. Now that I am back in Germany, it occurs to me that maybe the same principle can work for me. Bare-skinned connection with the site of my loss. Contact and release. Hungarian exorcism.

Lying awake in Goebbels's bed, I realize that I need to do what Margaret did, to perform the rite of grief that has eluded me all my life.

I decide to return to Auschwitz.

CHAPTER 19

Leave a Stone

I can't imagine going back to hell without Magda. "Fly to Kraków tonight," I beg Magda the next morning from the phone in the Hotel zum Türken lobby. "Please come back to Auschwitz with me."

I wouldn't have survived without her. I can't survive returning to our prison now unless she is beside me, holding my hand. I know it's not possible to relive the past, to be who I used to be, to hug my mother again, even once. There is nothing that can alter the past, that can make me different from who I am, change what was done to my parents, done to me. There is no going back. I know this. But I can't ignore the feeling that there is something waiting for me in my old prison, something to recover. Or discover. Some long-lost part of me.

"What kind of a crazy masochist do you think I am?" Magda says. "Why the hell would I go back there? Why would you?"

It's a fair question. Am I only punishing myself? Reopening a wound? Maybe I will regret it. But I think I will regret it more if I don't go back. No matter how many ways I try to convince her, Magda refuses. Magda is choosing never to return, and I respect her for it. But I will make a different choice.

* * *

Béla and I already have an invitation to visit Marianne's old host family in Copenhagen while we are in Europe, and we continue there from Berchtesgaden as planned.

We travel to Salzburg, where we tour the cathedral constructed on the ruins of a Roman church. It has been rebuilt three times, we learn—most recently after a bomb damaged the central dome during the war. There is no evidence of the destruction. "Like us," Béla says, taking my hand.

From Salzburg, we go to Vienna, traveling over the same ground Magda and I marched across before we were liberated. I see ditches running alongside roads, and I imagine them as I once saw them, spilling over with corpses, but I can also see them as they are now, filling up with summer grass. I can see that the past doesn't taint the present, the present doesn't diminish the past. Time is the medium. Time is the track, we travel it. The train goes through Linz. Through Wels. I am a girl with a broken back who learns to write a capital *G* again, who learns again to dance.

We spend the night in Vienna, not far from the Rothschild Hospital where we first lived when we were waiting for our visas to America, and where, I have since learned, my mentor Viktor Frankl was the chief of neurology before the war. In the morning we board another train north.

I think Béla assumes my desire to return to Auschwitz might wane, but our second morning in Copenhagen I ask our friends for directions to the Polish embassy. They caution me, as Marianne already has, about their survivor friends who visited the camp and then died. "Don't retraumatize yourself," they plead. Béla, too, looks worried. "Hitler didn't win," I remind him.

I thought that choosing to return would be the biggest hurdle. But at the Polish embassy, Béla and I learn that labor riots have broken out across Poland, that the Soviets might intervene to suppress the demonstrations, that the embassy has been advised to stop issuing travel visas to Westerners. Béla is ready to console me, but I brush him away. I feel the force of will that led me once to the prison warden in Prešov with a diamond ring in my hand, to a medical examiner's office in Vienna with my brother-in-law posing as my husband. I have come this far in my life and my healing. I can concede to no obstacle now.

"I'm a survivor," I tell the embassy clerk. "I was a prisoner at Auschwitz. My parents and grandparents died there. I fought so hard to survive. Please don't make me wait to go back." I don't know that within a year Polish–American relations will have deteriorated, that they will stay frozen for the rest of the decade, that this is in fact the last chance for me and Béla to go to Auschwitz together. I only know that I can't let myself be turned back.

The clerk eyes me, expressionless. He steps away from the counter, returns. "Passports," he says. Into our blue American passports he has inserted travel visas good for one week. "Enjoy Poland," he says.

This is when I start to feel afraid. On the train to Kraków I feel that I'm in a crucible, that I am reaching the point at which I will break or burn, that fear alone could turn me into ash. *This is here, this is now.* I try to reason with the part of me that feels that with every mile I travel I lose a layer of skin. I will be a skeleton again by the time I get to Poland. I want to be more than bones.

"Let's get off at the next stop," I tell Béla. "It's not important to go all the way to Auschwitz. Let's go home."

"Edie," he says, "you're going to be fine. It's only a place. It can't hurt you."

I stay on the train for another stop, and another, through Berlin, through Poznań. I think of Dr. Hans Selye—a fellow Hungarian—who said stress is the body's response to any demand for change. Our automatic responses are to fight or to flee—but in Auschwitz, where we endured more than stress, where we lived in *dis*tress, the stakes life and death, never knowing what would happen next, the options to fight or flee didn't exist. I would have been shot if I'd fought back, electrocuted if I'd tried to run away. So I learned to flow, I learned to stay in the situation, to develop the only thing I had left, to look within for the part of me that no Nazi could ever murder. To find and hold on to my truest self. Maybe I'm not losing skin. Maybe I am only stretching. Stretching to encompass every aspect of who I am—and have been—and can become.

When we heal, we embrace our real and possible selves. I had a patient who was obese, and she was cruel to herself every time she saw her reflection or stepped on a scale. She called herself a cow, disgusting. She believed her husband found her disappointing and her children found her embarrassing, that the people who loved her deserved better. But for her to be the person she wanted to be she first had to love herself for who she was. We sat in my office and I would ask her to pick a part of her body—a toe, a finger, her stomach, her neck, her chin—and talk about it in a loving way. *It looks like this, it feels like this, it is beautiful because . . .* It was awkward at first, even painful. It was easier for her to bash herself than to spend time attentively, willingly, in her own skin. We went slowly, we went gently. I began to notice little changes. She came to see me one day wearing a beautiful bright new scarf. Another day she had treated herself to a pedicure. Another day she told me she had called the sister she had grown distant from. Another time she had discovered that she loved walking on the trail around the park where her daughter played soccer. As she practiced loving all parts of herself, she discovered more joy in her life, and more ease. She also began to lose weight. Release begins with acceptance.

To heal, we embrace the dark. We walk through the shadow of the valley on our way to the light. I worked with a Vietnam veteran who came home desperate to resume the life he had before the war. But he returned with physical and psychological wounds: He was impotent, he couldn't find a job. His wife left him. When he sought my help, he was lost in the chaos of divorce and what felt to him like the death of his sexuality and identity. I gave him all of my compassion, but he was stuck, he was angry, caught in the quicksand of his loss. I felt powerless to help him out. The more I tried to love him back from the pit of despair, the deeper he sank.

As a last resort I decided to try hypnotherapy. I regressed him back to the war, when he was a bomber pilot, when he was in control, before he came home and lost it all. In his hypnotic state, he told me, "In Vietnam, I could drink as much as I wanted to. I could fuck as much as I wanted to." He got red in the face and screamed, "And I could kill as much as I wanted to!" In the war he wasn't killing people; he was killing "gooks," he was killing subhumans. Just as the Nazis weren't killing people at the death camps; they were eradicating a cancer. The war had brought about his injury and altered his life, and yet he missed the war. He missed the sense of power he gained in fighting an enemy, in feeling himself to be in an invulnerable class, above another nationality, above another race.

None of my unconditional love did any good until I gave him permission to express the part of him that he was grieving, the part that was both powerful and dark, the part he could no longer express. I don't mean that he needed to kill again in order to be whole. I mean that to find his way out of victimhood he needed to come to terms with his impotence *and* his power, the ways he had been injured *and* the ways he had hurt, his pride *and* his shame. The only antidote to brokenness is the whole self.

Maybe to heal isn't to erase the scar, or even to make the scar. To heal is to cherish the wound.

It is the middle of the afternoon when we reach Kraków. We will sleep here tonight—or try to. Tomorrow we will take a cab to Auschwitz. Béla wants to tour the Old Town, and I try to pay attention to the medieval architecture, but my mind is too heavy with expectation—a strange mix of promise and dread. We pause outside St. Mary's Church to hear the trumpeter play the *hejnał* that marks the top of every hour. A group of teenage boys jostles past us, joking loudly in Polish, but I don't feel their merriment, I feel anxious. These young men, a little older than my grandchildren, remind me how soon the next generation will come of age. Has my generation taught the youth well enough to prevent another Holocaust from occurring? Or will our hard-won freedom capsize in a new sea of hate?

I have had many opportunities to influence young people—my own children and grandchildren, my former students, the audiences I address around the world, individual patients. On the eve of my return to Auschwitz, my responsibility to them feels especially potent. It isn't just for myself that I'm going back. It's for all that ripples out from me.

Do I have what it takes to make a difference? Can I pass on my strength instead of my loss? My love instead of my hatred?

I've been tested before. A fourteen-year-old boy who had participated in a car theft was sent to me by a judge. The boy wore brown boots, a brown shirt. He leaned his elbow on my desk. He said, "It's time for America to be white again. I'm going to kill all the Jews, all the niggers, all the Mexicans, all the chinks."

I thought I would be sick. I struggled not to run from the room. *What is the meaning of this?* I wanted to shout. I wanted to shake the boy, say, *Who do you think you're talking to? I saw my mother go to the gas chamber.* I would have been justified. And maybe it was my job to set him straight, maybe that's why God had sent him my way. To nip his hate in the bud. I could feel the rush of righteousness. It felt good to be angry. Better angry than afraid.

But then I heard a voice within. *Find the bigot in you*, the voice said. *Find the bigot in you.*

I tried to silence that voice. I listed my many objections to the very notion that I could be a bigot. I came to America penniless. I used the "colored" bathroom in solidarity with my fellow African American factory workers. I marched with Dr. Martin Luther King Jr. to end segregation. But the voice insisted: *Find the bigot in you*. Find the part in you that is judging, assigning labels, diminishing another's humanity, making others less than who they are.

The boy continued to rant about the blights to America's purity. My whole being trembled with unease, and I struggled with the inclination to wag my finger, shake my fist, make him accountable for his hate—without being accountable for my own. This boy didn't kill my parents. Withholding my love wouldn't conquer his prejudice.

I prayed for the ability to meet him with love. I summoned every image I had of unconditional love. I thought of Corrie ten Boom, one of the Righteous Gentiles. She and her family resisted Hitler by hiding hundreds of Jews in their home, and she ended up in a concentration camp herself. Her sister perished there—she died in Corrie's arms. Corrie was released due to a clerical error one day before all of the inmates at Ravensbrück were executed. And a few years after the war, she met one of the most vicious guards at her camp, one of the men who were responsible for her sister's death. She could have spit on him, wished him death, cursed his name. But she prayed for the strength to forgive him, and she took his hands in her own. She says that in that moment, the former prisoner clasping the hands of the former guard, she felt the purest and most profound love. I tried to find that embrace, that compassion, in my own heart, to fill my eyes with that quality of kindness. I wondered if it was possible that this racist boy had been sent to me so I could learn about unconditional love. What opportunity did I have in this moment? What choice could I make right then that could move me in the direction of love?

I had an opportunity to love this young person, just for him, for his singular being and our shared humanity. The opportunity to welcome him to say anything, feel any feeling, without the fear of being judged. I remembered a German family that was stationed for a while at Fort Bliss, how the girl would climb into my lap and call me Oma—Grandma—and this little benediction from a child felt like the answer to the fantasy I'd had as I passed through German towns with Magda and the other inmates, as the children spat at us, when I dreamed of a day when German children would know they didn't have to hate me. And in my own lifetime, that day came to pass. I thought of a statistic I read, that most of the members of white supremacist groups in America lost one of their parents before they were ten years old. These are lost children looking for an identity, looking for a way to feel strength, to feel like they matter.

And so I gathered myself up and I looked at this young man as lovingly as I could. I said three words: "Tell me more."

I didn't say much more than that during his first visit. I listened. I empathized. He was so much like me after the war. We had both lost our parents—his to neglect and abandonment, mine to death. We both thought of ourselves as damaged goods. In letting go of my judgment, in letting go of my desire for him to be or believe anything different, by seeing his vulnerability and his yearning for belonging and love, in allowing myself to get past my own fear and anger in order to accept and love him, I was able to give him something his brown shirt and brown boots couldn't—an authentic image of his own worth. When he left my office that day, he didn't know a thing about my history. But he had seen an alternative to hate and prejudice, he was no longer talking about killing, he had shown me his soft smile. And I had taken responsibility that I not perpetuate hostility and blame, that I not bow to hate and say, *You are too much for me.*

Now, on the eve of my return to prison, I remind myself that each of us has an Adolf Hitler and a Corrie ten Boom within us. We have the capacity to hate and the capacity to love. Which one we reach for—our inner Hitler or inner ten Boom—is up to us.

In the morning, we hire a cab to drive us the hour to Auschwitz. Béla engages the driver in chitchat about his family, his children. I take in the view I didn't see when I was sixteen, when I approached Auschwitz from within the dark of a cattle car. Farms, villages, green. Life continues, as it did all around us when we were imprisoned there.

The driver drops us off, and Béla and I are alone again, standing before my former prison. The wrought-iron sign looms: ARBEIT MACHT FREI, work will set you free. My legs shake at the sight, at the memory of how these words gave my father hope. We will work until the end of the war, he thought. It will last for just a little while, and then we'll be free. *Arbeit Macht Frei.* These words kept us calm until the gas chamber doors locked around our loved ones, until panic was futile. And then these words became a daily, an hourly irony, because here nothing could set you free. Death was the only escape. And so even the idea of freedom became another form of hopelessness.

The grass is lush. The trees have filled in. But the clouds are the color of bone, and beneath them the man-made structures, even the ones in ruins, dominate the landscape. Miles and miles of relentless fence. A vast expanse of crumbling brick barracks and bare rectangular patches where buildings used to stand. The bleak horizontal lines—of barracks, fence, tower—are regular and orderly, but there is no life in this geometry. This is the geometry of systematic torture and death. Mathematical annihilation. And then I notice it again, the thing that haunted me those hellish months when this was my home: I can't see or hear a single bird. No birds live here. Not even now. The sky is bare of their wings, the silence deeper because of the absence of their song.

Tourists gather. Our tour commences. We are a small group of eight or ten. The immensity crushes. I sense it in our stillness, in the way we almost stop breathing. There is no fathoming the enormity of the horror committed in this place. I was here while the fires burned, I woke and worked and slept to the stench of burning corpses, and even I can't fathom it. The brain tries to contain the numbers, tries to take in the confounding accumulation of things that have been assembled and put on display for the visitors—the suitcases wrested from the soon to be dead, the bowls and plates and cups, the thousands upon thousands of pairs of glasses amassed in a tangle like a surreal tumbleweed. The baby clothes crocheted by loving hands for babies who never became children or women or men. The 67-foot-long glass case filled entirely with human hair. We count: 4,700 corpses cremated in each fire, 75,000 Polish dead, 21,000 Gypsies, 15,000 Soviets. The numbers accrue and accrue. We can form the equation—we can do the math that describes the more than one million dead at Auschwitz. We can add that number to the rosters of the dead at the thousands of other death camps in the Europe of my youth, to the corpses dumped in ditches or rivers before they were ever sent to a death camp. But there is no equation that can adequately summarize the effect of such total loss. There is no language that can explain the systematic inhumanity of this human-made death factory. More than one million people were murdered right here where I stand. It is the world's biggest cemetery. And in all the tens, hundreds, thousands, millions of dead, in all the possessions packed and then forcibly relinquished, in all the miles of fence and brick, another number looms. The number zero. Here in the world's biggest cemetery, there is not one single grave. Only the empty spaces where the crematories and gas chambers, hastily destroyed by the Nazis before liberation, stood. The bare patches of ground where my parents died.

We complete the tour of the men's camp. I still must go to the women's side, to Birkenau. That is why I am here. Béla asks if I want him to come with me, but I shake my head. This last piece of the journey I must travel alone.

I leave Béla at the entrance gate and I am back in the past. Music plays through the loudspeakers, festive sounds that contradict the bleak surroundings. *You see*, my father says, *it can't be a terrible place. We'll only work a little, till the war's over.* It is temporary. We can survive this. He joins his line and waves to me. Do I wave back to him? O memory, tell me that I waved to my father before he died.

My mother links her arm in mine. We walk side by side. "Button your coat," she says. "Stand tall." I am back inside the image that has occupied my inward gaze for most of my life: three hungry women in wool coats, arms linked, in a barren yard. My mother. My sister. Me.

I am wearing the coat that I put on that April dawn, I am slim and flat-chested, my hair tucked back under a scarf. My mother scolds me again to stand tall. "You're a woman, not a child," she says. There is a purpose to her nagging. She wants me to look every day of my sixteen years and more. My survival depends on it.

And yet, I won't for the life of me let go of my mother's hand. The guards point and shove. We inch forward in our line. I see Mengele's heavy eyes ahead, the gapped teeth when he grins. He is conducting. He is an eager host. "Is anyone sick?" he asks, solicitous. "Over forty? Under fourteen? Go left, go left."

This is our last chance. To share words, to share silence. To embrace. This time I know it is the end. And still I come up short. I just want my mother to look at me. To reassure me. To look at me and never look away. What is this need I hand to her again and again, this impossible thing I want?

It's our turn now. Dr. Mengele lifts his finger. "Is she your mother or your sister?" he asks.

I cling to my mother's hand, Magda hugs her other side. Although none of us knows the meaning of being sent left, of being sent right, my mother has intuited the need for me to appear my age or older, for me to look old enough to get through the first selection line alive. Her hair is gray but her face is as smooth as mine. She could pass for my sister. But I don't think about which word will protect her: "mother" or "sister." I don't think at all. I only feel every single cell in me that loves her, that needs her. She is my mother, my mama, my only mama. And so I say the word that I have spent the rest of my life trying to banish from my consciousness, the word that I have not let myself remember, until today.

"Mother," I say.

As soon as the word is out of my mouth, I want to pull it back into my throat. I have realized too late the significance of the question. *Is she your mother or your sister?* "Sister, sister, sister!" I want to scream. Mengele points my mother to the left. She follows behind the young children and the elderly, the mothers who are pregnant or holding babies in their arms. I will follow her. I won't let her out of my sight. I begin to run toward my mother, but Mengele grabs my shoulder. "You'll see your mother very soon," he says. He pushes me to the right. Toward Magda. To the other side. To life.

"Mama!" I call. We are separated again, in memory as we were in life, but I will not let memory be another dead end. "Mama!" I say. I will not be satisfied with the back of her head. I must see the full sun of her face.

She turns to look at me. She is a point of stillness in the marching river of the other condemned. I feel her radiance, the beauty that was more than beauty, that she often hid under her sadness and disapproval. She sees me watching her. She smiles. It's a small smile. A sad smile.

"I should have said 'sister'! Why didn't I say 'sister'?" I call to her across the years, to ask her forgiveness. That is what I have returned to Auschwitz to receive, I think. To hear her tell me I did the best with what I knew. That I made the right choice.

But she can't say that, or even if she did, I wouldn't believe it. I can forgive the Nazis, but how can I forgive myself? I would live it all again, every selection line, every shower, every freezing-cold night and deadly roll call, every haunted meal, every breath of smoke-charred air, every time I nearly died or wanted to, if I could only live this moment over, this moment and the one just before it, when I could have made a different choice. When I could have given a different answer to Mengele's question. When I could have saved, if even for a day, my mother's life.

My mother turns away. I watch her gray coat, her soft shoulders, her hair that is coiled and shining, receding from me. I see her walk away with the other women and children, toward the locker rooms, where they will undress, where she will take off the coat that still holds Klara's caul, where they will be told to memorize the hook number where they've stored their clothes, as though they will be returning to that dress, to that coat, to that pair of shoes. My mother will stand naked with the other mothers—the grandmothers, the young mothers with their babies in their arms—and with the children of mothers who were sent to the line that Magda and I joined. She will file down the stairs into the room with showerheads on the walls, where more and more people will be pushed inside until the room is damp with sweat and tears and echoing with the cries of the terrified women and children, until it is packed and there is not enough air to breathe. Will she notice the small square windows in the ceiling through which the guards will push the poison? For how long will she know she is dying? Long enough to think of me and Magda and Klara? Of my father? Long enough to say a prayer to her mother? Long enough to feel angry at me for saying the word that in one quick second sent her to her death?

If I'd known my mother would die that day, I would have said a different word. Or nothing at all. I could have followed her to the showers and died with her. I could have done something different. I could have done more. I believe this.

And yet. (This "and yet" opening like a door.) How easily a life can become a litany of guilt and regret, a song that keeps echoing with the same chorus, with the inability to forgive ourselves. How easily the life we didn't live becomes the only life we prize. How easily we are seduced by the fantasy that we are in control, that we were ever in control, that the things we could or should have done or said have the power, if only we had done or said them, to cure pain, to erase suffering, to vanish loss. How easily we can cling to—worship—the choices we think we could or should have made.

Could I have saved my mother? Maybe. And I will live for all of the rest of my life with that possibility. And I can castigate myself for having made the wrong choice. That is my prerogative. Or I can accept that the more important choice is *not* the one I made when I was hungry and terrified, when we were surrounded by dogs and guns and uncertainty, when I was sixteen; it's the one I make now. The choice to accept myself as I am: human, imperfect. And the choice to be responsible for my own happiness. To forgive my flaws and reclaim my innocence. To stop asking why I deserved to survive. To function as well as I can, to commit myself to serve others, to do everything in my power to honor my parents, to see to it that they did not die in vain. To do my best, in my limited capacity, so future generations don't experience what I did. To be useful, to be used up, to survive and to thrive so I can use every moment to make the world a better place. And to finally, finally stop running from the past. To do everything possible to redeem it, and then let it go. I can make the choice that all of us can make. I can't ever change the past. But there is a life I can save: It is mine. The one I am living right now, this precious moment.

I am ready to go. I take a stone from the ground, a little one, rough, gray, unremarkable. I squeeze the stone. In Jewish tradition, we place small stones on graves as a sign of respect for the dead, to offer mitzvah, or blessing. The stone signifies that the dead live on, in our hearts and memories. The stone in my hand is a symbol of my enduring love for my parents. And it is an emblem of the guilt and the grief I came here to face— something immense and terrifying that all the same I can hold in my hand. It is the death of my parents. It is the death of the life that was. It is what didn't happen. And it is the birth of the life that is. Of the patience and compassion I learned here, the ability to stop judging myself, the ability to respond instead of react. It is the truth and the peace I have come here to discover, and all that I can finally put to rest and leave behind.

I leave the stone on the patch of earth where my barrack used to be, where I slept on a wooden shelf with five other girls, where I closed my eyes as "The Blue Danube" played and I danced for my life. *I miss you*, I say to my parents. *I love you. I'll always love you.*

And to the vast campus of death that consumed my parents and so very many others, to the classroom of horror that still had something sacred to teach me about how to live—that I was victimized but I'm not a victim, that I was hurt but not broken, that the soul never dies, that meaning and purpose can come from deep in the heart of what hurts us the most—I utter my final words. *Goodbye*, I say. And, *Thank you*. Thank you for life, and for the ability to finally accept the life that is.

* * *

I walk toward the iron gate of my old prison, toward Béla waiting for me on the grass. Out of the corner of my eye I see a man in uniform pacing back and forth under the sign. He is a museum guard, not a soldier. But it is impossible, when I see him marching in his uniform, not to freeze, not to hold my breath, not to expect the shout of a gun, the blast of bullets. For a split second I am a terrified girl again, a girl who is in danger. I am the imprisoned me. But I breathe, I wait for the moment to pass. I feel for the blue American passport in my coat pocket. The guard reaches the wrought-iron sign and turns around, marching back into the prison. He must stay here. It is his duty to stay. But I can leave. I am free!

I leave Auschwitz. I skip out! I pass under the words ARBEIT MACHT FREI. How cruel and mocking those words were when we realized that nothing we could do would set us free. But as I leave the barracks and the ruined crematories and the watch houses and the visitors and the museum guard behind me, as I skip under the dark iron letters toward my husband, I see the words spark with truth. Work *has* set me free. I survived so that I could do my work. Not the work the Nazis meant—the hard labor of sacrifice and hunger, of exhaustion and enslavement. It was the inner work. Of learning to survive and thrive, of learning to forgive myself, of helping others to do the same. And when I do this work, then I am no longer the hostage or the prisoner of anything. I am free.

PART IV

Healing

CHAPTER 20

The Dance of Freedom

One of the last times I saw Viktor Frankl was at the Third World Congress on Logotherapy, in Regensburg in 1983. He was almost eighty; I was fifty-six. In many ways I was the same person who had fallen into a panic in an El Paso lecture hall when I put a little paperback book into my bag. I still spoke English with a thick accent. I still had flashbacks. I still carried painful images and mourned the losses of the past. But I no longer felt like I was the victim of anything. I felt—and will always feel—tremendous love and gratitude for my two liberators: the GI who pulled me from a heap of bodies at Gunskirchen, and Viktor Frankl, who gave me permission not to hide anymore, who helped me find words for my experience, who helped me to cope with my pain. Through his mentorship and friendship, I discovered a purpose in my suffering, a sense of meaning that helped me not only to come to peace with the past but also to emerge from my trials with something precious worth sharing: a path to freedom. The last night of the conference, we danced. There we were, two aging dancers. Two people enjoying the sacred present. Two survivors who had learned to thrive and be free.

My decades-long friendship with Viktor Frankl, and my healing relationships with all of my patients, including those I've been describing, have taught me the same important lesson that I began studying at Auschwitz: Our painful experiences aren't a liability—they're a gift. They give us perspective and meaning, an opportunity to find our unique purpose and our strength.

There is no one-size-fits-all template for healing, but there are steps that can be learned and practiced, steps that each individual can weave together in his or her own way, steps in the dance of freedom.

My first step in the dance was to take responsibility for my feelings. To stop repressing and avoiding them, and to stop blaming them on Béla or other people, to accept them as my own. This was a vital step in Captain Jason Fuller's healing too. Like me, he was in the habit of cutting his feelings off, of running from them until they got big enough to control him, instead of the other way around. I told him that he couldn't avoid pain by avoiding his feelings. He had to take responsibility for experiencing—and eventually expressing—them safely, and then for letting them go.

In those early weeks of treatment, I taught him a mantra for managing his emotions: *notice, accept, check, stay.* When a feeling started to overwhelm him, the first action toward managing the feeling was to notice—to acknowledge—that he was having a feeling. He could say to himself, *Aha! Here I go again. This is anger. This is jealousy. This is sadness.* (My Jungian therapist taught me something that I find quite comforting—that although it feels like the palette of human feelings is limitless, in fact every emotional shade, like every color, is derived from just a few primary emotions: sad, mad, glad, scared. For those just learning an emotional vocabulary, as I was, it's less overwhelming to learn to identify only four feelings.)

Once he could name his feelings, Jason needed to accept that those feelings were his own. They might be triggered by someone else's actions or speech, but they were his. Lashing out at someone else wasn't going to make them go away.

Then, once he was there with the feeling, he was to check his body response. *Am I hot? Cold? Is my heart racing? How's my breathing? Am I okay?*

Tuning into the feeling itself, and to how it was moving in his body, would help him stay with it until it passed or changed. He didn't have to cover, medicate, or run from his feelings. He could choose to feel them. They were only feelings. He could accept them, bear them, stay with them—because they were temporary.

Once Jason was more adept at tuning in to his feelings, we practiced how to respond to them, instead of reacting. Jason had learned to live like he was in a pressure cooker. He kept himself under tight control—until he burst. I helped him learn to be more like a teapot, to vent off the steam. Sometimes he'd come to a session and I'd ask him how he was feeling, and he'd say, "I feel like screaming." And I'd say, "Okay! Let's scream. Let's get it all out so it doesn't make you ill."

As Jason learned to accept and face his feelings, he also began to see that in many ways he was re-creating the fear, repression, and violence of his childhood in his current family. The need to control his feelings, learned at the hand of an abusive father, had translated into a need to control his wife and his children.

Sometimes our healing helps us to repair our relationships with our partners; sometimes our healing releases the other person to do his or her own growth. After a few months of joining him for couples counseling, Jason's wife told him that she was ready to separate. Jason was shocked and furious. I was concerned that his grief over the failed marriage would govern how he treated his children. At first Jason was vindictive and wanted to fight for full custody, but he was able to shift his all-or-nothing mind-set, and he and his wife worked out an agreement to share custody. He was able to mend and nurture his relationships with the people who had inspired him to drop the gun: his kids. He ended the legacy of violence.

Once we are recognizing and taking responsibility for our feelings, we can learn to recognize and take responsibility for our role in the dynamic that shapes our relationships. As I learned in my marriage, and in my relationships with my children, one of the proving grounds for our freedom is in how we relate to our loved ones. This is something that comes up frequently in my work.

Jun wore pressed slacks and a button-up shirt the morning I met him. Ling stepped through the door in a perfectly tailored skirt and blazer, her makeup expertly applied and her hair carefully coiffed. Jun sat at one end of the couch, his eyes going over the framed diplomas and photographs on my office walls, looking everywhere except at Ling. She perched neatly on the edge of the couch and looked right at me. "This is the problem," she said without preamble. "My husband drinks too much."

Jun's face reddened. He seemed on the verge of speaking, but he kept quiet.

"It has to stop," Ling said.

I asked what "it" was. What were the behaviors she found so objectionable?

According to Ling, over the last year or two, Jun's drinking had gone from an occasional evening or weekend activity to an everyday ritual. He began before he came home, with a scotch at a bar near the university campus where he was a professor. That drink was followed at home by another, and another. By the time they sat down for dinner with their two children, his eyes were a little glassy, his voice a little too loud, his jokes a little too off-color. Ling felt lonely and burdened by the responsibility of marching the kids through cleanup and bedtime routines. By the time she was ready for sleep, she was simmering with frustration. When I asked about their intimate life, Ling blushed, and then told me that Jun used to initiate sex when they went to bed, but often she was too upset to reciprocate. Now he usually fell asleep on the couch.

"That's not all," she said. She was listing all the evidence. "He breaks dishes because he's drunk. He comes home late. He forgets things that I tell him. He's driving drunk. He's going to get in an accident. How can I trust him to drive the kids?"

As Ling spoke, Jun seemed to disappear. His eyes dropped to his lap. He looked hurt, reserved, ashamed—and angry, but his hostility was directed inward. I asked Jun for his perspective on their daily life.

"I'm always responsible with the kids," he said. "She has no right to accuse me of putting them in danger."

"What about your relationship with Ling? How do you see your marriage working?"

He shrugged. "I'm here," he said.

"I notice a big space between you on the couch. Is that an accurate indication of a big gulf between you?"

Ling gripped her purse.

"It's accurate," Jun said.

"It's because he drinks!" Ling interjected. "That's what's making this distance."

"It sounds like there's a lot of anger there pushing you apart."

Ling looked quickly at her husband before nodding.

I see a lot of couples locked in the same dance. She nags, he drinks. He drinks, she nags. That's the choreography they've chosen. But what if one of them changes the steps? "I wonder," I began. "I wonder if your marriage would survive if Jun stopped drinking."

Jun's jaw clenched. Ling loosened her hold on her purse. "Exactly," she said. "This is what needs to happen."

"What would really happen if Jun stopped drinking?" I asked.

I told them about another couple I know. The husband was also a drinker. One day, he'd had enough. He didn't want to drink anymore. He wanted to get help. He decided that rehab was the best option, and he started working hard on his sobriety. This was precisely what his wife had been praying would happen. They both expected his sobriety to be the solution to all their problems. But as his recovery progressed, their marriage got worse. When the wife visited the rehab facility, angry and bitter feelings would surface. She couldn't stop herself from rehashing the past. *Remember five years ago when you came home and threw up all over my favorite rug? And that other time you ruined our anniversary party?* She couldn't keep from reciting a litany of all the mistakes he'd made, all the ways he'd hurt and disappointed her. The better her husband got, the worse she became. He felt stronger, less toxic, less ashamed, more in touch with himself, more tuned in to his life and relationships. And she grew more and more enraged. He let go of the drinking, but she couldn't let go of the criticism and blame.

I call this the seesaw. One person's up, and one person's down. Lots of marriages and relationships are built this way. Two people agree to an unspoken contract: One of them will be good and one of them will be bad. The whole system relies on one person's inadequacy. The "bad" partner gets a free pass to test all the limits; the "good" partner gets to say, *Look how selfless I am! Look how patient I am! Look at everything I put up with!*

But what happens if the "bad" one in the relationship gets sick of that role? What if he shows up to audition for the other part? Then the "good" one's place in the relationship is no longer secure. She's got to remind him how bad he is so she can keep her position. Or she might become bad—hostile, explosive—so that they can still balance the seesaw even if they switch positions. Either way, blame is the pivot that keeps the two seats joined.

In a lot of cases, someone else's actions really do contribute to our discomfort and unhappiness. I'm not suggesting that we should be okay with behavior that is hurtful or destructive. But we remain victims as long as we hold another person responsible for our own well-being. If Ling says, "I can only be happy and at peace if Jun stops drinking," she leaves herself vulnerable to a life of sorrow and unrest. Her happiness will always be a bottle or a swig away from disaster. Likewise, if Jun says, "The only reason I drink is because Ling is so nagging and critical," he gives up all of his freedom of choice. He isn't his own agent. He is Ling's puppet. He might get the temporary relief of a buzz as a protection against her unkindness, but he won't be free.

So often when we are unhappy it is because we are taking too much responsibility or we are taking too little. Instead of being assertive and choosing clearly for ourselves, we might become aggressive (choosing for others), or passive (letting others choose for us), or passive-aggressive (choosing for others by preventing them from achieving what they are choosing for themselves). It gives me no pleasure to admit that I used to be passive-aggressive with Béla. He was very punctual, it was important to him to be on time, and when I was annoyed with him, I would stall when it was time to leave the house. I would intentionally find a way to slow us down, to make us late, just to spite him. He was choosing to arrive on time, and I wouldn't let him get what he wanted.

I told Ling and Jun that in blaming each other for their unhappiness, they were avoiding the responsibility of making their own joy. While on the surface they both seemed very assertive—Ling always on Jun's case, Jun doing what he pleased instead of what Ling asked him to do—they were both experts at avoiding an honest expression of "I want" or "I am." Ling used the *words* "I want"—"I want my husband to stop drinking"—but in wanting something for someone else, she escaped having to know what she wanted for herself. And Jun could rationalize his drinking by saying that his drinking was Ling's fault, a way to assert himself against her oppressive expectations and criticisms. But if you give up the authority of your own choices, then you are agreeing to be a victim—and a prisoner.

In the Haggadah, the Jewish text that tells the story of liberation from slavery in Egypt and teaches the prayers and rituals for seder, the special Passover feast, there are four questions that the youngest member of the family traditionally gets to ask—the questions it was my privilege to ask at my childhood seders, that I asked the last night I spent with my parents in our home. In my therapeutic practice I have my own version of the four questions, which I developed years ago with the help of several colleagues when we were sharing strategies for beginning a session with a new patient. These are the questions I asked Ling and Jun to answer now, in writing, so they could liberate themselves from their victimhood.

1. *What do you want?* This is a deceptively simple question. It can be much more difficult than we realize to give ourselves permission to know and listen to ourselves, to align ourselves with our desires. How often when we answer this question do we say what we want for someone else? I reminded Ling and Jun that they needed to answer this question for themselves. To say *I want Jun to stop drinking* or *I want Ling to stop nagging* was to avoid the question.

2. *Who wants it?* This is our charge and our struggle: to understand our own expectations for ourselves versus trying to live up to others' expectations of us. My father became a tailor because his father wouldn't allow him to become a doctor. My father was good at his profession, he was commended and awarded for it—but he was never the one who wanted it, and he always regretted his unlived dream. It's our responsibility to act in service of our authentic selves. Sometimes this means giving up the need to please others, giving up our need for others' approval.

3. *What are you going to do about it?* I believe in the power of positive thinking—but change and freedom also require positive action. Anything we practice, we become better at. If we practice anger, we'll have more anger. If we practice fear, we'll have more fear. In many cases, we actually work very hard to ensure that we go nowhere. Change is about noticing what's no longer working and stepping out of the familiar, imprisoning patterns.

4. *When?* In *Gone with the Wind,* my mother's favorite book, Scarlett O'Hara, when confronted with a difficulty, says, "*I'll think about it tomorrow. . . . After all, tomorrow is another day.*" If we are to evolve instead of revolve, it's time to take action now.

Ling and Jun finished their responses to the questions, folded up their papers, handed them to me. We would look at them together the following week. As they got up to leave, Jun shook my hand. And then, walking out the door, I saw the reassurance I needed that they were willing to try to bridge the distance they had let damage their marriage, to get off the seesaw of blame. Ling turned back to Jun and gave him a hesitant smile. I couldn't see if he returned it—his back was to me—but I did see him gently pat her shoulder.

When we met the following week, Ling and Jun discovered something they wouldn't have predicted. In response to the question "What do you want?" they had each written the same thing: *A happy marriage.* Just speaking this desire, they were already on their way to having what they wanted. All they needed was some new tools.

I asked Ling to work on changing her behavior in the moments after Jun got home each day. This was the time when she usually felt most angry and vulnerable and frightened. Would he be drunk? How drunk would he be? How drunk would he get? Was there any possibility of closeness between them, or would it be another evening of distance and hostility? She had learned to manage her fear by trying to exert control. She would sniff Jun's breath, make accusations, pull away. I taught her to greet her husband the same way whether he was sober or drunk— with kind eyes and a simple statement: "I'm happy to see you. I'm glad you're home." If he was drunk, and she was hurt and disappointed, she was allowed to talk about those feelings. She could say, "I can see you've been drinking, and that makes me feel sad because it's hard to feel close to you when you're drunk" or "that makes me feel worried about your safety." And she was allowed to make choices for herself in response to his choice to drink. She could say, "I was hoping to talk to you tonight, but I can see you've been drinking. I'm going to do something else instead."

I talked to Jun about the physiological components of addiction, and told him that I could help him heal whatever pain he was trying to medicate with alcohol, and that if he chose to get sober, he would need additional support in treating his addiction. I asked him to go to three AA meetings and see if he recognized himself in any of the stories he heard there. He did go to the assigned meetings, but as far as I know he never went back. In the time that I worked with him, he didn't stop drinking.

When Ling and Jun ended their therapy, some things were better for them and some things weren't. They were better able to listen to each other without the need to be right, and they were spending more time on the other side of anger, where they could acknowledge their sadness and fear. There was more warmth between them. But a loneliness remained. And the fear that Jun's drinking would spiral out of control.

Their story is a good reminder that it isn't over till it's over. As long as you live, there's the risk that you might suffer more. There's also the opportunity to find a way to suffer less, to choose happiness, which requires taking responsibility for yourself.

Trying to be the caretaker who sees to another person's every need is as problematic as avoiding your responsibility to yourself. This is something that has been an issue for me—as it is for many psychotherapists. I had an epiphany about this when I was working with a single mother of five who was unemployed and physically challenged in addition to being depressed. She had a hard time leaving the house. I was happy to step in to pick up her welfare checks and get her children to their appointments and activities. As her therapist, I felt it was my responsibility to help her in any way possible. But one day as I stood in line at the welfare office, feeling benevolent and generous and worthy, a voice inside me said, "Edie, whose needs are being met?" I realized the answer wasn't "my dear patient's." The answer was "mine." In doing things for her, I felt very good about myself. But at what cost? I was fueling her dependence—and her hunger. She had already been depriving herself for a long time of something she could find only within, and while I thought I was sustaining her health and well-being, I was actually sustaining her deprivation. It's okay to help people—and it's okay to need help—but when your enabling allows others not to help themselves, then you're crippling the people you want to help.

I used to ask my patients, "How can I help you?" But that kind of question makes them Humpty Dumpty, waiting around on the pavement to be put back together again. And it makes me the king's horses and the king's men, ultimately powerless to fix another person. I've changed my question. Now I say, "How can I be useful to you?" How can I support you as you take responsibility for yourself?

* * *

I've never met a person who would consciously choose to live in captivity. Yet I've witnessed again and again how willingly we hand over our spiritual and mental freedom, choosing to give another person or entity the responsibility of guiding our lives, of choosing for us. A young couple helped me understand the consequences of abdicating this responsibility, of turning it over to someone else. They struck a special chord in me because of their youth, because they were in the phase of life when most of us are hungry for autonomy—and, ironically, the time when we may be particularly anxious about whether we are ready for it, strong enough to bear the weight of it.

When Elise sought my help, she had reached suicidal despair. She was twenty-one years old, her curly blond hair gathered in a ponytail. Her eyes were red from crying. She wore a man's large athletic jersey that came almost to her knees. I sat with Elise in the bright October sun as she tried to explain the roots of her anguish: Todd.

A charismatic, ambitious, handsome basketball player, Todd was a near celebrity on campus. She had met him two years ago, when she was a freshman in college and he was a sophomore. Everyone knew Todd. The revelation for Elise was that he wanted to get to know *her*. He was physically attracted to her, and he liked that Elise didn't try too hard to impress him. She wasn't superficial. Their personalities seemed complementary— she was quiet and shy, he was talkative and outgoing; she was an observer, he a performer. They hadn't been dating long before Todd asked her to move in with him.

Elise brightened as she recounted the early months of their relationship. She said that in the spotlight of Todd's affection, for the first time she felt not just good enough, she felt extraordinary. It wasn't that she had ever felt neglected or deprived or unloved as a child or in her earlier relationships, but Todd's attention made her feel alive in a new way. She loved the feeling.

Unfortunately, it was a feeling that came and went. Sometimes she felt insecure in their relationship. Especially at basketball games and parties, when other women flirted with Todd, she would feel chills of jealousy or inadequacy. Sometimes she scolded Todd after parties if he had appeared to flirt back. Sometimes he would reassure her, sometimes he would express irritation at her insecurities. She tried not to be the nagging girlfriend. She tried to find ways to be indispensable to him. She became his main academic support. He struggled to maintain the passing grades that his athletic scholarship required. At first Elise helped him study for tests. Then she started helping with his homework. Soon she was writing his papers for him, staying up late to do his work in addition to her own.

Consciously or not, Elise found a way to make Todd dependent on her. The relationship would have to last, because he needed her in order to maintain his scholarship and everything it enabled. The feeling of being indispensable was so intoxicating and soothing that Elise's life became organized around one equation: The more I do for him, the more he'll love me. Without realizing it, she had begun to equate her sense of self-worth with having his love.

Recently, Todd had confessed something that Elise had always feared would happen: He had slept with another woman. She was angry and hurt. He was apologetic and tearful. But he hadn't been able to break things off with the other woman. He loved her. He was sorry. He hoped he and Elise could still be friends.

Elise could barely force herself to leave the apartment that first week. She had no appetite. She couldn't get dressed. She was terrified of being alone, and she was ashamed. She realized how completely she had let her relationship direct her life—and at what cost. Then Todd called. He wanted to know if she could do a huge favor for him if she wasn't too busy. He had a paper due on Monday. Could she write it?

She wrote the paper for him. And the next one. And the next one.

"I gave him everything," she said. She was crying.

"Honey, that was your first mistake. You martyred yourself to him. What was in it for you?"

"I wanted him to be successful, and he was so happy when I helped."

"And what's happening now?"

She told me that yesterday she had learned from a mutual friend that Todd and the new woman had moved in together. And he had a paper due the next day that she had agreed to write.

"I know he's not coming back to me. I know I have to stop doing his homework. But I can't stop."

"Why not?"

"I love him. I know I can still make him happy if I do his work for him."

"And how about you? Are you becoming the best you can be? Are you making yourself happy?"

"You make me feel like I'm doing the wrong thing."

"When you stop doing what's best for you and start doing what you think someone else needs, you are making a choice that has consequences for you. It has consequences for Todd too. What does your choice to devote yourself to helping him say to him about his ability to meet his own challenges?"

"I can help him. I'm there for him."

"You really have no confidence in him either."

"I want him to love me."

"At the cost of his growth? At the cost of your life?"

I was very worried about Elise when she left my office. Her despair was profound. But I didn't believe she would take her own life. She wanted to change, which was why she had come to seek help. Still, I gave her my home phone number and the number to a suicide hotline and asked that she check in with me every day until her next appointment.

When Elise returned the next week, I was surprised to see that she brought a young man with her. It was Todd. Elise was all smiles. Her depression was over, she said. Todd had broken up with the other woman and she and Todd had reconciled. She felt renewed. She could see now that her neediness and insecurity had pushed him away. She would try harder to trust in the relationship, to show him how committed she was.

During the session, Todd looked impatient and bored, glancing at the clock, shifting in his seat as though his legs were falling asleep.

"There is no such thing as getting back together without a new beginning. What's the new relationship you want? What are you willing to give up to get there?" I asked.

They stared at me.

"Let's start with what you have in common. What do you love to do together?"

Todd looked at the clock. Elise scooted closer to him.

"Here's your homework," I said. "I want you to each find one new thing you like to do by yourself, and one new thing you like to do together. It can't be basketball or homework or sex. Do something fun and get out of the familiar."

Elise and Todd returned to my office occasionally over the next six months. Sometimes Elise came alone. Her main focus continued to be on preserving their relationship, but nothing she did was enough to erase her insecurities and doubts. She wanted to feel better, but she wasn't yet willing to change. And Todd, when he came to the appointments, seemed stuck too. He was getting everything he thought he wanted—admiration, success, love (not to mention good grades)—but he looked sad. He slumped, he receded. It was as if his self-respect and self-confidence had atrophied because of his dependence on Elise.

Eventually, Elise and Todd's visits tapered off, and I didn't hear from either of them for many months. And then one day

I received two graduation announcements. One was from Elise. She had finished her degree and been accepted to a master's program in comparative literature. She thanked me for the time we spent together. She said that one day she woke up, and she had had enough. She stopped doing Todd's schoolwork. Their relationship ended, which had been very hard, but now she was grateful that she hadn't settled for whatever she had been choosing in place of love.

The other graduation announcement was from Todd. He was graduating—a year late, but he was graduating. And he wanted to thank me too. He told me that he had almost dropped out of school when Elise stopped doing his homework for him. He was indignant and furious. But then he took responsibility for his own life, hired a tutor, and accepted that he was going to have to put in some effort on his own behalf. "I was a punk," he wrote. He said that without realizing it, the whole time he had relied on Elise to do his work for him, he'd been depressed. He hadn't liked himself. Now he could look in the mirror and feel respect instead of contempt.

Viktor Frankl writes, *Man's search for meaning is the primary motivation in his life. . . . This meaning is unique and specific in that it must and can be fulfilled by him alone; only then does it achieve a significance which will satisfy his own* will *to meaning.* When we abdicate taking responsibility for ourselves, we are giving up our ability to create and discover meaning. In other words, we give up on life.

CHAPTER 21

The Girl Without Hands

The second step in the dance of freedom is learning how to take risks that are necessary to true self-realization. The biggest risk I took on that journey was to return to Auschwitz. There were people on the outside—Marianne's host family, the clerk at the Polish embassy—telling me not to go. And there was my internal gatekeeper, the part of me that wanted to be safe more than I wanted to be free. But the night I lay awake in Goebbels's bed, I intuited the truth that I wouldn't be a complete person until I went back, that for my own health I needed to be in that place again. Taking risks doesn't mean throwing ourselves blindly into danger. But it means embracing our fears so that we aren't imprisoned by them.

Carlos began to work with me when he was a high school sophomore, struggling with social anxiety and self-acceptance. He was so afraid of being rejected by his peers that he wouldn't risk initiating friendships or relationships. One day I asked him to tell me about the ten most popular girls at his school. And then I gave him an assignment. He was to ask each of these girls out on a date. He told me that was impossible, that he would be committing social suicide, that they would never go out with him, that he would be laughed at for the rest of his high school days for having been so pathetic. I told him, yes, it's true, you might not get what you want—but even if you don't, you'll still be better off than you were before, because you'll know where you stand, you'll have more information, and you'll be seeing what's actually real instead of a reality created by your fear. Finally, he agreed to the assignment. And to his surprise, four of the most popular girls accepted! He'd already made up his mind about his worth, he'd already rejected himself five hundred times in his own head, and that fear had been coming through in his body language—in eyes that were hooded and averted instead of sparkling, connecting. He had made himself unavailable for joy. Once he embraced his fear and his choices and took a risk, he discovered possibilities that he hadn't known existed.

A few years later, on an autumn day in 2007, Carlos called me from his college dorm room. Anxiety pinched his voice. "I need help," he said. Now he was a sophomore at a Big Ten university in the Midwest. When I heard from him out of the blue, I thought that perhaps his social anxieties had again become overwhelming.

"Tell me what's happening," I said.

It was pledge week on campus, he said. I already knew that it had been his dream since he was in high school to belong to a fraternity. Once he began college, the dream had become even more important to him, he told me. Greek life was a significant piece of his university's social fabric, and all of his friends were pledging, so being in a frat seemed necessary to his social survival. He had heard rumors about inappropriate hazing rituals at other fraternities, but he had chosen his fraternity carefully. He liked the racial diversity of the members and the fraternity's emphasis on social service. It seemed like a perfect fit. While many of his friends were anxious about the hazing process, Carlos wasn't worried about it. He believed that hazing had a purpose, that it helped the young men to bond more quickly, as long as it wasn't over the top.

But pledge week was not turning out as Carlos had imagined.

"What's different?" I asked.

"My pledge master's on a power trip." He told me that the pledge master was incredibly aggressive, seeking out every pledge's weak spots and pushing hard on them. He called one young man's taste in music "gay." During a pledge meeting, he looked at Carlos and said, "You look like a guy who should be mowing my lawn."

"How did you feel when he said that?"

"I was so mad. I wanted to punch him in the face."

"What did you do?"

"Nothing. He was just trying to get me worked up. I didn't react."

"What happened next?"

Carlos told me that that morning, the pledge master ordered him and the other pledges to clean the frat house, assigning them different jobs. He handed Carlos a toilet brush and a bottle of cleaner. Then he gave Carlos a huge sombrero. "You're going to wear this while you scrub the toilets. You're going to wear this when you leave and go to class. And the only words you're allowed to say all day are, '*Sí, señor.*'" It was a public shaming, an appalling act of racism, but if Carlos wanted to join the fraternity, he would have to force himself to endure it.

"I felt like I couldn't say no," Carlos told me. His voice shook. "It was awful. But I did it. I didn't want to lose my spot just because the pledge master's an asshole. I didn't want to let him win."

"I can hear how angry you are."

"I'm furious. And embarrassed. And confused. I feel like I should have been able to take it without it upsetting me."

"Tell me more."

"I know it's not the same at all, but while I was scrubbing toilets in the sombrero, I thought about that story you told me about when you were at the death camp, when you were forced to dance. I remember you said that you were scared, and you were in prison, but you felt free. That the guards were more imprisoned than you. I know the pledge master's an idiot. Why can't I just do what he wants me to do and still feel free inside? You've always told me it's not what's happening outside that matters, it's what's inside. I'm proud of my Mexican identity. Why should his bullshit matter to me? Why can't I just rise above it?"

It was a beautiful question. Where does our power reside? Is it enough to find our inner strength, our inner truth, or does empowerment also require that we take action on the outside? I do believe it's what's happening inside that matters most. I also believe in the necessity of living in congruence with our values and ideals—with our moral selves. I believe in the importance of defending what is right and defying what is unjust and inhumane. And I believe in choices. Freedom lies in examining the choices available to us and examining the consequences of those choices. "The more choices you have," I said, "the less you're going to feel like a victim. Let's talk about your choices."

We made a list. One choice was for Carlos to wear the sombrero around campus the rest of the day, saying only, "*Sí, señor.*" He could agree to submit to whatever other humiliations his pledge master devised.

Another choice was to object. He could tell the pledge master he refused to comply.

Or he could withdraw his application to the fraternity. He could put down the sombrero and the scrub brush and walk away.

Carlos didn't like the consequences of any of these choices. He didn't like the shame and powerlessness he felt in capitulating to a bully, especially when the humiliations were racist. He felt he couldn't continue to play the racist caricature without eroding his self-respect—if he continued giving in to a bully, he would make the bully stronger and himself weaker. But outright defiance of the pledge master could be physically dangerous and socially isolating. Carlos was afraid of being assaulted—and of responding in kind. He didn't want to get swallowed by violent urges, he didn't want to fall into the pledge master's trap of trying to rile him, he didn't want to participate in a public showdown. He was also afraid of being ostracized by the fraternity and the other pledges—the very community whose acceptance he was trying to court. The third choice—to walk away—wasn't any better. He would have to give up his dream, give up his desire of belonging, and he wasn't willing to do that.

In sifting through the available options, Carlos discovered a fourth choice. Instead of confronting the pledge master directly in what he feared would become a violent fight, he could file a complaint with someone who had more authority. Carlos decided that the best person to approach was the fraternity president. He knew he could bring the issue higher up the ladder, to a university dean, if necessary, but he preferred to keep the conversation more local at first. We practiced what he was going to say, and how he would say it. It was hard for him to remain calm while he rehearsed, but he knew from our years of work together that when you lose your temper, you might feel strong in the moment, but really you are handing your power over. Strength isn't reacting, it's responding—feeling your feelings, thinking them over, and planning an effective action to bring you closer to your goal.

Carlos and I also talked about the possible consequences of his conversation. It was possible that the fraternity president would tell Carlos that the pledge master's behavior was acceptable, and that Carlos could take it or leave it.

"If that's how the president sees it, I guess I'd rather know than not know," Carlos said.

Carlos called me after his meeting with the fraternity president.

"I did it!" His voice rang with triumph. "I told him what was happening, and he said it was disgusting and he wouldn't tolerate it. He's forcing the pledge master to stop the racist hazing."

Of course I was happy that Carlos was being validated and supported, and happy that he did not have to give up his dream. But I believe it would have been a triumphant encounter no matter the fraternity president's response. Carlos had embraced his power to stand up and speak his truth at the risk of being excluded and criticized. He had chosen not to be a victim. And he had taken a moral stand. He had acted in alignment with a higher purpose: to combat racism, to protect human dignity. In defending his own humanity, he protected everyone's. He paved a way for all of us to live in keeping with our moral truth and ideals. Doing what is right is rarely the same as doing what is safe.

I think that a certain amount of risk is always inseparable from healing. It was true for Beatrice, a sad woman when I met her, her brown eyes distant, closed off, her face pale. Her clothes were loose and formless, her posture slumping and hunched over. I immediately recognized that Beatrice had no idea how beautiful she was.

She stared straight ahead, trying hard not to look at me. But she couldn't stop herself from shooting me quick glances that seemed to probe me for secrets. She had recently heard me give a talk about forgiveness. For more than twenty years, she had believed that there was no way to achieve forgiveness over her stolen childhood. But my speech about my own journey of forgiveness had sparked questions for her. *Should I forgive? Can I forgive?* Now she assessed me carefully, as though trying to discover if I was real, or just an image. When you're listening to someone up on a stage tell a story about healing, it can seem too good to be true. And to some extent, it is. In the hard work of healing, there's no catharsis when forty-five minutes are up. There's no magic wand. Change happens slowly, sometimes disappointingly slowly. *Is your story of freedom genuine?* her darting glances seemed to ask. *Is there any hope for me?*

Because she had been referred to me by another psychologist—a dear friend of mine, the same person who had encouraged Beatrice to come hear me speak—I already knew some of Beatrice's history. *When did your childhood end?* I often ask my patients. Beatrice's childhood had ended almost as soon as it began. Her parents had been extremely neglectful of her and her siblings, sending them to school unwashed and unfed. The nuns at Beatrice's school spoke sharply to her and blamed her for her unkempt appearance, scolding her to clean up and eat breakfast before she came to school. Beatrice internalized the message that her parents' neglect was her fault.

Then, when she was eight, one of her parents' friends began molesting her. The molestations continued, though she tried to resist. She also tried to tell her parents what was happening, but they accused her of making it up. On her tenth birthday, her parents let their friend, who by then had been touching her inappropriately for two years, take her on a "date" to the movies. After the movie he took her to his home and raped her in the shower. When Beatrice began her treatment with me, at age thirty-five, the smell of popcorn still triggered flashbacks.

At age eighteen Beatrice had married a recovering addict who was emotionally and physically cruel to her. She had escaped her family drama only to re-enact it, reinforcing her belief that being loved meant being hurt. Beatrice was eventually able to divorce her husband and had been finding a way forward in her life, with a new career and a new relationship, when she was raped on a trip to Mexico. She came home devastated.

At the insistence of her girlfriend, Beatrice began therapy with my colleague. She was ridden with anxiety and phobias and could hardly get out of bed. She felt a constant heavy, oppressive dread, and lived on high alert, afraid to leave her house for fear of being assaulted again, and afraid of the smells and associations that triggered debilitating flashbacks.

In her first sessions with my colleague, Beatrice agreed to get up every morning, take a shower, make her bed, and then sit on a stationary bike in her living room for fifteen minutes with the TV on for comfort. Beatrice wasn't in denial about her trauma, as I had once been. She had been able to talk about the past and to process it intellectually. But she hadn't yet grieved for her interrupted life. Over time, on the exercise bike, Beatrice learned to sit with the emptiness, to trust that grief is not an illness (though it can feel like one), and understand that when we anesthetize our feelings, with eating or alcohol or other compulsive behaviors, we just prolong our suffering. At first, during the fifteen minutes a day on the exercise bike, Beatrice didn't pedal. She just sat. A minute or two into her sit she would begin to cry. She cried until the timer rang. As the weeks passed, she spent a little longer on the bike—twenty minutes, then twenty-five. By the time she was sitting for thirty-minute stretches, she started to move the pedals. And little by little, day by day, she bicycled her way into her body's caches of pain.

By the time I met Beatrice, she had already done a tremendous amount of work in the service of her healing. Her grief work had diminished her depression and anxiety. She felt much better. But after hearing my speech at the community center event, she had wondered if there was more she could do to free herself from the pain of her trauma. The possibility of forgiveness had taken root.

"Forgiveness isn't you forgiving your molester for what he did to you," I told her. "It's you forgiving the part of yourself that was victimized and letting go of all blame. If you are willing, I can help guide you to your freedom. It will be like going over a bridge. It's scary to look down below. But I'll be right here with you. What do you think? Do you want to continue?"

A dim light sparked in her brown eyes. She nodded her head.

Several months after she began therapy with me, Beatrice was ready to take me mentally into her father's study, where the molestations had occurred. This is an extremely vulnerable stage in the therapeutic process, and there is an ongoing debate in the psychology and neuroscience communities about how useful or harmful it is for a patient to mentally relive a traumatic situation, or physically return to a site of trauma. When I received my training, I learned to use hypnosis in order to help survivors re-experience the traumatic event in order to stop being hostage to it. In more recent years, studies have shown that putting someone mentally back in a traumatic experience can be dangerous—psychologically reliving a painful event can actually retraumatize a survivor. For example, after the September 11 attacks on the World Trade Center, it was discovered that the more times people saw the image of the towers going down on TV, the more trauma they had years later. Repeated encounters with a past event can reinforce rather than release the fearful and painful feelings. In my practice and in my own experience, I have seen the effectiveness of mentally reliving a traumatic episode, but it must be done with absolute safety, and with a well-trained professional who can give the patient control over how long and how deeply he or she stays in the past. Even then, it isn't the best practice for all patients or all therapists.

For Beatrice, it was essential to her healing. To free herself from her trauma, she needed permission to feel what she hadn't been allowed to feel when the abuse was taking place, or in the three decades since. Until she could experience those feelings, they would scream for her attention, and the more she tried to suppress them, the more violently they would beg to be acknowledged, and the more terrifying they would be to confront. Over many weeks, I guided Beatrice gently, slowly, to get closer to those feelings. Not to be swallowed by them. To see they are just feelings.

As Beatrice had learned from doing the grief work, finally allowing herself to feel her immense sorrow had given her some relief from the depression, stress, and fear that had imprisoned her in her bed. But she hadn't yet allowed herself to feel her anger about the past. There is no forgiveness without rage.

As Beatrice described the small room, the way the door squeaked when her father's friend closed it, the dark plaid curtains he would make her draw shut, I watched her body language, ready to bring her back to shore if she was in distress.

Beatrice stiffened as she mentally closed the curtains in her father's study. As she sealed herself in the room with her attacker.

"Stop there, honey," I said.

She sighed. She kept her eyes closed.

"Is there a chair in the room?"

She nodded.

"What does it look like?"

"It's an armchair. Rust colored."

"I want you to put your father in that chair."

She grimaced.

"Can you see him sitting there?"

"Yes."

"What does he look like?"

"He has his glasses on. He's reading a newspaper."

"What is he wearing?"

"A blue sweater. Gray pants."

"I'm going to give you a big piece of duct tape, and I want you to put it over his mouth."

"What?"

"Cover his mouth with this tape. Did you do it?"

She nodded. She gave a faint smile.

"Now here's a rope. Tie him to that chair so he can't get up."

"Okay."

"Did you tie it tight?"

"Yes."

"Now I want you to yell at him."

"Yell how?"

"I want you to tell him how angry you are."

"I don't know what to say."

"Say, 'Dad, I'm so angry at you for not protecting me!' But don't say it. *Yell it!*" I demonstrated.

"Dad, I'm so angry at you," she said.

"Louder."

"Dad, I'm so angry at you!"

"Now I want you to punch him."

"Where?"

"Right in the face."

She raised a fist and swatted the air.

"Punch him again."

She did it.

"Now kick."

Her foot flew up.

"Here's a pillow. You can punch this. Really whack it." I handed her a cushion.

She opened her eyes and stared at the pillow. Her punches were timid at first, but the more I encouraged her, the stronger they became. I invited her to stand up and kick the pillow if she wanted to. To throw it across the room. To scream at the top of her lungs. Soon she was down on the floor, pounding on the pillow with her fists. When her body began to fatigue, she stopped punching and collapsed on the floor, breathing fast.

"How do you feel?" I asked her.

"Like I don't ever want to stop."

The following week I brought in a punching bag, a red one on a heavy black stand. We established a new ritual—we'd begin our sessions with some rage release. She'd mentally tie someone up in a chair—usually one of her parents—and scream while delivering a savage beating: *How could you let that happen to me? I was just a little girl!*

"Are you done?" I'd ask.

"No."

And she would keep punching until she was.

That Thanksgiving, after returning home from a dinner with friends, Beatrice was sitting on the couch, petting her dog, when her whole body started tingling. Her throat dried up, her heart began palpitating. She tried deep breathing to get her body to relax, but the symptoms got worse. She thought she was dying. She begged her girlfriend to take her to the hospital. The doctor who examined her in the emergency room said nothing was medically wrong. She had suffered a panic attack. When Beatrice saw me after the episode, she was frustrated and scared, discouraged to be feeling worse instead of better, and worried that she would have another panic attack.

I did everything I could to applaud her progress, to validate her growth. I told her that in my experience, when you release rage, you often feel much worse before you begin to feel better.

She shook her head. "I think I've gone as far as I can go."

"Honey, give yourself some credit. You had a terrifying night. And you got through it without harming yourself. Without running away. I don't think I could have coped as well as you did."

"Why do you keep trying to convince me that I'm a strong person? Maybe I'm not. Maybe I'm sick and I'll always be sick. Maybe it's time to stop telling me I'm someone I won't ever be."

"You're holding yourself responsible for something that isn't your fault."

"What if it is my fault? What if there's something different I could have done, and he would have left me in peace?"

"What if blaming yourself is just a way of maintaining the fantasy that the world is in your control?"

Beatrice rocked on the couch, her face streaked in tears.

"You didn't have choices then. You have choices now. You can choose not to come back here. That is always your choice. But I hope you can learn to see what a remarkable survivor you are."

"I'm barely holding on to my life. That doesn't seem very remarkable to me."

"Was there ever a place you went, when you were a girl, where you felt safe?"

"I only felt safe when I was alone in my room."

"Would you sit on your bed? Or by the window?"

"On my bed."

"Did you have any toys or stuffed animals you'd play with?"

"I had a doll."

"Did you talk to her?"

She nodded.

"Can you close your eyes and sit on that safe bed now? Hold your doll. Talk to her now like you talked to her then. What would you say?"

"How can I be loved in this family? I need to be good, but I'm bad."

"Do you know all that time you spent alone as a child, feeling so sad and isolated, you were building a huge store of strength and resilience? Can you applaud that little girl now? Can you take her in your arms? Tell her, 'You were hurt, and I love you. You were hurt, and you're safe now. You had to pretend and hide. I see you now. I love you now.'"

Beatrice held herself tightly and shook with sobs. "I want to be able to protect her now. I couldn't then. But I don't think I will ever feel safe unless I can protect myself now."

This is how Beatrice decided to take her next risk. Beatrice acknowledged that she wanted to feel safe, that she wanted to be able to protect herself. She had learned about a women's self-defense class beginning soon at the nearby community center. But she delayed registering. She feared she might not be up to the challenge of fighting off an attack, that a physical confrontation, even in the safe and empowering environment of a self-defense class, might trigger a panic attack. She came up with all kinds of reasons not to pursue what she wanted, in an effort to manage her fear—the class might be too expensive, or it might already be full, or it might not have enough participants and might be canceled. With me, she began to work through the fears underlying her resistance to pursuing what she wanted. I asked her two questions: *What's the worst that can happen?* and *Can you survive it?* The worst scenario she could imagine was experiencing a panic attack in class, in a room full of strangers. We confirmed that the medical release form she would be asked to fill out when she registered for the class would give the staff the information they needed to support her in the event of an attack. And we discussed the fact that she had experienced a panic attack before. If it happened again, she might not be able to stop it or control it, but at least she would know what was going on. And she already knew from experience that a panic attack, though frightening and unpleasant, wasn't deadly. She could survive it. So Beatrice registered for the class.

But once she was there in the room, in her sweatpants and sneakers, surrounded by the other women, she lost her nerve. She felt too self-conscious to participate. She was afraid of making mistakes, afraid of calling attention to herself. But she couldn't bring herself to leave after getting so close to her goal. She leaned against the wall and watched the class. She returned for each session after that, dressed to participate, but still too afraid. One day the instructor noticed her watching from the sidelines and offered to coach her one-on-one after class. Afterward, she came to see me, her face triumphant. "I could throw him against the wall today!" she said. "I pinned him. I picked him up. I threw him against the wall!" Her cheeks were flushed. Her eyes glistened with pride.

Once she had the confidence that she could protect herself, she began taking other risks—adult ballet classes, belly dancing. Her body began to change. It was no longer a container for her fear. It was an instrument of joy. Beatrice became a writer, a ballet teacher, a yoga instructor. She decided to choreograph a dance based on a Brothers Grimm tale she remembered reading as a child, "The Girl Without Hands." In the story, a girl's parents are tricked into giving their daughter to the devil. Because she is innocent and pure, the devil can't possess her, but in revenge and frustration, he cuts off her hands. The girl wanders the world, with stumps where her hands used to be. One day she walks into a king's garden, and when he sees her standing among the flowers, he falls in love with her. They get married and he makes her a pair of silver hands. They have a son. One day she saves their young son from drowning. Her silver hands disappear and are replaced with real hands.

Beatrice held out her hands as she told me about this story from her childhood. "My hands are real again," she said. "It wasn't someone else I saved. It was me."

CHAPTER 22

Somehow the Waters Part

Time doesn't heal. It's what you do with the time. Healing is possible when we choose to take responsibility, when we choose to take risks, and finally, when we choose to release the wound, to let go of the past or the grief.

Two days before his sixteenth birthday, Renée's son Jeremy came into the den where she and her husband were watching the ten o'clock news. In the flickering lights from the TV, his dark face looked troubled. Renée was about to reach for her son, wrap him up in the cuddly kind of hug that he would still consent to on occasion, when the phone rang. It was her sister in Chicago, who was going through a bad divorce and often called late at night. "I've got to take this," Renée said. She gave her son's cheek a quick pat and turned her attention to her distressed sister. Jeremy muttered a good night and headed toward the stairs. "Sweet dreams, baby," she called to his retreating back.

The next morning, Jeremy wasn't up by the time she was putting breakfast on the table. She called up the stairs to her son but got no response. She buttered the last piece of toast and went up to knock on his bedroom door. Still he didn't answer. Exasperated, she opened his door. The room was dark, the blinds still closed. She called to him again, confused to find that his bed was already made. A sixth sense drove her toward the closet door. She opened it, a gust of cold dread at her back. Jeremy's body hung from the wooden rod, a belt around his neck.

On his desk she found a note: *It's not you, it's me. Sorry to disappoint you.* —*J*

When Renée and her husband, Greg, first came to see me, Jeremy had been dead for only a few weeks. The loss of him was so fresh that they weren't grieving yet. They were in shock. The person they had buried wasn't gone to them. It felt as though they had put him in the ground alive.

During those early visits, Renée sat and sobbed. "I want to turn back the clock!" she cried. "I want to go back, go back." Greg cried too, but quietly. Often he would look out the window while Renée wept. I told them that men and women often grieve differently, and that the death of a child could be a rift or an opportunity in their marriage. I urged them to take good care of themselves, to let themselves rage and weep, to kick and cry and scream and get the feelings out so that they didn't make Jeremy's sister, Jasmine, pick up the tab for their grief. I invited them to bring in pictures of Jeremy so that we could celebrate his sixteen years of life, the sixteen years his spirit had resided with them. I gave them resources on support groups for survivors of suicide. And I worked with them as the what-if questions rose up like a tidal wave. *What if I'd been paying more attention? What if I hadn't answered the phone that night, if I'd given him that huge hug? What if I'd worked less and been at home more? What if I hadn't believed the myth that white kids are the only ones who commit suicide? What if I'd been on the lookout for signs? What if I'd put less pressure on him to perform in school? What if I'd checked in on him before I went to bed?* All the what-ifs reverberated, an unanswerable echo: *Why?*

We want so much to understand the truth. We want to be accountable for our mistakes, honest about our lives. We want reasons, explanations. We want our lives to make sense. But to ask *why?* is to stay in the past, to keep company with our guilt and regret. We can't control other people, and we can't control the past.

At some point during their first year of loss, Renée and Greg came to see me less and less frequently, and after a while their visits tapered off altogether. I didn't hear from them for many months. The spring that Jeremy would have graduated from high school, I was happy and surprised to get a call from Greg. He told me he was worried about Renée and asked if they could come in.

I was struck by the changes in their appearance. They had both aged, but in different ways. Greg had put on weight. His black hair was flecked with silver. Renée didn't look run-down, as Greg's concern for her had led me to believe she might. Her face was smooth, her blouse crisp, her hair freshly straightened. She smiled. She made pleasantries. She said she felt well. But her brown eyes held no light.

Greg, who had so often been silent in their sessions, spoke now, with urgency. "I have something to say," he said. He told me that the previous weekend he and Renée had attended a high school graduation party for their friend's son. It was a fraught event for them, full of land mines, devastating reminders of what the other couples had that they didn't have, of Jeremy's absence, of the seeming eternity of grief, every day a new host of moments that they would never experience with their son. But they forced themselves into nice clothes and went to the party.

At some point during the evening, Greg told me, he realized that he was having a good time. The music the DJ played made him think of Jeremy, and the old R&B albums his son had taken an interest in, playing them on the stereo in his room when he did homework or hung out with friends. Greg turned to Renée in her elegant blue dress and was struck by how clearly he could see Jeremy in the slope of her cheeks, the shape of her mouth. He felt swept away by love—for Renée, for their son, for the simple pleasure of eating good food under a white tent on a warm evening. He asked Renée to dance. She refused, got up, and left him alone at the table.

Greg cried as he recounted this. "I'm losing you too," he said to his wife.

Renée's face darkened, her eyes looked blacked out. We waited for her to speak.

"How dare you," she finally said. "Jeremy doesn't get to dance. Why should you? I can't turn my back on him so easily."

Her tone was hostile. Venomous. I expected Greg to wince. He shrugged instead. I realized this wasn't the first time that Renée had perceived his experience of happiness as a desecration of their son's memory. I thought of my mother. Of all the times I had seen my father try to nuzzle her, kiss her, and how she would rebuff his affection. She was so stuck in the early loss of her own mother that she hid herself in a shroud of melancholy. Her eyes would sometimes light up when she heard Klara play the violin. But she never gave herself permission to laugh from the belly, to flirt, to joke, to rejoice.

"Renée, honey," I said. "Who's dead? Jeremy? Or you?"

She didn't answer me.

"It doesn't do Jeremy any good if you become dead too," I told Renée. "It doesn't do you any good either."

Renée wasn't in hiding from her pain, as I had once been. She had made it her husband. In marrying herself to her loss, she was in hiding from her life.

I asked her to tell me how much space she was allowing for grief in her daily life.

"Greg goes to work. I go to the cemetery," she said.

"How often?"

She looked insulted by my question.

"She goes every day," Greg said.

"And that's a *bad* thing?" Renée snapped. "To be devoted to my son?"

"Mourning is important," I said. "But when it goes on and on, it can be a way of avoiding grief." Mourning rites and rituals can be an extremely important component of grief work. I think that's why religious and cultural practices include clear mourning rituals—there's a protected space and structure within which to begin to experience the feelings of loss. But the mourning period also has a clear end. From that point on, the loss isn't a separate dimension of life—the loss is integrated into life. If we stay in a state of perpetual mourning, we are choosing a victim's mentality, believing *I'm never going to get over it.* If we stay stuck in mourning, it is as though our lives are over too. Renée's mourning, though it was painful, had also become a kind of shield, something that fenced her off from her present life. In the rituals of her loss she could protect herself from having to accept it. "Are you spending more time and emotional energy with the son who is dead, or with the daughter who is alive?" I asked.

Renée looked troubled. "I'm a good mother," she said, "but I'm not going to pretend I'm not in pain."

"You don't have to pretend anything. But you are the only person who can stop your husband and your daughter from losing you too." I remembered my mother talking to her mother's picture above the piano, crying, "My God, my God, give me strength." Her wailing frightened me. Her fixation on her loss was like a trapdoor she would lift and fall through, an escape. I was like the child of an alcoholic, on guard against her disappearance, unable to rescue her from the void but feeling that it was somehow my job.

"I used to think that if I let grief in, I would drown," I told Renée. "But it's like Moses and the Red Sea. Somehow the waters part. You walk through them."

I asked Renée to try something new to shift her mourning into grief. "Put a picture of Jeremy in the living room. Don't go to the cemetery to mourn his loss. Find a way to connect with him right there in your house. Set aside fifteen or twenty minutes every day to sit with him. You can touch his face, tell him what you're doing. Talk to him. And then give him a kiss and go on about your day."

"I'm so scared of abandoning him again."

"He didn't kill himself because of you."

"You don't know that."

"There are an infinite number of things you could have done differently in your life. Those choices are done, the past is gone, nothing can change that. For reasons we will never know, Jeremy chose to end his life. You don't get to choose for him."

"I don't know how to live with that."

"Acceptance isn't going to happen overnight. And you're never going to be glad that he's dead. But you get to choose a way forward. You get to discover that living a full life is the best way to honor him."

Last year I received a Christmas card from Renée and Greg. It shows them standing by the Christmas tree with their daughter, a beautiful girl in a red dress. Greg embraces his daughter in one arm, his wife in the other. Over Renée's shoulder, a picture of Jeremy sits on the mantel. It's his last school picture, he wears a blue shirt, his smile larger than life. He isn't the void in the family. He isn't the shrine. He is present, he is always with them.

My mother's mother's portrait now lives in Magda's house in Baltimore, above her piano, where she still gives lessons, where she guides her students with logic and heart. When Magda had surgery recently, she asked her daughter, Ilona, to bring our mother's picture to the hospital so that Magda could do what our mother taught us: to call on the dead for strength, to let the dead live on in our hearts, to let our suffering and our fear lead us back to our love.

"Do you still have nightmares?" I asked Magda the other day.

"Yes. Always. Don't you?"

"Yes," I told my sister. "I do."

I went back to Auschwitz and released the past, forgave myself. I went home and thought, "I'm done!" But closure is temporary. It's not over till it's over.

Despite—no, because of—our past, Magda and I have found meaning and purpose in different ways in the more than seventy years since liberation. I have discovered the healing arts. Magda has remained a devoted pianist and piano teacher, and she has discovered new passions: bridge and gospel music. Gospel, because it sounds like crying—it is the strength of all the emotion let out. And bridge, because there's strategy and control—a way to win. She is a reigning bridge champion; she hangs her framed awards on the wall in her house opposite our grandmother's portrait.

Both of my sisters have protected and inspired me, have taught me to survive. Klara became a violinist in the Sydney Symphony Orchestra. Until the day she died—in her early eighties, of Alzheimer's—she called me "little one." More so than Magda or I did, Klara remained immersed in Jewish Hungarian immigrant culture. Béla and I loved to visit her and Csicsi, to enjoy the food, the language, the culture of our youth. We weren't able to be together, all of us survivors, very often, but we did our best to gather up for major events—more celebrations our parents would not be present to witness. In the early 1980s, we met in Sydney for Klara's daughter's wedding. The three of us sisters had awaited this reunion with happy anticipation, and when we were finally together again, we went into a frenzy of embraces as emotional as the ones we shared in Košice when we found one another alive after the war.

No matter that we were now middle-aged women, no matter how far we had come in our lives, once in one another's company it was funny how quickly we fell into the old patterns of our youth. Klara was in the spotlight, bossing us around, smothering us with attention; Magda was competitive and rebellious; I was the peacemaker, hustling between my sisters, soothing their conflicts, hiding my own thoughts. How easily we can make even the warmth and safety of family into a kind of prison. We rely on our old coping mechanisms. We become the person we think we need to be to please others. It takes willpower and choice not to step back into the confining roles we mistakenly believe will keep us safe and protected.

The night before the wedding, Magda and I came upon Klara alone in her daughter's childhood bedroom, playing with her daughter's old dolls. What we witnessed was more than a mother's nostalgia over her grown child. Klara was caught up in her make-believe game. She was playing as a child would. My sister had never had a childhood, I realized. She was always the violin prodigy. She never got to be a little girl. When she wasn't performing onstage, she performed for me and Magda, becoming our caretaker, our little mother. Now, as a middle-aged woman, she was trying to give herself the childhood she had never been allowed. Embarrassed to have been discovered with the dolls, Klara lashed out at us. "It's too bad I wasn't at Auschwitz," she said. "If I'd been there, our mother would have lived."

It was terrible to hear her say it. I felt all my old survivor's guilt rushing back, the horror of the word I spoke that first day of Auschwitz, the horror of remembering it, of confronting that old, long-buried belief, however erroneous, that I had sent our mother to her death.

But I wasn't a prisoner anymore. I could see my sister's prison at work, hear her guilt and grief clawing through the blame she threw at me and Magda. And I could choose my own freedom. I could name my own feelings, of rage, worthlessness, sorrow, regret, I could let them swirl, let them rise and fall, let them pass. And I could risk letting go of the need to punish myself for having lived. I could release my guilt and reclaim my whole pure self.

There is the wound. And there is what comes out of it. I went back to Auschwitz searching for the feel of death so that I could finally exorcise it. What I found was my inner truth, the self I wanted to reclaim, my strength and my innocence.

CHAPTER 23

Liberation Day

In the summer of 2010, I was invited to Fort Carson, Colorado, to address an Army unit returning from combat in Afghanistan, a unit with a high suicide rate. I was there to talk about my own trauma—how I survived it, how I survived the return to everyday life, how I chose to be free—so the soldiers might also adjust more easefully to life after war. As I climbed up to the podium, I experienced a few brief internal skirmishes of discomfort, the old habits of being hard on myself, of wondering what a little Hungarian ballet student has to offer men and women of war. I reminded myself that I was there to share the most important truth I know, that the biggest prison is in your own mind, and in your pocket you already hold the key: the willingness to take absolute responsibility for your life; the willingness to risk; the willingness to release yourself from judgment and reclaim your innocence, accepting and loving yourself for who you really are—human, imperfect, and whole.

I called on my parents for strength, and my children and grandchildren and great-grandchildren too. Everything they've taught me, everything they've compelled me to discover. "My mama told me something I will never forget," I began. "She said, 'We don't know where we're going, we don't know what's going to happen, but no one can take away from you what you put in your own mind.'"

I have said these words countless times, to Navy SEALs and crisis first responders, to POWs and their advocates at the Department of Veterans Affairs, to oncologists and people living with cancer, to Righteous Gentiles, to parents and children, to Christians and Muslims and Buddhists and Jews, to law students and at-risk youth, to people grieving the loss of a loved one, to people preparing to die, and sometimes I spin when I say them, with gratitude, with sorrow. This time as I said the words, I almost fell from the stage. I was overcome by sensations, by sense memories I've stored deep inside: the smell of muddy grass, the fierce sweet taste of M&M's. It took me a long moment to understand what was triggering the flashback. But then I realized: flanking the room were flags and insignias, and everywhere I saw an emblem I hadn't thought about consciously for many, many years, but one that is as significant to me as the letters that spell my own name—the insignia the GI who liberated me on May 4, 1945, wore on his sleeve—a red circle with a jagged blue 71 in the center. I had been brought to Fort Carson to address the Seventy-first Infantry, the unit that sixty-five years ago had liberated me. I was bringing my story of freedom to the survivors of war who once brought freedom to me.

I used to ask, *Why me? Why did I survive?* I have learned to ask a different question: *Why* not *me?* Standing on a stage surrounded by the next generation of freedom fighters, I could see in my conscious awareness something that is often elusive, often invisible: that to run away from the past or to fight against our present pain is to imprison ourselves. Freedom is in accepting what is and forgiving ourselves, in opening our hearts to discover the miracles that exist now.

I laughed and wept on the stage. I was so full of joyful adrenaline that I could barely get out the words: "Thank you," I told the soldiers. "Your sacrifice, your suffering, have meaning— and when you can discover that truth within, you will be free." I ended my speech the way I always do, the way I always will, as long as my body will let me: with a high kick. *Here I am!* my kick says. *I made it!*

And here you are. Here you are! In the sacred present. I can't heal you—or anyone—but I can celebrate your choice to dismantle the prison in your mind, brick by brick. You can't change what happened, you can't change what you did or what was done to you. But you can choose how you live *now.*

My precious, you can choose to be free.

Acknowledgments

I believe that people don't come to me—they are sent to me. I offer my eternal gratitude to the many extraordinary people who have been sent to me, without whom my life wouldn't be what it is, and without whom this book wouldn't exist:

First and foremost, my precious sister Magda Gilbert—who is ninety-five years old and still blossoming, who kept me alive in Auschwitz—and her devoted daughter Ilona Shillman, who fights for the family like no other.

Klara Korda—who was larger than life, who truly became my second mom, who made every visit to Sydney a honeymoon, who created Friday night dinners like our mother's, everything artfully done by hand—and Jeanie and Charlotte, the women following in her line. (Remember the Hungarian song? *No, no, we're not going away until you kick us out!*)

My patients, the unique and one-of-a-kind humans who have taught me that healing isn't about recovery; it's about discovery. Discovering hope in hopelessness, discovering an answer where there doesn't seem to be one, discovering that it's not what happens that matters—it's what you do with it.

My wonderful teachers and mentors: Professor Whitworth; John Haddox, who introduced me to the existentialists and phenomenologists; Ed Leonard; Carl Rogers; Richard Farson; and especially Viktor Frankl, whose book gave me the verbal capacity to share my secret, whose letters showed me I didn't have to run away anymore, and whose guidance helped me discover not only that I survived, but how I could help others to survive.

My amazing colleagues and friends in the healing arts: Dr. Harold Kolmer, Dr. Sid Zisook, Dr. Saul Levine, Steven Smith, Michael Curd, David Woehr, Bob Kaufman (my "adopted son"), Charlie Hogue, Patty Heffernan, and especially Phil Zimbardo, my "baby brother," who wouldn't rest until he'd helped find this book a publishing home.

The many people who have invited me to bring my story to audiences around the world, including: Howard and Henriette Peckett of YPO; Dr. Jim Henry; Dr. Sean Daneshmand and his wife, Marjan, of The Miracle Circle; Mike Hoge of Wingmen Ministries; and the International Conference of Logotherapy.

My friends and healers: Gloria Lavis; Sylvia Wechter and Edy Schroder, my treasured fellow Musketeers; Lisa Kelty; Wendy Walker; Flora Sullivan; Katrine Gilcrest, mother of nine, who calls me Mom, whom I can count on day and night; Dory Bitry, Shirley Godwin, and Jeremy and Inette Forbs, with whom I can talk so openly about the ages and stages of our lives and how to make the best out of what we have as we age; my doctors, Sabina Wallach and Scott McCaul; my acupuncturist, Bambi Merryweather; Marcella Grell, my companion and friend who has taken exceptional care of me and my home for the last sixteen years and who always tells me what she thinks right out.

Béla. Life mate. Soul mate. Father of my children. Loving, committed partner who risked it all to build a new life with me in America. You used to say, when I was consulting for the military and we traveled Europe together, "Edie works, and I eat." Béla, it was our rich life together that was the true feast. I love you.

All of my love and gratitude to my children: my son, John Eger, who has taught me how not to be a victim and who has never given up the fight for people living with disabilities; my daughters, Marianne Engle and Audrey Thompson, who have offered me unceasing moral support and loving comfort during the many months of writing, and who understood, perhaps before I did, that it would be more difficult for me to relive the past than it was to survive Auschwitz. In Auschwitz, I could think only about my survival needs; to write this book required that I feel all of the feelings. I couldn't have taken the risk without your strength and love.

And thank you to my children's and grandchildren's beautiful spouses and life partners, the people who keep adding branches to the family tree: Rob Engle, Dale Thompson, Lourdes, Justin Richland, John Williamson, and Illynger Engle.

My nephew Richard Eger—my Dickie-boy—and his wife, Byrne, thank you for being true relatives, for watching over me and my health and celebrating holidays together.

When our first grandchild was born Béla said, "Three generations—that's the best revenge to Hitler." Now we are four! Thank you to the next generation, to Silas, Graham, and Hale. Every time I hear you call me GG Dicu my heart goes pitter-patter.

Eugene Cook, my dancing partner and soul mate, a gentle man and a gentleman. Thank you for reminding me that love isn't what we feel—it's what we do. You're there for me always, every step and every word. Let's keep dancing the boogie-woogie as long as we're able.

Finally, the people who word by word and page by page helped me bring this book into being, a collaboration that from the beginning has felt meant to be:

The talented Nan Graham and Roz Lippel and their able staff at Scribner. How lucky I am to have been sent the most qualified editors with hearts as brilliant as their minds. Your editorial wisdom, persistence, and human compassion helped this book become what I always hoped it could be: an instrument of healing.

Esmé Schwall Weigand, my co-writer—you didn't just find the words. You became me. Thank you for being my ophthalmologist, for your ability to see my healing journey from so many different perspectives.

Doug Abrams, world-class agent and world's truest mensch, thank you for being a person with the backbone and character and soul to commit himself to make the world a better place. Your presence on the planet is an absolute gift.

To all: In my ninety years of life I have never felt so blessed and grateful—or so young! Thank you.

Index

365